Sexology
The Basis of Endocrinology
and Criminology

Sexology
The Basis of Endocrinology and Criminology

Samael Aun Weor

Sexology, the Basis of Endocrinology and Criminology
A Glorian Book / 2017

Originally published in Spanish as "Nociones
Fundamentales de Endocrinología y Criminología" (1953).

Print ISBN 978-1-943358-03-8

Glorian Publishing is a non-profit organization. All proceeds
go to further the distribution of these books. For more
information, visit our website.

gnosticteachings.org

Contents

Part One: Sexology

Part Two: Endocrinology

Part Three: Perception

Part Four: Criminology

Illustrations

Editor's Notes

When preparing a new edition of Samael Aun Weor's *Fundamental Notions of Endocrinology and Criminology* (1958) for publication in English, we contemplated some facts about the modern reader:

1. People judge books by their titles, and this one sounded like a college textbook—something dull, intellectual, and lacking practicality, none of which are qualities of this book. Our first printing of the book literally sat on the shelf, undeservedly finding no readers, because of the title. We were determined to find a way for readers to discover the valuable content of the book, but we also did not want to rename the book entirely, out of respect to the author.

2. The book was the nineteenth book Samael Aun Weor wrote, and thus was written when he had many readers who already knew the core message of his earlier writings: knowledge of sexuality. Thus in this book he did not repeat what he explained thoroughly in those previous books. For new readers, the book lacked that context and the foundation it is based upon, and we felt that if this book were to be the only one someone were to read, they should at least be introduced to that foundation.

Therefore, in order to craft a title suitable both for the content and the modern reader, and help new readers understand the main body of the book, we expanded the book by drawing from his lectures. We added a section called "Sexology" with three lectures that explain the sexual foundations, and later in the book we added the lecture "Perception of Reality" as a bridge between the two original sections. We hope you agree that this added material makes the book more understandable and interesting, and we hope you like the new title, *Sexology, the Basis of Endocrinology and Criminology.* Hopefully, it will invite more readers into these valuable studies.

In addition, the chapter "Supraconsciousness" was written in 1959 but revised in 1977 or so by Samael Aun Weor for inclusion in *Tarot and Kabbalah* (1978). We have included his updated chapter here.

May all beings be happy!

Part One
Sexology

"In the view of tantra, the body's vital energies are the vehicles of the mind. When the vital energies are pure and subtle, one's state of mind will be accordingly affected. By transforming these bodily energies we transform the state of consciousness."
—The 14th Dalai Lama

Chapter 1
Love and Sex

Allow me to speak a bit about love and sex.
Love begins with a flash of delectable affinity. It is substantiated with infinite tenderness, and it is synthesized with supreme adoration...

A perfect marriage is the union of two beings (male and female), one who loves more and the other who loves better. Love is the best religion available...

Hermes Trismegistus, the thrice-great god ibis of Thoth, author of *The Emerald Tablet*, wrote the following sentence,

"I give you love, within which is contained all the sum of wisdom..."

Indeed, love is the extract of all sapience. It is written that in its final synthesis wisdom is summarized as love, and love as happiness.

The Power of Love

When human beings are in love they become noble, charitable, helpful, philanthropic; they are in a state of ecstasy, and if the being they adore is absent, a simple handkerchief or a portrait or a ring or any love-memory of them will be enough in order to fall into a state of ecstasy; that is what love is...

Indeed, love is an effusion, an energetic emanation that flows within the deepest depths of the consciousness; it is, we would say, a superlative sense of the consciousness.

The cosmic energy that flows from within the bottom of our heart stimulates the endocrine glands of our body and puts them to work, then many hormones are produced that inundate the sanguineous channels and fill us with a great vitality. In ancient Greece the word "hormone" meant "longing of being," "strength of being"...

Let us observe an old decrepit man. It would be enough to put him in contact with a woman, it would be enough for him to fall in love with her for him to become mystically exalted; then his endocrine glands will produce abundant hormones which, flooding his sanguineous channels, will revitalize them extraordinarily; this is how love is...

Indeed, love truly revitalizes, love awakens in us the innate powers of the Being. When human beings are truly in love, they become intuitive, mystical. In such moments they forebode their future, afraid of what might happen to them, and often exclaim, "It seems to me that this is a dream; I fear that later you will find someone else on your way." Such intuitive hunches, throughout time and distance, become exactly fulfilled; that is love...

In Europe and the United States, there is a wonderful order; I refer to the Order of the Swan. Such an institution scientifically analyzes the various processes of that which is called "love."

In India, love has always been symbolized by the kala hamsa swan, which floats marvelously upon the waters of life. Indeed, the swan emphatically allegorizes the ineffable joys of love. Observe a crystalline lake, where the swan glides over the most pure waters where the sky is reflected. When a partner swan dies, the other succumbs with sadness, and it is because love is fed with love...

To love, how beautiful it is to love. Only great souls can and know how to love... So said a great thinker.

Observe the stars rotating around their centers of universal gravitation: they attract and repel according to the law of cosmic magnetization. They love and turn again to love each other...

Often, stars have been seen to approach each other, sparkling, shining in the starry night sky. Suddenly something happens, "A collision of stars," exclaim astronomers from their wonderful observatory towers... Love, yes! They have come too close, their masses have merged, have been integrated by the force of affection, they have become a new mass. Behold the miracle of love in the firmament...

Let us observe a flower: the atoms of the molecule in the scented, ambrosial rose, bathed by the rays of the moon in the starry night on the banks of the crystalline fountain, speaks of love...

And look at those atoms around their nuclear centers: obviously, the molecule resembles a miniature solar system. Why are there atoms rotating around their gravitational centers as the planets rotate around the Sun? It is because they are attracted by the wonderful force that is called love...

It is written that if all human beings without distinction of race, sex, caste, or color would even for a minute leave their resentments, vendettas, wars, hatred, and would dearly love each other, then even the venom of vipers would disappear. This is because love is a cosmic force, a force that surges from within the vortex of all atomic nuclei, a force that surges from the vortex of any solar system, a force that surges from the center of any galaxy. It is an extraordinary force that properly used can perform miracles and wonders, as those performed by the Divine Rabbi of Galilee when passing through the Earth. This is how love is...

The kiss itself (which some give in a morbid manner) is indeed the mystical consecration of two souls eager to express in a sensory way what they live inside...

The sexual act is the consubstantiation of love in the psychophysiological reality of our nature...

In Asia, they never built monuments to great heroes, not even to Genghis Khan with his bloody battles, but to love and to women. And it is because the Asians understood that only through the marvelous force of love we can transform ourselves radically.

Maternity, love, woman — lo and behold something grandiose that resonates in the coral of space in an always perennial manner. Woman is the most beautiful thought of the Creator made flesh, blood, and life...

We males are fascinated by a beautiful painting, or are enchanted by a beautiful sunset, or are captivated when observing an eclipse through an observatory. But the woman immediately provokes in us the craving of possessing her, the urge of becoming one with her, the drive of integrating with her, in order to participate in the plentitude of the universe.

ADAM AND EVE IN THE GARDEN OF EDEN

Nevertheless, we must not, in any way, look at love or at women in a morbid manner; we must remember that love in itself is pure, holy, and noble.

When a male defiles a woman with his perverse gaze,[1] indubitably he marches on the path of degeneration.

We must learn to see woman purely, in all of her natural beauty.

For us males, the woman, born for a holy destiny, is the only being that can liberate us from the chain of pain.

For women the male is something similar; she sees in the man all hope, all protection; she wants to be completed by the man. She sees in him precisely the masculine eternal principle, the force that has put into activity all that is, everything that has been, and all that will be.

Indeed, man and woman are truly the two pillars of the temple. These two columns must not be overly close nor exorbitantly away from each other; there must be a space so that the light can pass between them.

When the force of affection is studied, when one comprehends that which is called "love," we then feel that at the base of sex there might be something that can indeed bring us enlightenment, a mystical relevance that can transform us into superhumans.

There is no one that cannot be changed by means of love. Indeed, it is only by means of this wonderful force that one can be changed.

Adam and Eve left the terrestrial paradise together, and together, hugging each other, they must return to Paradise. Adam and Eve left Eden for having eating the forbidden fruit of which they were told, "Thou shall not eat of it..."[2]

It is obvious that by not eating the forbidden fruit we will come back into Eden.

---

1 "... whosoever looketh on a woman to lust after her hath committed adultery with her already in his heart." —Jesus, from Matthew 5:28

2 "And אלהים יהוה commanded the man, saying, Of every tree of the garden thou mayest freely eat: But of the tree of the knowledge of goodness and impurity, thou shalt not eat of it: for in the day that thou eatest thereof thou shalt surely die." —Genesis 2:16-17

If through the door of sex we came out of Eden, then only through that marvelous door can we return to Eden. Eden[3] is sex itself.

The atomic powers of good and evil fight for supremacy; they clash within the sacred sperm.[4]

The sacred sperm is indeed formidable. Within it are found the mystical, ethical, and scientific principles that could make us something different: a superhuman.

The Superhuman

Friedrich Nietzsche addressed the superhuman. Let us remember the words of Nietzsche when he said:

"When Zarathustra was thirty years old, he left his home and the lake of his home, and went into the mountains. There he enjoyed his spirit and his solitude, and for ten years did not weary of it. But at last his heart changed, and rising one morning with the rosy dawn, he went before the sun, and spoke to it thus: You great star! What would your happiness be, had you not those for whom you shine? For ten years have you climbed here to my cave: you would have wearied of your light and of the journey, had it not been for me, my eagle, and my serpent...

"Zarathustra went down the mountain alone, no one meeting him. When he entered the forest, however, there suddenly stood before him an old saint, who had left his holy hut to seek roots in the forest. And thus spoke the old saint to Zarathustra: "No stranger to me is this wanderer: many years ago he passed by. Zarathustra he was called, but he has changed. Then you carried your ashes up to the mountains: will you now carry your fire into the valleys? Do you not fear the arsonist's punishment? Yes, I recognize Zarathustra. Pure are his eyes, and no loathing lurks around his mouth. Does he not move like a dancer? Transformed is Zarathustra; Zarathustra has become a child; an awakened one is Zarathustra: what will you do in the land of the sleepers? As in the sea have you lived in solitude, and it has supported you. Alas, will you now go ashore? Alas, will you again haul your body by yourself?" Zarathustra answered: "I love mankind." "Why," said the saint, "did I go into the forest and the desert? Was it not because I loved men far too well? Now I love God; men I do not love. Man is a thing too imperfect for me. Love of man would be fatal to me." Zarathustra answered: "Did I talk of love? I am

---

3   The Hebrew word עֵדֶן Eden literally means "pleasure, delight."
4   From Greek sperma, "seed," whether male and female

bringing a gift to men." "Give them nothing," said the saint. "Instead, take part of their load, and carry it with them - that will be most agreeable to them: if only it is agreeable to you! If, however, you want to give something to them, give them no more than alms, and let them also beg for it!" "No," replied Zarathustra, "I give no alms. I am not poor enough for that." The saint laughed at Zarathustra, and spoke thus: "Then see to it that they accept your treasures! They are distrustful of hermits, and do not believe that we come with gifts. Our footsteps sound too lonely through the streets. And at night, when they are in bed and hear a man walking nearby long before sunrise, they may ask themselves: Where is this thief going? Do not go to men, but stay in the forest! Go rather to the animals! Why not be like me - a bear among bears, a bird among birds?" "And what does the saint do in the forest?" asked Zarathustra. The saint answered: "I make songs and sing them; and in making songs I laugh and weep and growl and hum: thus do I praise God. With singing, weeping, laughing, growling and humming do I praise the God who is my God...."

"Many fine things has Zarathustra said, especially for those who are young enough for them. Strange! Zarathustra knows little about women, and yet he is right about them! Does this happen, because with women nothing is impossible? And now accept a little truth by way of thanks! I am old enough for it! Swaddle it up and hold its mouth: otherwise it will scream too loudly, the little truth." "Give me, woman, your little truth!" said I. And thus spoke the old woman: "You go to women? Do not forget your whip!" —Thus Spoke Zarathustra

This painful phrase has been misinterpreted. Many have believed that Zarathustra will advise man to whip the woman or something like that, no! Nietzsche, the author of *Thus Spoke Zarathustra,* was very sweet and he loved woman very much. Indeed, truly, he only wanted to insinuate the idea of using the whip of willpower in order to overpower ourselves and not to get carried away by our animal passions. Therefore, the whip is not against woman, but against ourselves, since the whip is the symbol or allegory of willpower.

"When Zarathustra arrived at the nearest town which is close to the forest... Zarathustra spoke thus to the people: I teach you the superhuman. The human is something to be superseded. What have you done to supersede it?"

"Zarathustra, however, looked at the people and wondered. Then he spoke thus: The human is a rope stretched between the animal and the superhuman — a rope over an abyss. A dangerous crossing, a dangerous on-the-way, a dangerous looking-back, a dangerous trembling and stopping. What is great in the human is that it is a bridge and not a goal: what can be loved in the human is that it is an over-going and a down-going." –Thus Spoke Zarathustra

Well, Nietzsche spoke of the superhuman but he forgot to speak about the human.

First we must create the human within ourselves, then and only then we could afford the luxury of elevating ourselves to the level of the superhuman.

Indeed, it is necessary for the human to be born within us. Since, day by day, it is written that we are just "rational animals"... A professor of medicine exclaimed in Mexico, when addressing us saying, "We are just intellectual mammals"... Okay, they can name us as they please, but the truth is that we need to create the human being within ourselves; we need to have the necessary available elements for the creation of the human being. The human germs for the creation of the human being exist, and are located exactly within our sexual glands.

I know I am before a learned audience here in the Auditorium of Culture of Hermosillo, this is why when addressing these things, seemingly morbid, I do it with the absolute certainty that I am standing before a decent, learned audience. Therefore, truthfully, if I say that we are intellectual animals, I do not think that anyone would be offended by it, since we have always heard that we are rational animals, thus, if instead of rational we say intellectual, we understand that both terms have the same meaning.

Thus, truthfully, we need to have the necessary available elements for the creation of the human being, that is clear. Again, the human germs [seeds] are within our sexual endocrine glands. These human germs could become developed or permanently lost. If we develop them, the human being will then be born within us, but if we do not work on ourselves, these human germs will be definitively lost. The human being must be formed within us in the same way that the butterfly is formed within the chrysalis, and this metamorphosis is only possible by means of the marvelous force of love and sex.

I said it and I repeat again: The sexual act is the consubstantiation of love within the psychophysiological reality of our nature...

So, we will become transformed by developing the human germs.

Undoubtedly, these human germs can and must grow within us, by means of love and scientific procedures.

Transmutation and Elevation

In these moments, the Sun[5] is making a new creation. The Sun wants to create human beings.

During the time of Abraham, the Sun did a test within the test tube of Nature, and achieved some human creations. During the first eight centuries of Christianity, the Sun made further experiments and managed to create a group of human beings. And at these precise moments of global crisis and bankruptcy of all principles, the Sun is performing a new effort within the laboratory of Nature. The Sun wants to create human beings. Thus, the creation of human beings is possible; what is important is knowing the clue, the system, the method.

Regarding transcendental sexology, the Oneida Society in the United States, controlled by illustrious doctors, was conducting remarkable experiments: twenty-five couples were subjected to scientific observation. Those twenty-five couples were taught the sexual act by which the transformation of the creative energy is possible. Unquestionably, that sexual act is based on the following clue:

"Inmissum membrum virile in vaginam feminae sine eiaculatione seminis."

In other words, during chemical copulation the connection of the lingam-yoni can be achieved, but, the doctors from the Oneida Society said, without the ejaculation of the end seminis, meaning without the spilling the cup of Hermes Trismegistus, the thrice great God Ibis of Thoth. This signifies

---

5   The divinity who brings life and love into being, symbolized in many religions by the solar gods, such as Christ, Avalokitesvara, etc.

that during the sexual act the couple must not complete the consummation of it. "Coitus interruptus," exclaim the doctors of medicine. Some of them pronounce themselves against this formula, yet others accept it. Those who accept it can transmute the sacred sperm into creative energy. This very fine type of energy will reach the brain through certain nervous canals that relate to the vagus and the sympathetic. When the sacred sperm is transmuted into energy, the brain is then seminized and the semen is cerebrated.

Behold a way for an extraordinary revitalization, a path that can transform us radically. Behold a method in order to produce sexual energy. That type of energy is more powerful than electricity. That energy flows in everything that is, in everything that has been, and in all that will be. That type of energy put the universe into existence. That type of energy put our solar system into existence. That type of energy, flowing from every nuclei, placed into activity the galaxy in which we live. Thus, truthfully, the creative energy of the universe has a formidable power.

We might say that in our organism there is a complete power plant by means of which it is possible to drive that very fine type of energy towards our brain mass. Comprehend that this does not mean that we raise the sacred sperm towards the brain, because if we did that then the mind would go crazy, thus that would be absurd. The main point here is to transmute the sperm into energy, and that is different.

As the wise Einstein stated:

"Mass is transformed into energy, energy is transformed into mass."

It is possible to transform the seminal mass into creative energy in order to dynamize the brain and awaken transcendent faculties that are in our organic physiology.

Those who accept this wonderful, formidable clue will be transformed into true human beings.

The human germs must be developed in order to give rise to the human being.

By human germs, I mean, for example, the germ of the astral body. When the sacred sperm is transformed into ener-

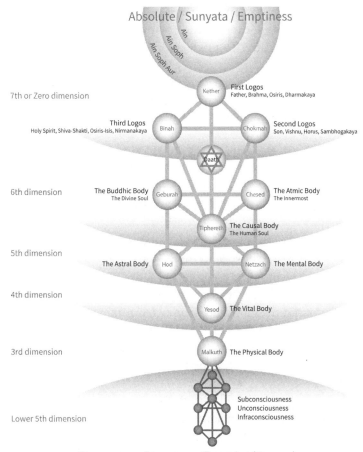

Absolute / Sunyata / Emptiness

Ain
Ain Soph
Ain Soph Aur

7th or Zero dimension — Kether — First Logos
Father, Brahma, Osiris, Dharmakaya

Third Logos
Holy Spirit, Shiva-Shakti, Osiris-Isis, Nirmanakaya — Binah — Chokmah — Second Logos
Son, Vishnu, Horus, Sambhogakaya

Daath

6th dimension — The Buddhic Body
The Divine Soul — Geburah — Chesed — The Atmic Body
The Innermost

Tiphereth — The Causal Body
The Human Soul

5th dimension — The Astral Body — Hod — Netzach — The Mental Body

4th dimension — Yesod — The Vital Body

3rd dimension — Malkuth — The Physical Body

Lower 5th dimension — Subconsciousness
Unconsciousness
Infraconsciousness

DIMENSIONS AND BODIES ON THE TREE OF LIFE (KABBALAH)

gy in a higher octave, then an astral human germ develops, and comes to crystallize in the wonderful and splendorous form of the astral body.[6] That sidereal body is related to the grand sympathetic nervous system. One knows that one has an astral body when one can use it, when you can leave the physical body at will, when one can travel with that vehicle through the unalterable infinite.

When the sperm is transmuted into energy in an even higher, second octave, then it comes to crystallize within our organism in the extraordinary and marvelous form of the

---

6   The solar astral body, which is related to the fifth dimension and the sephirah Hod on the Tree of Life.

mental body.[7] One knows that one has a mental body when one can apprehend, capture the great cosmic truths contained within Nature. To possess a mental body is something extraordinary.

Thereafter, when the sacred sperm is transmuted into mystical energy, it then comes to finally crystallize in an even higher, third octave, in the most magnificent form of the cognizant body of will.[8]

Thus, when we possess the physical, astral, mental and causal bodies, we then receive our psychic and spiritual principles and become true human beings. Before that moment we are not humans; before that moment we only are "intellectual mammals."

Now, not all human beings achieve integration with the divine. Obviously, those who manage to do so become superhumans in the most transcendental sense of the word.

The human beings who want to reach the heights of the superhuman must eliminate from within themselves all of their psychological defects; in other words, we would say: they must eliminate the psychological "I" from within themselves. But first it is necessary for the true human being to be born within us.

Nevertheless, as I said, the seed-germs for the human being may be lost, and what is normal is for them to be lost. But when one works with those human germs, one then manages to not lose them, thus they germinate and the human being is born within us.

The human being is the king or queen of creation. The human being has power over fire, air, water, and earth...

A handful of humans was enough in order to produce the blackout of New York.[9] Remember, my dear friends, that case about the New York blackout... Really, two spaceships appeared in the atmosphere of the United States. Then the US armed forces sent against them airplanes heavily armed with

---

7   The solar mental body, which is related to the fifth dimension and the spehirah Netzach on the Tree of Life.

8   The solar causal body, which is related to the sixth dimension and the spehirah Tiphereth on the Tree of Life.

9   Described fully in *Cosmic Ships* by Samael Aun Weor.

machine guns and atomic rockets, etc. The two ships floated in the atmosphere, and when they saw that they were strafed, they separated. One was lost in the firmament; the other descended very gently to an electric power tower, then came the New York blackout, which was extraordinary: the traffic was interrupted, there were many accidents, people seemed crazy throughout the streets and avenues of that skyscraper city. They immediately investigated with electronic brains in order to see where the damage was, but they did not find it; there was no damage of any kind, and nonetheless the lights went out. Full of despair, the generals of the United States said, "Behold here the Achilles heel of our mighty American nation..." Indeed, what would all of their rockets serve for, if they do not have electricity? Extraterrestrials, a group of humans (true human beings) in a cosmic ship, were strong enough in order to paralyze the United States and part of Canada.

Thus, this is how the human being is: a king, a lord, with power (as it is written) over all of Nature. Yet, another thing is the intellectual animal. The rational mammals have no power; they are victims of circumstances. They are weak. They are born, die, fight, suffer, weep. They are unhappy creatures...

We need for the human being to be born within us, and that is only possible by means of the love between a man and a woman in the sexual act.

The Degeneration of Sex

The time has arrived to learn how we must forever stop desecrating sex. It is horrifying to see how we look at sex, namely, pornographic magazines, lust, etc., as if sex were, indeed, something filthy.

True human beings never desecrate sex. True human beings know that sex is sacred. Human beings know that wonderful force put the universe into existence. They know that the day the sexual energy ceases to flow in nature the plants and animals would cease to reproduce, all that exists would disappear, the Earth would become a desert.

So, why should we see perversity in sex? Why do we spit on the holy shrine of love? Why do we look lustfully at what is sacred, that is, the chemical or metaphysical copulation?

Let us reflect a little; it is time to reflect. The time has arrived when we must learn how to transmute the sacred sperm into creative energy.

Unfortunately, the world has entered into a descending, devolving cycle. Right now, there are countries where homosexuality has spread alarmingly. There is a country where 95 percent of people are bisexual, homosexual, or lesbian.

Yes, the world has entered into a descending, devolving wave. Authentic masculinity is being lost. Males now have the tendency to become feminized, and females tend to become masculinized.

It is necessary for the woman to return and become the queen of home in order to instruct her children. It is necessary for the man to reconquer his masculine values and to express himself with the potentiality of a male. The man should be very manly, and the woman must be truly very womanly.

So, the moment has arrived to realize that we must learn how to transmute in order for the human germs to be developed within us, here and now.

Again, right now, the Sun is performing a great experiment within the laboratory of Nature. The Sun wants to create solar humans.

Any human race on the face of the Earth has only one goal: to serve for the experiment of the Sun, a very difficult experiment. If we do not cooperate with the Sun, then it is impossible for the human being to be born within us. If we do not cooperate with the Sun, we fail.

Unfortunately, present humanity has become frighteningly mechanistic, lunar. In these times, all interest in solar ideas is being lost. Now people think only of bank accounts and the latest technology. Unfortunately, even the songs about love seem to flee. Now marriages think only about bank account calculations and the latest technology, and that is all.

Young men and women in Russia do not want to get married. That is unfortunate. The Russian government is alarmed, and I understand these young people, since they have been submitted to so many regulations again and again that they have lost interest in marriage.

Instead, degeneration, homosexuality, lesbianism are multiplying in all the countries of the Earth, and there is supreme pain. Soon we will see a Third World War and a great atomic holocaust. This is because when the sexual energies are not truly properly channeled, all that is brought on the face of the Earth are wars and bitterness.

We all are guilty of the future World War III, since all of us are channeling the creative energies in the wrong way. All males have stopped seeing in the woman the beauty of love, and have only converted her into a pornographic figure. The humanoids of these times wallow in the Procrustean bed. Venereal diseases spread everywhere. This is infinitely regrettable.

There are countries where there is a kind of memory of what the charms of love were in times of yore. Let us remember the geishas in Japan. With infinite decency, they attended men. Their mission was exclusively in knowing how to serve them, and for that they prepared themselves for many years; they were polyglots, etc. When a geisha loved a man, she took him to a crystalline fountain filled with flowers, and there she bathed him, massaged him with lotions and wonderful ointments from the Eastern world. She venerated him, and religiously took him to her chamber for the chemical copulation.[10] But this copulation was not the brutal, violent sexual act of the Western world, since it was preceded by many mystical ceremonies. This is how Japan was. Unfortunately, the

---

10 In ancient times, priestesses (vestals, geishas) performed this sacred duty for unmarried initiates. "There were many vestals ready to work in the Great Work with the celibate initiates. The married initiates practiced in their homes with their priestess wives. The vestals were duly prepared for the priesthood of love. They had great lady masters who prepared them, and they were submitted to great ordeals and penances. These were precisely the sacred prostitutes about which many authors speak. Today it would be impossible to have vestals of this type... The world has become so corrupted, that the result would be to further corrupt that which is already corrupted." —Samael Aun Weor, *The Perfect Matrimony*

Western world has entered that country, and before long even the most beautiful fragrance of Japan will be gone.

Remember that thirty years ago the men and women of Japan bathed naked in public. They did not have perversity. No one felt lust when contemplating the opposite sex. They seemed like older children frolicking on the beaches. But, one day Douglas MacArthur arrived and banned bathing naked on the shores of Japan, arguing "principles of morality." The Japanese, who had never thought of perversity, looked at themselves and were like the biblical book of Genesis states, "And the eyes of them both were opened, and they knew that they were naked." And as the book of Genesis continues, "And they sewed fig leaves together, and made themselves aprons." So, likewise the Japanese covered their flesh. Thus, it was from that time when they began to see what they did not see before: perversity in sex. Before that they saw sex with respect, they did not feel lust. Now, everything has changed. The Western world is corrupting, damaging Japan.

I do not know why people want to see taboo, sin, where there is none. I do not know why they want to see in sex something undignified and perverse.

Let us observe the flowers. Their sexual organs are in their center. They rise toward the Sun and show to the Sun their creative organs without perversity of any kind. Why would we be lower than flowers? Why do we not understand the holiness of sex and love? Why do we not want to understand that sex, the creative energy, is a marvelous force whose original source is divine, the Holy Spirit, as we would say in pure Christianity?

Unfortunately, people march down on the descending, devolving path. The face of the Earth is rotten even to the marrow of the bones. Corruption has reached the breaking point. The fact that there are countries where 95 percent of people are bisexual, homosexual, and lesbian is horrible, monstrous in the most tremendous sense of the word. The time has arrived when we must understand these issues...

VESTALS

In these moments where I address these sexual matters to you, I also remember how the priestesses of love in Rome[11] made sex a sacred worship. Likewise even the very women who were part of those ceremonies in Athens looked at love with deep respect. Never were man and woman thrown into the Procrustean bed in the brutal and ruthless manner of the people in this twentieth century.

Diverse sacred rituals that were practiced by the Vestals always preceded the wonderful charm of love and the sexual act. In ancient times, sex was always seen with great respect and profound veneration.

I am certain that if men and women learned how to love, the world would be completely transformed...

Lemuria and Atlantis

At this moment, Lemuria comes into my memory, Lemuria, that old extraordinary continent that was once located in the Pacific Ocean. Lemuria was inhabited. It is clear that when that giant planet Hercolubus arrived — which also now is approaching again in order to end our Aryan root race[12] — it produced catastrophic events on the old continent Mu. The fire of volcanoes erupted to the surface. All over, the liquid fire burned the face of the Earth. Terrible earthquakes and horrific tidal waves ended the great cities of the Lemurian

---

11 Vestals, Vestal Virgins
12 In esotericism, the word Aryan refers not to "white people" or to an ancient, dead civilization, but instead refers to to the vast majority of the popluation of this planet. See glossary.

continent. And finally, it gradually sank in the raging waves of the Pacific Ocean. Easter Island and Oceania are remnants of Lemuria.

During the time of the third Lemurian subrace, it happened at certain times that men and women who loved each other were guided to the sacred temples of mysteries. Then, under the direction of the great sages they sexually united in order to create and again to create anew. Yet, in those times of Arcadia where the rivers of pure water of life flowed with milk and honey, the sexual act was an ineffable sacrament. In those ancient ages, no one dared to perform the sexual act outside of the temples. Even the kings and queens of the various walled cities attended those holy places in order to copulate before the altar, since for them the sexual act was sacred.

Then, human beings reproduced by Kriyashakti, the power of will and yoga.[13] No one spilled the sacred sperm. Men and women withdrew from the sexual act without spilling the semen.[14] Then, their sperm was transformed into creative energy that awakened extraordinary powers in those Cyclopean men and women... It was another time...

In these moments, there are already devices that will prove the reality of what I am stating. Soon the sound waves of

13 Through this method, a single masculine sperm is guided to the female body. There is no orgasm or loss of energy or matter.
14 **Jewish / Christian:** "When any man hath an ejaculation of semen out of his flesh, because of his ejaculation he is filthy." — Leviticus 15. **Buddhism:** "Being able to have sexual contact without releasing semen is something needed when you practice the advanced stages of the complete stage." - The 14th Dalai Lama (Berzin Archives). "Actually, [..] the sexual organ is utilized, but the energy movement which is taking place is, in the end, fully controlled. The energy should never be let out. This energy must be controlled and eventually returned to other parts of the body. And here we can see there is a kind of special connection with celibacy." - Quoted from "The Good Heart," H.H. the Dalai Lama. **Hinduism:** "Through practice, the sexual matter that others discharge [via orgasm] is drawn upwards [into the spinal column]. One can restrain and preserve one's own sexual matter." —Hatha Yoga Pradipika. "Ejaculation of semen [orgasm] brings death, preserving it within brings life. Therefore, one should make sure to retain the semen within. One is born and dies through semen; in this there is no doubt. Knowing this, the Yogi must always preserve his semen. When the precious jewel of semen is mastered, anything on earth can be mastered." —Shiva Samhita

PADMASAMBHAVA, WHO BROUGHT TANTRA TO TIBET, WITH HIS CONSORT YESHE TSOGYAL.
"Lustful people do not enter the path of liberation."
—Padmasambhava, from oral instructions to Lady Tsogyal

Lemuria will be found and transformed into images. Through television sets they will demonstrate with concrete facts the reality of these affirmations.

Indeed, truthfully, in Lemuria sex was sacred. Any spermatozoon could escape from the endocrine glands of the man in order to fecundate the female womb. So, this is how the children of wisdom, the children of will and yoga were born into the world.

In that ancient age, the rivers of pure waters of life flowed with milk and honey. Everything belonged to everyone, and everyone could eat from the tree of the neighbor without fear. That was the paradisiacal epoch, the epoch of the Titans. Humans had not degenerated yet. They had a sixth sense that allowed them to see the aureola of the stars, and to communicate with people of other worlds.

Let us say that they were "giants," yes, they were about four meters tall. We have stone representations of them in the wonderful sculptures of Tula. They have said that those sculptures are Atlantean sculptures, but indeed, these monuments remind us of the Lemurian humanity, the children of wisdom; they remind us those people who spoke delightfully in the great universal language, which like a river of gold always flows as the golden light of the sun.

There was no pain. This was the epoch in which humanity still lived in a paradisiacal state. It was the epoch in which the one who knew how to play the lyre sang with its delicious melodies. In that ancient age, the lyre of Orpheus had not yet fallen to the floor of the temple and smashed into pieces. It was the age in which humanity was considered one family. Woman did not suffer during childbirth. She enjoyed bringing a new creature into the world. There was no hatred on the face of the Earth. There were no wars. Everything was love and spiritual beauty.

But when those humans began to fornicate, when they started spilling the cup of Hermes Trismegistus, then they degenerated, they lost their precious faculties, and left Eden.

What I am stating will be corroborated one day, when certain devices currently being refined capture the waves of the continent Mu and transform them into images.

Friends, that humanity degenerated on the continent Mu towards the end of that continent, when people began to reproduce themselves in a manner similar to this present humanity. Then, they no longer attended the temples for the sexual act, no. They began to reproduce themselves in their huts, in their homes, in their palaces, ejaculating the ens seminis. Thus, it was from that time that the descending, devolving human process began.

When Lemuria sank into the Pacific Ocean, then the famous Atlantis sung of by Plato emerged from the Atlantic Ocean. Atlantis was located from the south to the north pole; it had a powerful civilization with atomic rockets that could

cross the infinite space and descend not only on the Moon
but on other planets of our solar system. The lighting system
of Atlantis was atomic. Their amphibious or aerial vehicles
were impelled or propelled by solar energy.

In the beginning, the Atlanteans also had a great spiritual
culture. They did not know wars. Love reigned everywhere.
Men and women made of love a worship. They remembered
the previous Lemurian epochs and in no way they wanted to
fall back into devolution. Unfortunately, at the end of Atlantis
(as we right now are at the end of our Aryan root race), they
frightfully degenerated and delivered themselves also to sexual orgies. Then, it so happened that on a given day, when the
planet Hercolubus came in the starry space, there was a revolution of the axis of the Earth. Then the seas changed their
beds, and Atlantis with all its millions of inhabitants sank
into the stormy ocean waves that bear its name.

A little time later the new earth emerged, which are these
continents where we currently live perversely. In the beginning, our race was beautiful, exquisite. Let us remember the
paradisiacal people of ancient Mexico. Let us remember also
the powerful spiritual cultures of the central plateau of Tibet.
Likewise let us now remember ancient Ithaca...

There is no doubt that at that time the gods of the Aryans
communicated with people, and happiness reigned everywhere. But the diverse historical cycles were changing, and in
these times of worldwide crisis and bankruptcy of all principles, humanity is finally rushing down the path of sexual
degeneration.

What Determines Our Future

Obviously, we need to transform ourselves before it is too
late. We can and should give birth to the human being within ourselves. We must cooperate with the Sun. We must care
about the solar ideas. We must become solar humans in the
fullest sense of the word.

Since the dawn of creation, love has emerged. This world,
this universe, sprang from the Chaos by means of the mar-

velous force of love. The Army of the Voice,[15] the Army of the Word, also knew how to love, and it was at the dawn of creation and within the same Chaos when ineffable beings gave rise to this current universe. Obviously, only by means of love could this creation emerge. It would have been impossible for this universe to emerge from within the Chaos without the magnificent force of love.

As a proof that love was the cause of the existence of this universe, we have that love flows, as I told you, from the center of each atomic nucleus, flower, solar system, and galaxy.

Ineffable beings have come here to this world by means of love — namely Gautama, the Buddha Shakyamuni, came here because of love, and gave a message of love to humanity; he had his wife Yasodhara. He was happy with his wife. He loved her. And what we will say about Quetzalcoatl? He also knew how to love. And what about Hermes Trismegistus, the thrice great God Ibis of Thoth? He also loved, and this is why he said, "I give you love, within which is contained all the sum of wisdom..." Or what will we say about other men, like Krishna? We know very well how much he loved his wife. All great initiates that have come into the world have known how to love. But this humanity has poisoned some of them: they poisoned Gautama Buddha Shakyamuni. They poisoned Milarepa, the great holy Tibetan. Other great initiates were poisoned. Those who were not poisoned were stabbed or hanged, killed, banished, etc., like Apollonius of Tyana. Finally, the great Kabir Jesus of Nazareth was sent to us, and he was crucified.

Next to the great enlightened men of the past a woman was never missing. The most wonderful Mary Magdalene shines next to Jesus, as Yasodhara, the wife-disciple of Gautama the Buddha Shakyamuni tremendously shines. Great women have always been next to great men. Women have animated them. Women have given them life. Women have incited them to fight. Women have raised them upon the pedestal. Women have guided them to make gigantic works...

15 A term describing Christ, which is not an individual but the combined love and intelligence of all the most divine beings. "The Central Sun is the Great Breath. The Great Breath is the Army of the Voice. The Army of the Voice is a host of divine beings." —Samael Aun Weor

Woman, as I said, is the most beautiful thought of the Creator made flesh, blood, and life.

Woman is born for a holy predestination, which is to bring children to Earth, to educate them, to guide them along the path of revitalization of the solar principles so that they may achieve self-realization together...

Chapter 2
Sexology

"In matters of sexuality we are at present, every one of us, ill or well, nothing but hypocrites." —Sigmund Freud, Sexuality in the Aetiology of the Neuroses (1898)

Certainly, we can study sexology from two different angles, namely from the merely official point of view as taught in the universities, in the faculty of medicine, etc., and from the gnostic point of view.

Allow me to explain sexology in the light of universal Gnosticism.

First of all, gnosis means "knowledge." The word gnosis is used by the official science. For example, you can see the word gnosis in the etymology of diagnosis, diagnostic...

The well-established gnostic currents know sexology in depth. In the name of the truth, I have to tell you that Sigmund Freud started an epoch of extraordinary transformations with his psychoanalysis. In the field of sexology, Sigmund Freud innovated the field of medicine, and this is known by all of those who have studied Freud. Alfred Adler was certainly one of his best disciples. Carl Gustav Jung was also his disciple, and many other psychologists, psychoanalysts, and parapsychologists.

Sex itself is the center of gravity of all human activities. All the aspects of social life gravitate around sex. For instance, let us observe a dance club, a party: the entire party gravitates around sex. The same in a café: everything gravitates around sex.

Today, sex has begun to be studied by some wise people with transcendental purposes.

Unfortunately, however, sex is indeed very popular through pornography, where sex is deviated to merely sensual activities.

There are different types of sex, namely:

· ordinary, common, normal sexuality

· infrasexuality

· suprasexuality

What do we understand as normal sexuality? Let us understand that normal sexuality is the sexual activity oriented towards the reproduction of the species.

Yet, infrasexuality is different. There are two types of infrasexuality that in the field of Kabbalah are described as the two wives of Adam, namely Lilith and Nahemah. Lilith is represented as one of these two spheres of infrasexuality. In Lilith's sphere we find pederasts, homosexuals, lesbians, etc., In the sphere of Nahemah we find the abusers of sex, the pornography addicts, those who deliver themselves completely to lust without restrictions or conditions of any kind. So these are the two spheres of infrasexuality.

Normal sex, therefore, I repeat, is concerned with the reproduction of the species.

In regard to sexual pleasure, this in itself is a legitimate human joy. Therefore, those who consider sexual pleasure as a sin, those who qualify it as taboo, or those who have the tendency to consider it as reason for shame or concealment are absolutely mistaken. I repeat, sexual pleasure is a legitimate human joy, and must not be despised, undermined, or qualified as taboo. By nature, humans have the right to sexual enjoyment.

But let us now study suprasexuality or superior sex. Undoubtedly, supra-sexuality is for geniuses, for transcendental men, for ineffable women, etc. For instance, supra-sexual humans include Jesus of Nazareth, Buddha, Hermes Trismegistus, Mohammed, Lao Tze in China, Quetzalcoatl among the Mexicans, Pythagoras, etc.

All of us can enter into the kingdom of suprasexuality. Nonetheless and first of all, normal sex is necessary first in order to enter into the sphere of suprasexuality.

Infrasexuality

Infrasexuals like lesbians, homosexuals, pederasts, and masturbators are not prepared in order to enter into the kingdom of supra-sexuality. If an infrasexual wants to be regenerated, they must first begin to attain normal sexuality. Once it has been attained, then they can enter wholly into the path of suprasexuality.

For homosexuals and lesbians — who belong to the sphere of infrasexuality — regeneration is something very difficult. Not long ago an homosexual came to visit me; he travelled from Honduras. That man has a very high intellectual culture and liked the revolutionary ideas of sexology as they are divulged by universal Gnosticism, thus he told me with honesty his tragic history as an homosexual. However, he told me about his desire to regenerate so he could enter into the field of normal sexuality and afterwards into the path of suprasexuality. I said to him, "My friend, you have no alternative but to attain normal sexuality. In this moment you are an effeminate, so you have to begin by getting a woman. First of all, get a woman, get married, regenerate yourself, become a normal man. Thus, the day you become a normal male, the day that you truly like females, then you will be prepared to enter the field of suprasexuality. Before that, it is not possible. Since presently you are walking on the path of degeneration, you are a degenerated one..." Well, the man did not get offended. He frankly understood that common sense was on my side. He said to me, "I will get a woman and I will get married, and I will indeed try to become of the normal sex," because he wanted to enter one day into the transcendental spheres of suprasexuality. I hope my friend will regenerate himself. I hope.

On another occasion, a lesbian came to me and said that she needed my counsel, because frankly, women captivated her very much, and therefore she was facing a very serious problem because she was spending a lot of money courting a certain lady, but that lady was, as people say, "fooling around." Well, certainly the lady of her dreams had been seen with other ladies in the street, and of course that situation made her very jealous. That wretched lesbian suffered exactly like a man; she cried, begged, and asked me for counsel as if she was a man. (Between parentheses, she was a horrible, old woman. I do not deny that. It was difficult for me to physically transform the feeling of an extreme repugnance towards her.). Well, I gave her some advice. I told her that the best thing for her was to regenerate herself, to get a man, to enter into the path of normal sexuality, etc. I do not know if that wretched old woman regenerated herself, since she did not seem to have desires of regeneration because she was extremely jealous, feeling jealousy about her lady, jealous of the other ladies who were courting her lady. She felt herself drawn to be nothing more, nothing less, than a hell of a man.

Behold how horrible is the path of degeneration, the infrasexual path. Nevertheless, infrasexuals are not only lesbians, homosexuals, masturbators, etc. No! Infrasexuals are also those who abuse sex, those males who at any moment, at any opportunity, are switching their partner, those males who copulate even 10 to 15 times a day (yes, there are males like that; I know them). Undoubtedly, males like that are degenerate, they are infrasexuals, even if they believe they are very manly. But indeed, they are degenerated.

Normal Sexuality

Let us enter now the path of normal sexuality. In itself, normal sexuality is something beautiful: the man and the woman get together, love each other, reproduce their species, live a moderate life, etc. Nonetheless, they live according to the interests of nature, according to the economy of nature.

Each of us is a little machine – and we cannot deny this — that captures different types and subtypes of comic energy. Each little machine — meaning, each of us — after capturing those types of cosmic or universal energy, transforms those energies automatically, subconsciously, and thereafter transmits them to the inner layers of the Earth. So, the Earth is a living organism that is nourished through us.

Likewise, plants fulfill the same function. It is clear that each plant according to its own kind captures particular types of cosmic vibrations that it then transforms and transmits to the inner layers of the Earth. Regarding animal organisms, it happens likewise: they capture specific types of energy to transform and transmit to the inner layers of the planetary organism. So, the Earth is a living organism.

We incessantly reproduce ourselves by means of normal sexuality because it is necessary for the economy of nature. Sexual pleasure is therefore a legitimate human joy. It is not a crime, an unlawful act as many sanctimonious, self-righteous, pietistic hypocrites suppose. Nonetheless, day by day though our normal sexuality we are just living according to the economical interests of nature.

So, suprasexuality is another subject-matter; this is definitive. To enter into the suprasexual field means to enter into the path of extraordinary transformations. Friedrich Nietzsche in his book *Thus Spoke Zarathustra* speaks frankly about the superhuman [Übermensch]. He said:

> "Behold, the hour of the superhuman is here. The human is a rope tied between beast and superhuman — a rope over an abyss. A dangerous crossing, a dangerous wayfaring, a dangerous looking-back, a dangerous shuddering and stopping. What is great in the human is that it is a bridge and not an end.... Behold, I am a herald of the lightning and a heavy drop from the cloud; but this lightning is called the superhuman... the hour of the superhuman is here..."

Well, Hitler interpreted Nietzsche in his own way. During the Second World War even the most insignificant German police was a "superhuman"; none of them felt small. Yes, in the times of Hitler in Germany, everybody believed they were superhuman. It seems that Hitler, even with very good intentions, did not know how to interpret Nietzsche. I frankly manifest to you that I believe in the superhuman, yet it seems to me that Hitler interpreted Nietzsche in the wrong way.

To attain the heights of the superhuman is possible, yet it is only possible by means of the transmutation of the sexual energies, since alchemy[1] belongs to the field of suprasexuality.

Compatibility Between Man and Woman

There are five fundamental centers in the human organism, namely:

- the intellectual center, which is in the brain, and the most utilized by people for studies.

1   The science of transmutations, whose heart doctrine is the transmutation of the base metal (lead, the impure sexual energy) into gold (Spirit).

- second, the emotional center related with the heart
- third, the motor center, which is located at the superior part of the dorsal spine
- fourth, the instinctual center, located at the inferior part of the dorsal spine
- and the fifth is properly said: the sexual center

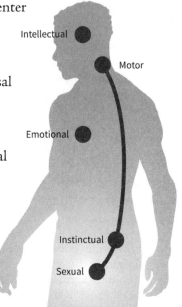

THE FIVE CENTERS OR THREE BRAINS

Again, I repeat, so you can record it well: intellectual, emotional, motor, instinctual, and sexual. Five centers in total. These centers are fundamental for all human activities.

About the sexual center, I want to properly say to you that it is the center around which all human activities gravitate.

Thought [the intellectual center] appears to be very fast but unfortunately is not; it is very slow. For example, if we are driving a car and suddenly in a moment of danger we start to analyze if we have to do this or that, if we have to move forward or backward, to turn to the right or to the left, we will crash and get involved in a catastrophe. The motor center is faster. When one is driving a car, one does not have time to think: one acts quickly and continues on. Yet, if in that moment one gets entangled in a thought, the outcome will be a crash. How many times does it happen that while driving a car, in a determined moment one is undecided if to turn towards the right or towards the left, and ends in a failure? So, the thought center is very slow; the movement center or motor center is faster.

The emotional center is also a fast center, but there is no center faster than the sexual center. When a man sees a woman, he knows in a thousandth of a second if she is sexually compatible with him or not. Amazingly, all of this happens in a thousandth of a second. Young men know this; when a young man is in front of a girl he instinctively, automatically knows if she matches his own "waves." This is done very fast. Therefore, the sexual center is a center that allows us to register the other sexual pole with an extraordinary speed. The sexual center is therefore, the fastest center that we have.

But let us enter in detail into some other factors. Oftentimes a man lives happily with his wife, he loves her, yet he feels that he lacks something. Certainly, it can happen that one does not feel complete with the woman with which one lives. It may be that she fills the activities of the emotional center but perhaps she is not compatible intellectually or maybe she is not compatible sexually; thus, when that man finds another lady that is compatible with him in other centers, the outcome is that which is called adultery.

Notwithstanding, I did not come here to praise adultery. On a certain occasion, there was a hall where some adulterous ladies were drinking heavily; suddenly one of them, a very beautiful woman inebriated with wine, sadly said, "Hail to adultery!" No! We must not praise adultery, because that would be absurd. But, let us study the causes of adultery.

Oftentimes, one member of the couple is not totally compatible with all five centers of their consort, thus since it is possible to find compatibility with another person, from this is derived that which is known as adultery.

Let us consider the case of a man that is emotionally compatible with a woman, but sexually is not; thus, he could find a lady that is compatible with him sexually. Let us suppose that a man is mentally compatible with a woman but emotionally is not; thus, it could happen that he finds a woman that is emotionally compatible with him. It could also be that in the range of habits a man is not compatible with his wife; thus it could happen that he may find in the sphere of habits (related with the motor center) another woman with whom he will really be compatible, with whom he will find affinity. So, this is the intrinsic cause of so many adulteries that result in divorces.

Again, as I already stated, I am not here to praise adultery, because that would be absurd, since I disagree with that lady who in that drunken revelry, orgy, screamed, "Hail to adultery!" No, my friends, I disagree with that. I am just here with you in partnership studying this sexual subject-matter, thus we cannot omit the problem of adultery.

I think that the best for a man is to find a woman compatible in the intellect, in emotion, in the motor center or range of habits, in the center of instincts, and in the sexual center — that is to say, the ideal couple, the perfect couple. And I believe that the ideal for a woman would be to find a man with whom she is compatible; this is how true happiness will emerge.

Sexual Temperaments

Sexual temperaments[2] are another grave hinderance to happiness.

It is impossible for a man of ardent temperament to be happy with a woman that is a block of ice; it simply cannot be. The very fact of wanting to kiss her and in the moment of the kiss he finds that she does not want be kissed, that indeed is detrimental. Now, what could we say if during copulation, during the moment for copulation, the woman is cold? Let us remember the book entitled *Sinuhe the Egyptian*. It was also filmed. It so happens that in Egypt there were places for mummification. As there were many places, filthy places where cadavers were mummified, those who worked in those places for mummification smelled awfully, thus wherever they went they left their stench. So women did not like that class

---

2   The four temperaments are commonly attributed as developments of the four humors of the Greek philosophers Aristotle, Hippocrates, and Galen, yet can also be traced to India, Egypt, and Mesopotamia, and are still used in many traditions today, such as Ayurveda, Unani Tibb, and Traditional Chinese Medicine. The temperaments describe basic qualities of health and psychology, and are combinations of the four elements (earth, water, air, and fire) and the four qualities (cold, hot, moist, and dry).
·   Earth / Melancholic / Bilious: cold and dry
·   Water / Phlegmatic: cold and moist
·   Fire / Choleric: hot and dry
·   Air / Sanguine: hot and moist

of men who smelled so horribly, since indeed, being among decomposing bodies, they smelled like putrefaction. So, do you know what those mummifiers did? Being around the putrefaction, do you know what that class of mummifiers used to do? They copulated with female cadavers that were brought to those places. Do you think that it is very pleasant, to copulate with the dead? Well, that happened in Egypt. Well then, what would we say about a man with an ardent temperament that has to copulate with a "woman of ice," with a cadaver? That is frightfully horrible.

Likewise, it is verily true, completely true, that there is also a temperament that is called bilious: lethargic and slow people. For example, for a woman of melancholic temperament that by nature is torpid in her movements, it is impossible for her to match a man with an nervous temperament. Impossible! Another impossible relationship is that of a man of a nervous temperament could match a woman with a completely ardent temperament.

So, this subject matter of temperaments is very important. Not only is it necessary to have affinity between the different centers of the organic machine — intellect, emotion, movement, instinct and sex — but moreover, affinity of temperaments is also necessary. Only by the affinity of temperaments and by a perfect interrelation between the different centers of the human machine can there be authentic affinity that will bring happiness.

Nevertheless, I am at this moment only addressing normal sexuality. My friends, suprasexuality is different.

Suprasexuality

In order to enter into the field of suprasexuality, first of all it is required to know how to transmute the creative energy. We must know that sex is not only something physiological. We must know what type of energy is within sex. To that end, Einstein said:

"Energy equals mass multiplied by the speed of light squared."

He also said:

"Energy transforms into mass and mass transforms into energy."

Is it possible to transform mass into energy? Indeed, it is possible! Observe what happens with a puddle of water on the road: with the heat of the sun the water evaporates, and finally becomes clouds, which eventually will become energy, namely from the clouds emerges lightning and thunder. All the waters from oceans and rivers become clouds and finally lightning and thunder, that is to say: energy.

The same happens with the ens seminis. What does ens seminis mean? It means "the entity of semen," that is to say, the sacred sperm. In this day and age, there is a tendency of considering the sperm just a substance excreted by our sexual endocrine glands. When the word "sacred" is applied to the sperm, it looks "topsy-turvy." However, if we carefully study the psychoanalysis of Sigmund Freud we will see that he says the following:

"In the last synthesis, all religions are sexual in their origin."

I agree with Freud in that sense. If you agree with him, good, yet you can disagree, too. Yet, I indeed agree with him.

For example, when one observes the aboriginal religions, that is, the religions of the different tribes of Indo-America or Africa or Asia, one can directly evidence that in all those religions, in all those cults, there is a mixture of sexuality with mysticism, that is to say, of what is religious with what is erotic.

One is amazed when seeing in India that type of temples or pagodas where gods and goddesses are found in erotic postures, copulating. What is the most intriguing is that those postures were sacred in the land of the Vedas. These carvings are dully classified and contribute marvelously in one or another form to eros, to eroticism in the Freudian manner or merely, we might say, lustful manner, but nonetheless they contribute to Freud's statement.

Another example is Crete, where great processions were celebrated where the priestesses walked with enormous phalluses made from sacred wood. In those times the phallus was not considered something vulgar like we do in this day and age, rather they rendered it true reverence. They also rendered reverence to the yoni, that is to say, to the sexual feminine organ.

There is no doubt that the lance — with which it is stated that Longinus wounded the side of Christ — is nothing else than a living representation of the phallus. There is no doubt also that the cup, chalice or Holy Grail — by whom the knights of the Middle Ages fought when they went to the Holy Land during the time of the eucharistic crusades — represents the feminine yoni, the eternal feminine. Indeed, the knights of the Middle Ages were seeking that chalice (symbol of the yoni) from which Christ drank in the last supper. Obviously, they never found it. Yet as a memory of that epoch and of the search of the Holy Grail and of the fight against the Moors, the olympic cup has remained, a cup that is delivered to the winners in the Olympic Games. It has its origins in that chalice. Do not forget that cup represents the yoni, that is to say the feminine sexual organ.

So, in the field of suprasexuality, the chalice and the lance are sacred.

The sperm is sacred because our personality is contained in the sperm. The sperm is sacred, because our divine personality is contained in the sperm.

In the sperm the medieval alchemists saw the Vitriol, that is to say:

Visita Interiora Terrae Rectificando Invenies Occultum Lapidem

"Visit the interior of the Earth, which by rectifying you will find the hidden stone."

But to what kind of stone were the medieval alchemists referring? It was the famous Philosophical Stone. That stone has to be fabricated, and there is no doubt that there are formulas for its fabrication. I believe in the Philosophical Stone, but it has to be made. By means of the sacred sperm and its transmutations it is possible to attain the Philosophical Stone.

The transmutation of the sexual libido (to transform the sperm into energy) is possible when one knows the clue. What is important is to know the clue.

Regeneration of the Brain

If with the ens seminis [seed, whether male or female] we can procreate a child, if with the ens seminis we can reproduce the species, if with the ens seminis we can fill the world with millions of people, then it is true and the whole truth that with the ens seminis — that is to say, with the entity of the semen — we can give life to ourselves and become true super-humans in the most complete sense of the word. Now, what is important is to achieve the transmutation of the sexual libido, because by means of the transmutation of the libido we cerebrate the semen and seminize the brain.

It is necessary to seminize the brain, ladies and gentlemen, because it is very well known by current scientists that not all the areas of the brain are presently exercising their functions. Today it is well known in medicine that only a minimal part of our brain is fulfilling its functions. Unquestionably, we have many areas, many parts of the brain that are inactive. If with this small amount of active brain we have reached the creation of atomic spaceships that travel to the Moon, if we have reached the creation of the atomic bomb with which the cities of Hiroshima and Nagasaki were destroyed, if we have created supersonic planes that travel at an extraordinary speed, what if we could regenerate our brain, what if we could place in activity all the parts of our brain, what if the totality of the encephalic mass worked? Then, we could transform this world and to make of it something marvelous. Therefore, it is necessary to regenerate the brain, to seminize it: to cerebrate the semen and to seminize the brain. Behold the clue.

To seminize the brain is possible, like the great musicians of the past accomplished, such as Beethoven, Chopin, or Liszt who were men who had their brains very well semi-nized, men who gave to their brains extraordinary capacities and who utilized the major percentage of their cerebral areas. Nevertheless, in this day and age things are very different: the human brain has degenerated a lot, and sadly we do not real-ize it.

If we are happy in the middle of a party, if we agree with the latest trends, if we are happily dancing and suddenly somebody takes off the popular music and plays the Ninth Symphony of Beethoven, how would you feel? We are sure that you would not continue enjoying the party. What would you do? Of course, you would not go to insult the host of the party, but you would leave the party, right? Why?

In earlier times, when the brain was not as degenerated as now, things were different; people used to dance waltzes, they rhythmically danced to classical music. The musicians were in the midst of dinner playing the most delicious symphonies. At that time, Mozart, Beethoven, Chopin, Liszt were very popular. But, ladies and gentlemen, those were the times of the previous ages, but now we are not in those ages. If somebody plays that type of music now we just say good-bye and leave the party! Why? Because we get bored. And why do we get bored? Let us be analytical, since we are here in order to analyze. We get bored because our brain is degenerated. There are certain areas of the brain that no can longer appreciate good music.

Why did the brain degenerate? It simply degenerated because for many centuries we have been extracting the entity of the semen from our organism. We have extracted the semen from our organism not only for procreation, to create life, to create new creatures, no! We have extracted the semen because we like to do so, because it gives us a great pleasure and that is all. We have been indulging in lechery on beds of pleasure, enjoying lust in an unrestrained way, and the one that has paid the consequences has been the brain. Now it so happens that many areas of the brain are not working. Is it possible to regenerate the brain? Yes, it is, but in order to regenerate the brain it is necessary to transmute the entity of the semen, to transform it into energy. Only thus can we cerebrate the semen.

The Method of Sexual Transmutation

What is missing in this lecture thus far is to say how the brain can be seminized. Well, I have the pleasure to explain unto you a very singular artifice that the medieval alchemists taught to their disciples. The artifice that I am going to teach you was also taught by men of modern science like Brown-Séquard in the United States. It was also taught by Krumm-Heller, Doctor Colonel of our glorious Mexican Army. It was also taught by Karl Jung, and by the Asian schools of eastern Tantra. This is not my invention. I learned it from those wise men, and I transmit it to you, not like an article of faith or an unbreakable dogma, no. If you want to accept it, do it. If you do not want to accept it, then do not do it. Many schools have accepted it, many schools have rejected it. Each one of us is free to think whatever they please. I am just giving you my modest opinion.

The artifice is formulated as fallows: connection of the lingam-yoni. Lingam: we already know that the lingam is the phallus. Yoni: we already know that the yoni is the uterus, the eternal feminine, the sexual organ of the woman. So, connection of the lingam-yoni without the ejaculation of the entity of the semen. Dr. Krumm-Heller used to teach the clue in Latin, so he said:

"Immissum Membrum Virile In Vaginam Feminae Sine Eiaculatione Seminis."

Some modern scientists have accepted this clue. The Oneida Community in United States experimented with this formula. Observe what they did in the Oneida Community: about twenty-five couples (man and woman) began experimenting with sex. During a certain period of time they were ordered to copulate but without the ejaculation of the entity of the semen. Thereafter they were submitted to clinical studies.

At that time in the United States, they achieved the observation of the complete seminizing of the brain, the increase of hormones in the blood, the complete improvement of the organism, the fortification of sexual potency and the disappearance of many illnesses. When the scientists decided that it was necessary for the couples to procreate children, then they allowed the couples to copulate with seminal ejaculation. Then, reproduction was easily attained. And, many similar experiments were done within the Oneida Community.

Anyway, the interesting point of this ancient artifice that constitute the secret secretorum of the medieval alchemists is that the sexual glands never degenerate.

We know very well that when the sexual glands are degenerated, then the hypophysis and other glands of internal secretion also degenerate. Then, the entire nervous system enters into processes of degeneration, and the final outcome is decrepitude and death. If we wonder why the body grows old, it is simply because the sexual glands enter into decrepitude. When the sexual glands become decrepit, all the endocrine glands also become decrepit, and thereafter the process of decrepitude and age appears.

However, if there was a system that avoided the degeneration and decrepitude of the sexual glands, then the entire nervous system could be preserved in perfect activity. Then there would be neither decrepitude nor aging; that is obvious.

Therefore, by means of this fine artifice — namely, the connection of the lingam-yoni without the ejaculation of the ens seminis as the famous doctors Arnold Krumm-Heller and Brown-Séquard stated — it is possible then to conserve the sexual glands actively for our entire life. This means that anyone who practices this system would reach the ages of 90 and 100 and still have the capacity to perform copulation, and freely enjoy sexual pleasure, which is a legitimate human joy, not a sin or a taboo, and that should not be a cause of shame or concealment, etc., since, again I repeat, it is a legitimate human joy.

Now then, extraordinary physiological changes are processed by means of the transmutation of the entity of the semen into energy, namely the pineal gland is developed. That gland was active in times of yore, in very ancient times of history. Back then the human being possessed the eye of which Homer wrote in his *Odyssey*, the eye of the Lacertidae, the eye of that terrible giant that threatened to devour Odysseus and his companions. The eye of the Lacertidae is not a mere legend without a foundation. By means of sexual transmutation, that gland is developed and becomes active again. The eye that allows us to perceive the ultra of everything is in the pineal gland.

Our world does not only have three dimensions as the learned ignoramuses believe; our world exists in a fourth dimension, and we can even affirm emphatically that it exists also in fifth, sixth, and seventh dimensions. This signifies that we have never seen our world as it truly is, and we have not seen it as it really is because our five senses are degenerated and because our pineal gland is atrophied.

There are other senses in us, but which are completely degenerated. We can perceive the other dimensions with those senses, yet they are degenerated. However, if we regenerate our human organism, we will then be able to perceive the world as it is with its seven dimensions.

Thus, the crude reality of the facts is that by means of sexual transmutation it is possible to regenerate the pineal gland and the other senses that are atrophied. This is how we could perceive and have access to a world of extraordinary knowledge and to the superior dimensions of nature and the cosmos. This is how we could see, hear, and touch the great realities of life and death. We could then apprehend through our senses the entire cosmic phenomena as they really are and not as they appear to be.

Transmutation of the sperm is the key, to change the sperm, to modify it into energy; lo and behold the fundamental. Therefore, the time has come to comprehend all of this in depth, integrally.

A Revolutionary Change

If man and woman commit themselves to fulfill that simple formula, the method taught by Brown-Séquard and Krumm-Heller and the medieval alchemists, I could emphatically say unto you with absolute certainty that in the long run the couple would transform themselves into superhumans.

All of us need and feel the necessity to change, of becoming something different. Indeed, this occurs in those who are not conformists, because those who are conservative, the retarded ones, do not want to change. Nonetheless, when one

is truly revolutionary, one wants to be different, one wants
to change fundamentally and to be transformed into something distinct, to be transformed into a superhuman, to make
Nietzsche's doctrine a reality. This radical change is possible
by means of sexual transmutation.

The sexual force placed us into the field of life, and you
cannot deny it. We exist, live, because of the sexual energy of
our father and mother. In the last synthesis, the root of our
life is found in the copulation of a man and a woman. If the
sexual force, the energy of sex, had the power to place us into
the field of existence, obviously it is the only energy that has
the power to transform us radically.

There are many ideologies and beliefs in the world, and
everybody is free to believe whatever they wish to believe, but
the only force that has the power to transform us is the energy
that created us, the energy that placed us in the field of life. I
am emphatically addressing the sexual force. So, to learn how
to handle the marvelous energy of sex signifies to transform
ourselves into lords of creation.

When the sacred sperm is transformed into energy,
extraordinary psychosomatic changes arise. We very well know
what those hormonal vessels of our gonads are, how they
work and how the hormones pass through from one vessel to
another vessel, how finally they reach the prostate along the
spermatic canals. We very well know how valuable the prostate
is, since within it occurs the great transformation of the entity
of the semen, and the hormones are produced to finally enter
into the blood stream.

The word hormone comes from a Greek root that means
"that which sets in motion," "impelling force." The hormones
have been studied by scientists. They are marvelous! For
instance, when the sexual hormones enter into the blood system, they generate wonders. When the sexual hormones touch
the endocrine glands, namely the thyroid, the parathyroids,
the suprarenal glands, thymus, etc., they stimulate them and
impel those tiny micro-laboratories to produce more and
more hormones, and all of those hormones produced by the
glands in general enrich the sanguineous torrent extraor-

dinarily; then pains and illnesses disappear. Unfortunately, in this day and age, the sperm that is duly prepared by the gonads and that ascends to the prostate is lecherously squandered, thus the priceless spermatozoids are not even allowed to metamorphosize into hormones, since they are always ejected from our organism [through the orgasm]. Often times the entity of the semen cannot even ascend from the testicles to the prostate since it is eliminated before it can ascend.

Now, what could we say in regard to masturbators? You very well know what the vice of masturbation is. Those who masturbate undoubtedly commit a crime against their own nature. After the ejaculation of the entity of the semen [through orgasm, whether male or female], there is a peristaltic movement in the sexual organ, and this is known by anyone. In copulation, the energy that the brain needs in order to be nourished is always absorbed from the sexual organ of the opposite sex by means of the peristaltic movement. However, during masturbation everything is different; the only thing that the sexual organ absorbs during masturbation through its peristaltic movement is "cold air" that rises to the brain, and this is how many faculties have vanished from our brains. Innumerable individuals have ended up in asylums because of the abominable vice of masturbation. A brain filled with "air" is a one hundred percent stupid brain. Therefore, we totally condemn the vice of masturbation.

To transmute the sacred sperm into energy is different, yet this is only possible during copulation and by avoiding at any cost the ejaculation of the ens seminis, because as it was stated by the best medieval wise men, within the ens seminis is found the ens virtutis of the fire, that is to say, the igneous entity of the fire.

To enrich the blood with hormones does not seem like a crime to me. To transmute the sperm into energy is very well documented by men like Sigmund Freud and many others. Then, what is important is to totally take advantage of the sexual potency in order to seminize the brain and to develop the pineal gland, and even the hypophysis and other endocrine glands. Thus, this is how a marvelous organic transformation can be achieved.

That which is sexual is intimately related with that which is psychosomatic. Thus, suprasexuality also implies, as a fact, something suprasexual within the psychosomatic. For this reason I say unto you with complete clarity that Hermes Trismegistus, Quetzalcoatl, Buddha, Yeshuah Ben Pandira (that is to say, the great Kabir Jesus) were suprasexual. These messengers were suprasexual. The suprasexual human is the superhuman of Nietzsche.

Man and woman can reach the heights of the superhuman by entering into the field of suprasexuality, by knowing how to enjoy love, by knowing how to enjoy sex, by knowing how to live with happiness, with more emotion and with less useless reasoning. Emotion is what counts, and is more valuable than anything.

So, from a revolutionary point of view, men can transform themselves into true god-men and women into true goddess-women, if that is what they want. For this, it would be enough to regenerate all the areas of our brain, and to place all of them to work; thus, this is how, indeed, we would make of this world something better.

Notwithstanding, I believe that it is indispensable to know that the clue for transmutation is also the clue for regeneration.

The Solar Fire

The wise of ancient times spoke to us about the solar fire that exists in a latent manner within all organic and inorganic matter. Naturally, that fire is inclosed within the seminal system of the human body. Naturally, this fire is not merely a physical fire, rather, we would say it is a type of supra-dimensional, psychological, and metaphysical kind of fire. That Fohat (a word that means fire) is a strictly sexual kind of fire that all of us feel during copulation. Men can unfold and develop that fire and make it ascend from their seminal system along the spinal medullar canal. When that fire ascends along the spinal medullar canal, powers awaken that we pres-

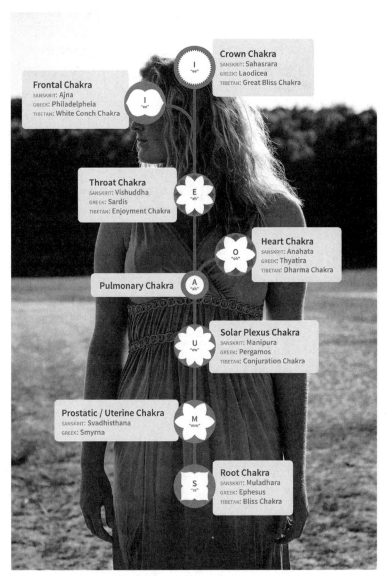

Crown Chakra
SANSKRIT: Sahasrara
GREEK: Laodicea
TIBETAN: Great Bliss Chakra

I
"ee"

Frontal Chakra
SANSKRIT: Ajna
GREEK: Philadelpheia
TIBETAN: White Conch Chakra

I
"ee"

Throat Chakra
SANSKRIT: Vishuddha
GREEK: Sardis
TIBETAN: Enjoyment Chakra

E
"eh"

Heart Chakra
SANSKRIT: Anahata
GREEK: Thyatira
TIBETAN: Dharma Chakra

O
"oh"

Pulmonary Chakra

A
"ah"

Solar Plexus Chakra
SANSKRIT: Manipura
GREEK: Pergamos
TIBETAN: Conjuration Chakra

U
"ew"

Prostatic / Uterine Chakra
SANSKRIT: Svadhisthana
GREEK: Smyrna

M
"mm"

Root Chakra
SANSKRIT: Muladhara
GREEK: Ephesus
TIBETAN: Bliss Chakra

S
"ss"

THE CHAKRAS OR CHURCHES OF ST. JOHN

ently ignore, extraordinary powers of perception or, better said, extrasensory powers of perception, power that divinize. But these fires awaken only by means of the transmutation of the libido, by knowing how to enjoy love. Women can also awaken those fires, by knowing how to enjoy their husband. Many prodigies are performed with that fire. That divine and marvelous fire is called Kundalini by Asian people.

The sages of ancient Mexico used to call that fire coatl, meaning "serpent," because they said it has the shape of a sacred serpent that rises through the spinal medullar canal.

In the east they talk about the existence of seven centers located in the dorsal spine, seven magnetic centers that can be perfectly studied with the help of very special films and magnetized needles and other methods of investigation. The first one is in the coccyx, and when it become active it grants us particular powers over the element earth. The second is at the level of the prostate and uterus, and grants us powers over the aqueous elements of our organism. The third is at the level of the navel, and once awakened allow us to control our ardent temperament and even to act over the universal fire. The fourth is at the level of the heart, and it is obvious it grants us certain extraordinary faculties such as telepathy, intuition, and many others. The fifth is at the level of the thyroid gland (that secretes biological iodine) and grants us certain extraordinary psychic powers, namely clairaudience, that is, the power to hear the sounds of the ultra. The sixth is at the level of the eyebrows, and grants us the power to perceive the superior dimensions of nature and the cosmos. The seventh is at the level of the pineal gland, and grants us the power to see for ourselves the mysteries of life and death.

So, all these faculties are in a latent state within our human organism and can be awakened with that extraordinary fire the Hindustani call "Kundalini," which that ascends through the medullar canal by means of sexual transmutation.

However, in order to reach those heights it is necessary to work with the secret secretorum for one's entire life. Those who do so will transform themselves into superhumans and will be able to enter the amphitheater of cosmic science, into the university of pure science, and will resolve problems that present science still is not able to resolve.

QUESTION: As you stated, copulation is done while trying to not ejaculate the entity of the semen, so what do you want to attain with the retention of the semen?

ANSWER: All one wants with this simple artifice taught by Brown-Séquard and the Oneida Community is to copulate without the ejaculation of the entity of the semen, because the wise men say that through this artifice one attains the transformation of the sacred sperm into energy. So, what ascends to the brain is not the sperm — otherwise we would become crazy — but the energy within the sperm. That is called transmutation. One can enjoy the sexual pleasure without debilitating oneself. Normally after copulation, one feels a bit of repugnance, but if one does not ejaculate, and transmutes the entity of the semen, after copulation one feels desire to repeat it millions of times and happily enjoys it always, without ever debilitating oneself. This is what the Oneida Community was teaching in the United States, and that is what Karl Jung taught. This is what the best wise people of the Earth are teaching in all the corners of the world. That is all!

QUESTION: What is the entity of the semen?

ANSWER: Well, when we speak about the entity of the semen, we are talking about the sacred sperm, the semen itself [the seed, whether male or female]. However, using a most delicate language it is called entity of the semen, and even in a most delicate form (so, people do not get scared) is called ens seminis.

QUESTION: Those individuals who are called masochists, in what kind of sexuality would they be classified?

ANSWER: Well, the masochist is somewhat similar to the sadist, but instead of abusing others like the sadistic — as the Marquis de Sade so happily spread it — the masochist feels pleasure by mortifying himself horribly. Certainly, speaking in the language of the ancient sages, the masochist is an infrasexual that belongs to the sphere of Lilith.

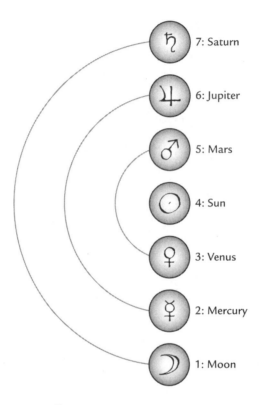

7: Saturn

6: Jupiter

5: Mars

4: Sun

3: Venus

2: Mercury

1: Moon

THE ORDER OF THE PLANETS IN ESOTERICISM

Chapter 3
Planetary Influences

The human being enters the maternal womb as a mere germinating seed to develop and evolve. After nine months, the same seed comes into life more developed, but not fully developed yet.

During the first seven years of childhood, we live under the influence of the Moon.[1] We enjoy the happiness of the home unless some negative karma harms these first years of our life. Yet, the seed is still not completely developed, it is still in the process of development. The fact that a germinating seed has been born, that a child came into life somewhat developed, does not mean that this seed, this child, has finished its development.

During the first seven years of our lives, in our organisms manifest, in the males, the first testicular layer that permits them to be, and in females, their ovaries produce certain cells, certain principles, that vitally sustain them.

Later, continuing its process of development, that seed enters under the influence of Mercury.[2] Then the child goes to school, studies, learns, plays, etc. The child can no longer remain at home at all times. Mercury moves him, agitates him, and makes him restless. The second testicular layer produces in the male particular cells that come to specify and to completely define his sex. The female's ovaries produce certain cells, certain principles, that come to specify and to completely define her sex.

In our development between fourteen and twenty-one years of age, we pass under the influence of Venus.[3] It is stated that this is the age of falling in love. Men and women begin to experience sexual restlessness, because the sexual glands

1   As a planetary influence, the Moon strongly affects conception and early development of all living things, and the basic functions of the body.
2   As a planetary influence, Mercury affects the development of the mind, the intellect.
3   As a planetary influence, Venus most affects the heart, emotion, social life.

become activated. The third testicular zone in the male develops and produces sperm, but it is still not sufficiently mature, because the male who is between fourteen and twenty-one years of age has not completed his process of development. The seed has not concluded its process of development. Therefore, it is very serious for a seed that has not finished its natural process of development to enter the field of sexual commerce.

Undoubtedly, sexual intercourse is not advisable for seeds that have not yet completed their development. It is not proper for a male to copulate in its second infancy (7-14) or adolescence (14-21). It is obvious that copulation between seeds that have not completed their development — in other words, by teenagers or adolescents — undoubtedly, irrefutably, seriously damages their physical and mental health. These damages, if not felt during youth, are felt during old age. This is how and why it is normal today for a man to begin losing his virility between the ages of forty and fifty years old. Why? Because of the abuse in his adolescence and during his second childhood. The first childhood is from birth to the age of seven and the second childhood is between seven and fourteen years of age.

Unfortunately, although it is pitiful to realize it, nowadays many children of twelve and thirteen years of age are already copulating. Moreover, those who are not yet copulating commit the crime of masturbation. Through masturbation they eliminate their hormones, degenerate their brains, and atrophy their pineal glands. This is how they become sure candidates for a mental home.

It is well known that after coitus, the phallus continues with certain peristaltic movements conducive to receiving vital energies from the feminine uterus in an attempt to replace its wasted creative principles. However, when there is masturbation, instead of assimilating vital feminine energies (useful principles for life) with those peristaltic movements, , the masturbator absorbs "cold air," which passes directly to the brain. The outcome of this is idiocy, mental degeneration, or insanity.

The vice of masturbation is, unfortunately, also very popular among the feminine sex. Obviously, with that vice, many women that could have been genial or good wives have prematurely become degenerated, have aged quickly, have lost their sexual potential, and have become true victims of life.

Therefore, it is important to know all these aspects of sex; it is important to know what sex is.

It is absurd for adolescents to have sex, because they are mere seeds which have not yet completed their development. Development concludes at the age of twenty-one. That is when adulthood really begins, the "responsible age" as it has already been called.

It is between twenty-one and forty-two years of age that we have to conquer our place under the Sun. Our vocation, whatever we are to be, remains forever decided.

Unfortunately, those who have reached adulthood ordinarily have not had a specific upright sexual education. They have squandered their hormone capital and wasted their virile potency without having completed their development as seeds that one day enter the maternal womb. Thus, on arriving at the age of twenty-one, they discover that they have very weak mental strength.

Obviously, the pineal gland and the sexual glands are intimately related. So, mental strength and mental force are radiated by the pineal gland. Yet, when this gland has been weakened by sexual abuses, then the outcome is that we are at a very disadvantageous position in trying to conquer our place under the Sun.

Consequently, when we are not capable of radiating our psychic waves with force due to the weakness of the pineal gland located in the upper part of our brain, we fail professionally, or the labor for our daily bread becomes more difficult. Our business fails and those people with whom we should establish commercial ties do not feel our drive, cancel their business with us and we are then hardly able to obtain our daily bread.

If the seed were to develop without interventions of any kind, if the seed were to evolve without interference of any sort, if there was no abuse of sex, then upon becoming twenty-one years old we would have extraordinarily energetic potential and we would conquer our little place under the Sun with great success.

It is good to know that many millions of inhabitants, many millions of people, are struggling to live. There are many millions of illiterate people who are suffering hunger and misery. One could protest against the government or governments and would solve nothing with those protests, because indeed, we should not blame others for our bad situation. We are the only ones responsible for our bad economic situation. We always blame the different political or economical systems, always accuse the president or presidents of the countries, and that is absurd, because we alone are the creators of our own destiny.

It is obvious that if we begin the struggle for life with weakness, if we do not possess the potent psychic-mental-erotic forces as to be able to carve out our niche in life, we will have to suffer hunger and misery.

If that seed that one day enters the maternal womb was allowed to harmoniously develop to the age of twenty-one, we would enter the path of life with great success, strong and powerful, full of health and energy. Yet, unfortunately, most of us have been copulating since our second infancy. That seed that once enters the maternal womb has not been allowed to successfully continue its processes of development without interference.

As to the feminine sex, I will state that women develop earlier than men. Because of this, she can certainly marry at a younger age. Yet, for a male teenager who is not yet a man but a seed in the process of development, to marry before twenty-one years of age, to be copulating from the age of fourteen, is absurd, criminal, and monstrous in the most complete sense of the word.

After the age of forty-two, that is to say, after the solar influence has elapsed during which we were to conquer our little place under the Sun, we enter the age of Mars, which begins at the age of forty-two and lasts up to the age of forty-nine. Whosoever ignores these cosmic cycles that repeat themselves in the human being, the microcosm, undoubtedly does not know how to take advantage of the cycle of Mars and he creates for himself a very miserable old age.

It is good that we think a little about old age, my dear friends; it is good that we begin preparing for old age. It is not right for us to wait until we are old men to then try to arrange our life. Just as in our childhood we had a cradle, a home, a father, a mother, likewise in our old age we also need a house, we need a home. We need to have a source of financial income, enough so as not to perish of hunger and misery. Between the ages of forty-two and forty-nine the cycle of Mars is present, and in this period we should work very intensely to the maximum. It is during this time that we should give a concrete form to that home we need for our old age. It is between the ages of forty-two and forty-nine, under the influence of Mars, that we should create an economic source that is absolutely secure for our old age.

Mars helps us with its energetic potential, but unfortunately, many have abused sex during the cycles of Venus and the Sun. When they arrive at the cycle of Mars, in spite of receiving the influence of this planet through their endocrine glands, they are totally worn out because of their sexual way of life, their abuses. Therefore, they in no way know how to take advantage, as they should, of their share of the potential. The result is lamentable, not taking advantage as they should of the cycle of Mars. Then, as a consequence or corollary, a miserable old age arrives.

Old age arrives and finds us without any secure source of income, and now, instead of being useful in some way or another, at least to our grandchildren, we undoubtedly become an obstacle for the entire world. All this because of not knowing how to live! Because of not knowing how to live! Because of not knowing how to live!

From forty-nine to fifty-six years of age, thundering Jupiter enters our life, almighty Jupiter, he who gives the scepter to kings, the staff to patriarchs, and the horn of abundance to whomever deserves it.

However, if we have not really worked during the cycle
of Mars, or if we have struggled at a disadvantage due to the
abuse of sex, if we have not taken proper advantage of the
solar influence and have not allowed the harmonious development of that seed that once entered that maternal womb, then
the influence of Jupiter, instead of becoming positive, instead
of granting us the scepter of kings, comes to give us misery.

Keep in mind that every planet has a dual aspect, positive and negative. If thundering Jupiter has as its ruler, the
angel Zachariel, it also has as its dark antithesis, Sanagabril.
Distinguish between Zachariel and Sanagabril; they are different. Distinguish between the horn of abundance and the
stick of the beggar. Obviously, whosoever has spent his sexual
potential has spent his vital values and his cosmic capital, and
reaps the consequences: misery, poverty, and humiliation in
the cycle of Jupiter.

Old age, properly defined, begins at the age of fifty-six
with Saturn, the Ancient of the Heavens, and ends at sixty-three. I do not necessarily mean that we must all die at the
age of sixty-three. No, rather, that the first cycle of Saturn
properly begins at fifty-six years and ends at sixty-three. Other
cycles follow.

For example, the cycle of Uranus would then follow, but
then only the internally developed individuals, the great initiates, grasp it. The cycle of Neptune with its seven years is
also for the great hierophants. A cycle of Pluto for mahatmas.
Beyond that follow two transcendental cycles, and lastly,
exquisite harmony and powers for those who have acquired
the Elixir of Long Life.

For the human being of the streets, the cycle of Saturn
lasts seven years. On arriving at the age of sixty-three the
cycle of Saturn ends. For the common human being comes
more combinations; for example: Saturn with the Moon, then
Saturn with Mercury. A similar change takes place every seven
years, Saturn with Venus, etc. That is why we see elderly people changing as the years go by. Take an old man or woman
between sixty-three and seventy years old, for example, with
Saturn and the Moon combining in him or her. They become

very infantile in their way of being. Between seventy and seventy-seven years, they would have a certain mercurial restlessness, certain desires to study or acquire knowledge, etc. In any case, during old age, Saturn is combining in one form or another with the other worlds.

It is obvious that Saturn, the Ancient of the Heavens, is the sword of justice that reaches us from heaven. If we do not know how to live harmoniously with each of the planetary cycles, we will reap the results with old Saturn, the ancient of the heavens.

Therefore, dear reader, these extraordinary, vital transformations of our life are marvelous.

The ordinary human being thinks that on becoming twenty-one, one has come of age. Normally, yes; the seed that was born, that one day entered the womb of life and was then born to live, concludes its development at the age of twenty-one, that is precisely so. Yet, if we were to fulfill our cosmic duty, as was done by our ancestors the Lemurians and the Atlanteans, we would be converted into genuine human beings.

Our Cosmic Duty

What is our cosmic duty? I will tell you what our cosmic duty is:

First: the intellect. Not to allow intellectual concepts to pass through our minds in a mechanical manner; in other words, I will state, to become conscious of all the intellectual data that comes to the mind.

How do we become conscious of this data? By means of meditation. When we read a book, we should meditate on it and try to comprehend it.

Second: the emotions. We should become conscious of all the activities of the emotional center. It is deplorable how people act under the impulse of emotions in a completely mechanical manner, without any control whatsoever. We should become conscious of all our emotions.

Third: the habits and customs of the motor center. We should become conscious of all activities, of all movements, of all our habits. Do nothing mechanically.

Fourth: instincts. We should take control of all of our instincts and subdue them. We should comprehend them in depth.

Fifth: transmute the sexual energy. By means of the Sahaja Maithuna,[4] we will unceasingly transmute our sexual energies.

Thus, in fulfilling our cosmic duty, it is obvious that our life will develop harmoniously. The superior existential bodies[5] of our Being will be formed, built in us, and thus, we will be in harmony with the infinite, attuned with the great law. We will be able to arrive at an old age full of ecstasy, and conquer mastery and perfection.

Before the great Atlantean catastrophe that had completely changed the physiognomy of the terrestrial globe, and even before the abominable Kundabuffer organ[6] of the continent of Mu[7] had been developed, human beings fulfilled their cosmic duty and could then live, dear reader, a thousand years.

When one fulfills his cosmic duty, life prolongs itself. Unfortunately, the intellectual animal mistakenly called a human being became totally degenerated when he developed in his inner constitution the abominable Kundabuffer organ.

4   Sanskrit for "original sexual union." A reference to superior sexuality in which the orgasm is abandoned and lust is replaced by love.

5   Sacred vehicles that the initiate must construct in order to ascend into the superior worlds. They include the physical, vital, astral, mental, and causal bodies that are created through the beginning stages of sexual alchemy (tantra) and that provide a basis for existence in their corresponding levels of nature, just as the physical body does in the physical world. These bodies or vehicles are superior due to being created out of solar (or Christic) energy, as opposed to the inferior, lunar bodies we receive from nature. They are also known as the Wedding Garment (Christianity), the Merkabah (Kabbalah), To Soma Heliakon (Greek), and Sahu (Egyptian).

6   Originally a useful organ that served the function of helping ancient humanity become focused on material, physical existence, it became corrupted by desire and the sexual fall, thus resulting in the emergence of the ego and the fortification of the sexual energy in a negative polarity, and has since been symbolized by the tail of the devils, the tail of Satan.

7   Lemuria

It is obvious that after having lost that organ, the consequences remained: the ego, the "I," the myself, within us. Once having these consequences, we became perverse, no longer wanting to carry out our cosmic duty, and life became miserably shortened. In other times, when humanity was not yet degenerated, when it still fulfilled its cosmic duty, it was clear that life could be prolonged. Any human being could reach an average of a thousand years of age. The results were that the superior existential bodies of the Being were formed in each creature, and it was during this era that many solar men and women, many devas, many divine humans appeared upon the face of the Earth. Today one rarely sees these beings, because people do not fulfill their cosmic duty.

It is therefore necessary to live attuned with the infinite, to fulfill our cosmic duty, to become conscious of ourselves, and to not waste our sexual energies.

We must teach our children to transmute the sperm into energy, warn them that it is a disgrace, a monstrosity, to copulate before the age of twenty-one. Let adolescents know that they have not yet completed their process of development and that it is monstrous for a seed to be copulating. Seeds are seeds, and they should develop.

Therefore, dear reader, meditate on all this. Utilize sexual alchemy[8] in yourselves so that you can accomplish these transmutations of the metallic planets within yourself.

It is through sexual alchemy, through the fulfilled cosmic duty, that we can transform old, aged Saturn into the divine Moon, into that juvenile child. It is by sexual alchemy, as I have already stated, that we can convert thundering Jupiter into the wise Mercury of secret philosophy. It is through alchemy that combative Mars can be transformed into a creature of love, and we can, thus, genuinely be born as adepts.

The important thing is, I repeat, for our seed to develop harmoniously and that it then continues with the processes of ultra development until it achieves the Innermost Self-realization of our Inner Being.

8   The esoteric knowledge contained within the ancient tradition of alchemy. The Western equivilent of tantra.

Part Two
Endocrinology

"Sexuality is the key to the problem
of the psychoneuroses and of
the neuroses in general. No one
who disdains the key will ever
be able to unlock the door."
—Sigmund Freud, Fragment of an
Analysis of a Case of Hysteria (1905)

PRIESTESS OF BACCHUS BY JOHN COLLIER, 1885–1889

Priests and priestesses of ancient times used a staff topped with a
pine cone to represent the pineal gland atop the spinal column.

Chapter 4
The Pineal Gland

The pineal gland is situated in the posterior part of the brain. This small gland is only five millimeters in diameter. A very important, fine, sand-like tissue surrounds it. The pineal gland is a small tissue of a red-grayish color. This small gland is intimately related with the sexual organs. The pineal gland secretes certain hormones that regulate the whole process of evolution and the development of the sexual organs.

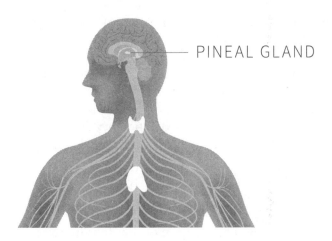

PINEAL GLAND

Conventional science assures that after these hormones have achieved their purpose, then this gland degenerates into a fibrous tissue. They state that after the total development of the sexual organs, the pineal gland is no longer capable of secreting any hormones.

Descartes[1] assured us that this gland is the "seat of the soul." Asians assure us that this gland is a dormant "third eye." When western medicine of the world discovered that this gland is only a red-grayish tissue situated in the posterior part of the brain, then it rejected the affirmation of Descartes and the Asians. It would have been better not to have created sci-

---

1 René Descartes, the famous philosopher and mathematician who said, "I think; therefore I am."

entific dogmas and to have studied instead all the concepts in an eclectic and didactic form.

The yogis of India assure us that the pineal gland is the window of Brahma, the diamond eye, the polyvoyant eye, that through some special training gives us the perception of the ultra.

Western science should study these concepts of Asian yoga. Western science is not the whole science. It is urgent also to study Asian science. We need a complete, integral culture.

The microscope allows us to perceive objectively that which is infinitely small. The telescope allows us to see the infinitely grand. If the pineal gland allows us to see the ultra of all things, then we should study the Asian yoga and develop that wonderful gland. The yogis of India have practices through which one can obtain a special superfunction of the pineal gland. Then we perceive the ultra. To deny this affirmation of Asian yoga is not scientific. It is necessary to study and analyze.

The Asian sages say that sexual potency depends on the potency of the pineal gland. Now we can explain to ourselves the scientific basis of chastity.[2]

There is no doubt that all the great Biblical prophets were great pinealists. Scientific chastity combined with certain practices permitted them to see the ultra of nature.

Gnostics state that the atom of the Holy Spirit[3] is found within the pineal gland.

Biology is resolved to investigate all these things.

The Asians affirmed that in the pineal gland is found the lotus flower of a thousand petals.[4] There is no doubt that this is the crown of saints.

THE PINEAL LOTUS
AND ITS SOUND

Human beings of great intelligence have their pineal gland highly developed. It has been discovered that the pineal glands of cretins are atrophied.

---

2 Sexual purity, whether as a single or a couple. See glossary.
3 This "atom" is a spiritual, non-physical creative power. See illustration
4 Chakra Sahasrara

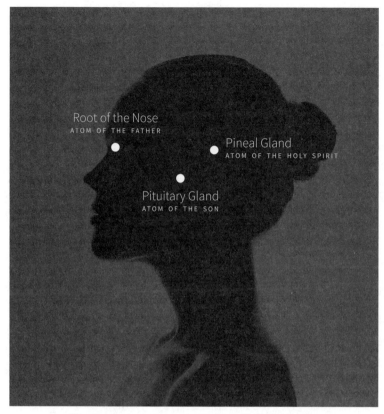

THREE SPIRITUAL ATOMS THROUGH WHICH OUR INNER TRINITY CAN HELP US.
1. FATHER, FIRST LOGOS, KETHER, BRAHMA, OSIRIS, DHARMAKAYA
2. SON, SECOND LOGOS, CHOKMAH, VISHNU, HORUS, SAMBHOGAKAYA
3. HOLY SPIRIT, THIRD LOGOS, BINAH, SHIVA, OSIRIS-ISIS, NIRMANAKAYA

The great phenomena through which the masses become fascinated, so common in India, is only possible when the authentic fakir[5] has the pineal gland full of great vigor.

The blood directly absorbs the secretions of the endocrine glands. The blood bears all the secretions of the endocrine glands to other organs and glands that are then forced to be pushed in a major effort to more intense work. The word hormone comes from a Greek word that means "to excite."

---

5   A fakir or faqir (from Arabic) is an ascetic who performs acts of endurance or the seemingly impossible (such as holding their arm upright for many years), apparantly in an effort to strengthen their willpower.

Indeed, the hormones have the power of exciting the whole organism and obligating it to work.

The secretions of the endocrine glands also have influence over the mind. We now see why the Hindustani dedicate themselves to control the mind. Through our mind we can regulate our hormonal functions.

Some Hindustani sages have remained buried for many months without dying.

Biology cannot remain indifferent to all this. Biologists need to investigate all these wonders of Asia.

Mr. Emmanuel Kant admits a "nissus formativus" to our physical body. The Asian sages believe that the "nissus formativus" is a fluidic body that is in contact with the autonomic nervous system and with the fluid [central] nervous system. There is no doubt that this fluidic body is the [protoplasmic] astral body[6] mentioned by medieval doctors. The human mind and all those purely psychic principles are within the astral body.

The senses of this astral body seem to bloom like lotus flowers from the very essence of the endocrine glands. The lotus of a thousand petals mentioned by yogis of India is a psychic sense of the astral body.

The special development of the pineal gland allows us to perceive the astral body and its psychic senses as lotus flowers bloom from the endocrine glands.

Medical science plays with the mechanism of phenomena, yet it does not know its vital depth. The special development of the pineal gland allows us to see the very vital depth.

---

6   "A sheath of radiant, fluidic atmosphere that envelops the physical form and is seen by the third eye. It registers our passions and desires and is a remnant of the past." —M, *The Dayspring of Youth*

Chapter 5
The Pituitary Gland

The pituitary gland is very small. Biology affirms that this gland is just the size of a pea and that it marvelously hangs from the very base of the brain and harmoniously rests over the sphenoid bone.

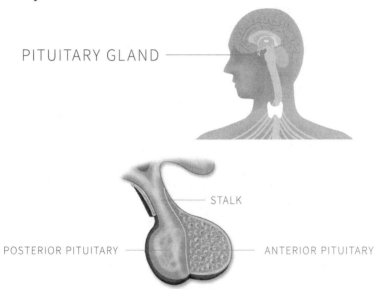

PITUITARY GLAND

STALK

POSTERIOR PITUITARY

ANTERIOR PITUITARY

We find a marvelous trinity related with this gland. The law of the triangle rules everything created.

Indeed, three parts, two lobes and a middle, form the pituitary gland. Behold, here is the triangle, marvelous law of all creation.

Biologists believe that life is absolutely impossible without the anterior or posterior lobe of the pituitary gland.

The anterior lobe of this gland is in charge of administering the size of the structure of the cellular community. Now then we must also know that within this administration there is also regulation and control. This is the only way we can explain to ourselves how life becomes impossible without the frontal lobes of the pituitary gland.

The hyperfunction of the anterior lobe of the pituitary originates gigantic human beings. When the function of the anterior lobe is insufficient, then dwarves are the outcome. Therefore, it is logical to suppose that without the anterior lobe of the pituitary gland, life would be impossible, since this gland regulates the size of the structure of the cellular community.

Some forms of idiocy and blindness are also due to some abnormalities of the frontal lobe of the pituitary.

The function of the posterior lobe of the pituitary gland is to wonderfully invigorate the involuntary muscles of the organism. The secretion of the pituitary also effects the excretion of water from the kidneys.

Doctors use the pituitary to aid them in cases of difficult birth.

Master H.P. Blavatsky stated that the pituitary gland is the page and light bearer of the pineal gland.

Dr. Krumm-Heller, professor of medicine at the University of Berlin, stated that between the pituitary and pineal glands there is a small, very subtle channel or capillary. This channel or capillary is not found in dead bodies. Thus, these two glands are found connected by this fine channel.

There is no doubt whatsoever about electrobiology and the bioelectromagnetic forces. Why then, is a bioelectromagnetic interchange between the pineal and pituitary glands not accepted? The time has come to start analyzing all mystical sensory and psychosomatic possibilities without fanaticisms, prejudices and dogmatisms.

The yogis of Hindustan state that the lotus of two petals[7] sprouts from the pituitary gland. The Western scientists, instead of laughing at these affirmations, should study them profoundly. To laugh at what we do not know is not scientific.

THE PITUITARY LOTUS
AND ITS SOUND

That lotus flower is found situated in the astral body exactly between the eyebrows. The sages of Hindustan give these lotus flowers the

7   Chakra Ajna

name of chakras ["wheels"]. The yogis assure us that the
pituitary chakra makes us clairvoyant. In the holy land of the
Vedas there are many secret practices for the development of
clairvoyance.[8] The Hindustani state that these chakras have
eight major powers and thirty-six minor.

The clairvoyant can perceive the ultra of nature. The clairvoyant can perceive the fourth dimension, and the clairvoyant
can also perceive the astral body. All the psychic and spiritual
principles of the human being are found within the astral
body.

Glandular energetics cannot be denied by biologists. The
bioelectromagnetic interchange of the pineal and pituitary
glands makes us clairvoyant.

There seems to be a certain relationship between copper
atoms and the pituitary gland. Some sages utilize the element
copper to develop clairvoyance. Nostradamus remained hours
gazing at the waters contained inside a receptacle of pure copper. This wise physician (Nostradamus) made prophecies that
have come true with exactitude over time. The astrologists
assure us that Venus influences the pituitary gland, and Venus
also influences copper. Only this way can we comprehend the
intimate relationship between copper and the pituitary gland.

When the Catholic priests who arrived from Spain during
the times of the Conquistadors came across a group of Aztec
priests, something very interesting occurred. Traditions state
that when the Catholic priests were catechizing some natives,
they told them of angels and archangels, etc. After their talk,
the autochthonous priests invited the Catholic priests to eat.
The story goes that among the foods that the Catholic priests
ate was a tasty cactus. This cactus momentarily gave clairvoyance to the Spanish priests. The Catholic priests then saw
angels and archangels; so terrific was their amazement that
they did not know what to do. Meanwhile, the autochthonous
priests smiling said, "These angels and archangels of which
you spoke, we already know them."

The account goes on to say that the Catholic priests had
every one of the Aztec priests killed, considering them wizards

8   French, "clear sight," a term meant to divert the naive away from the
      reality: clairvoyance is imagination, developed and enhanced.

and magicians. There is no doubt about the power that these cactuses have for the instantaneous awakening of clairvoyance to those who eat it. This cactus is the peyote.[9] In the state of Mexico one cannot find peyote that is usable for clairvoyance. Whosoever wishes to find it must look for it either in Chihuahua or San Luis Potosi, Mexico. One must chew on it. The only good peyote is the ripe one. If it is dry, it is useless.

Biology cannot underestimate the peyote nor assure in a dogmatic and intransigent way that clairvoyant perceptions are hallucinations. Similarly, if the first sages who were able to see germs with the microscope were told and assured that those germs did not exist, that what they were seeing through the lens was nothing more than hallucinations, then in this day and age we would still be ignoring the existence of germs. Therefore, we need to be less dogmatic and more studious. We need to be more eclectic and more didactic.

The pituitary gland secretes seven types of hormones.

The value of the pituitary gland in obstetrics is incalculable.

Dr. George Adoum, famous Gnostic writer and grand master of higher mysteries of the White Lodge,[10] stated that the atom of the Cosmic Christ[11] is found within the pituitary gland while the atom of the Father is found within the magnetic field at the root of the nose.

Biology analyzes and studies the scientific concepts of all sages. Biology came from the horrible materialism of the eighteenth century, thus now it is starting to study all the physical, psychic, and spiritual potencies of the internal secretions of the glands.

---

9   "We do not recommend the use of this marvelous cactus, which makes the astral body separate itself from the physical body and preserves the lucidity of consciousness while acting in the astral world. Indeed, what we recommend is practice, much practice [of conscious astral projection], and soon you will act and travel within the astral body." —Samael Aun Weor, *Aztec Christic Magic*

10   The ancient order of human beings of the highest quality from every race, culture, creed and religion, and of both sexes who maintain the highest and most sacred of sciences: white magic, white tantra. It is called "white" due to its purity and cleanliness.

11   These "atoms" are spiritual, non-physical powers. See illustration pg. 29

Chapter 6
The Thyroid Gland

The thyroid gland is of a beautiful dark red color. The thyroid has two lobes that the endocrinologists know very well. The biologists are amaze when observing these two beautiful lobes wisely united by a wonderful isthmus. Behold here the perfect triangle.

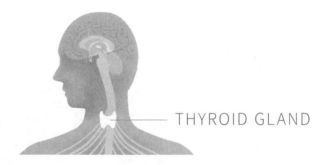

THYROID GLAND

The two lobes of the thyroid gland are found situated exactly at each side of the Adam's apple.

The thyroid gland is vulnerable to two fundamental sicknesses: hyperthyroidism and hypothyroidism; the first one is characterized by too much secretion, the second by too little secretion. Hyperthyroidism can be cured by surgery. Hypothyroidism cannot in any way be cured by surgery. Hypothyroidism is only possible to cure when the patient is given thyroxine (a principle of secretion of the thyroid gland). In reality, thyroxine is an iodine compound that is very important in medicine. Thyroxine is intimately related with all the metabolism of the physical body.

When the patient suffers hyperthyroidism, the excess thyroxine increases intensively the combustion of foods. The result is an increasing rhythm of normal respiration and heart rate.

In hypothyroidism, the metabolism becomes slower. If a child were to suffer hypothyroidism, body and brain development would retard horribly. When hypothyroidism is present in an adult, he becomes mentally weak. His nails and hair grow in a slow and abnormal form. Any physical strain fatigues him terribly and his skin becomes dry, flaky, and somewhat bulky.

Biological iodine disinfects the whole organism. Without the biological iodine of the thyroid, our human organism would not be able to live.

The Rosicrucian doctors assure us that Venus influences the thyroid gland and that Mars influences the parathyroid glands. The famous Dr. Arnold Krumm-Heller, professor of medicine at the University of Berlin, assures that between Venus and Mars there is a terrible struggle that repeats itself between the thyroid and parathyroid glands.

On a certain occasion, an old farmer who did not know how to read or write assured us that he had cured himself from the sickness of goiter by applying to himself a plaque of lead. The farmer told us that he made two small perforations with the purpose of tying a thread or cord. With that cord he tied the plaque around his neck, leaving the plaque over the root of the goiter. The farmer assured us that during the three months he wore the plaque, he was cured

A GOITER CAN BE CAUSED BY IODINE DEFICIENCY OR INFLAMMATION OF THE THYROID GLAND.

radically. He also mentioned to us that some family members also cured themselves with the plaque of lead.

Metal therapy is practically in an embryonic state. There is no doubt of the great possibilities of metal therapy.

We knew South American peasants that utilized salt and saliva, applying it during breakfast as the only remedy for a goiter. They mixed these two elements during the waning of

the moon and then applied it. This was their only remedy to
cure such an ugly sickness. Biology is willing to study profoundly all these therapeutic systems of the peasants, because
we are convinced that many of those formulas that our grandmothers used saved the lives of many illustrious personages.

The yogis of India state that the root of
the laryngeal chakra[12] comes out of the thyroid gland. The great doctor of the Hindustan
Sivananda assures us that the laryngeal chakra
has sixteen lotus petals.

THE THROAT LOTUS
AND ITS SOUND

Many Western scientists laugh at what they
do not know.

The Asian sages state that there is a super-
ear that is capable of registering the waves from
the ultra. They call that super-ear "clairaudience." The laryngeal chakra is the center of clairaudience. This demonstrates
to us the intimate relationship between the thyroid gland
and the mind. If the thyroid gland and the mind are found so
closely interrelated, why not admit that the Asian theses on
the chakra of the thyroid and its conceptual synthesis is valid?
The sages of India state that they acquire conceptual synthesis
by developing the laryngeal chakra.

Physics accepts the ether.[13] The Hindustani state that
ether is but a condensation of the tattva akasha.[14] The great
Asian yogis state that matter is the condensation of the ether,
and ether, at the same time, is a condensation of the tattva
akasha, in which they find the ultimate synthesis, the primordial root of matter. The Hindustani consider the akasha to be
the primordial sound, and that its instrument in the human
being is the creative larynx.

12 Chakra Vishuddha
13 A medium permeating all space through which light and other electro-
    magnetic radiation move; modern science has rejected the word "ether"
    and now uses other terms the explain the same function. "ETHER is
    the Astral Light, and the Primordial Substance is AKASA, the Upadhi
    of DIVINE THOUGHT. In modern language, the latter would be better
    named COSMIC IDEATION -- Spirit; the former, COSMIC SUB-
    STANCE, Matter." —H.P. Blavatsky, *The Secret Doctrine*
14 Akasha is the substance from which every other substance emerges; the
    primordial substance that inundates the entire space.

Dr. Sivananda assures us that with the development of the thyroid chakra, we can control akasha, and we can achieve life during the profound night of the great pralaya.

According to Dr. Sivananda, eminent endocrinologist and Hindustani yogi, by awakening the chakra of the thyroid gland, we achieve clairaudience. If one submerges into daily meditation with the purpose to hear a distant friend, then during the period of sleep one would be able to hear his words. With inner meditation, one can awaken clairaudience.

The secretions of the endocrine glands are intimately related with all the order and control of the autonomous nervous system of the so-called involuntary muscles. The glandular secretions govern, with great physiological-cosmic wisdom, all the wonderful metabolism of the physical body. The endocrine secretions control the growth and development of all the grand cellular community.

The secretions of the endocrine glands control the characteristics of sexuality.

The thyroid gland has an auric radiation that is truly wonderful.

Chapter 7
The Parathyroid Glands

The parathyroid glands should never be removed, because it has been proven that terrible convulsions and inevitable death can occur.

In a very amazing, knowledgeable way the two pairs of parathyroid glands normally regulate all the calcium values that are abundant in the cells and blood. The secretions of the four wonderful parathyroid glands have to carry out the whole labor of calcium control in the cells and the blood. This difficult job is possible thanks to the secretions of the four parathyroid glands.

THYROID GLAND

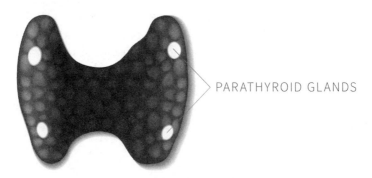

PARATHYROID GLANDS

Indeed, these glands are very small and are situated on each side of the thyroid. Observing attentively, the biologists would be able to see a pair of small bodies the size of a pea.

Astrology sustains that Mars regulates these glands.

Conventional science only sees the glands from a very materialistic point of view. The science of the Gnostic sages goes beyond.

In all atoms there is a triad of matter, energy, and consciousness. Every cell is a triad composed of matter, energy, and consciousness.

Each gland of internal secretion is a truly microcosmic laboratory. The interrelation between the glands of secretion, the wise interchange of biochemical products, and the infinite perfection in which the glands work is showing us to satiation the existence of certain intelligent coordinates whose root we must search for in the cosmic consciousness.

Wherever there is life, there is consciousness. Consciousness is as inherent to life as humidity is to water.

The yearning for consciousness and spirituality cannot be repressed. In Soviet Russia today there are fifteen million Muslims. It is evident that the materialism of Marx has failed totally.

Every machine is organized according to laws. Every machine has its rudder, its lever from which it is governed, and a pilot who controls it and conducts it. Why then should our human organism be an exception?

The human body is a perfect machine built in the workshop of Nature by the cosmic consciousness. This machine has its rudder and lever from which it is governed and conducted. That rudder is the autonomic nervous system.[15] The pilot that controls this machine is the Innermost (the Holy Spirit). Therefore, by means of the autonomic nervous system lever, the Innermost wrapped in the astral body controls the whole organism and all the hormonal secretions.

---

15 The aspect of the nervous system that functions without conscious control to manage the endocrine system (glands), heart, digestive system, respiratory system, skin, etc. The autonomic nervous system has two parts: the sympathetic nervous system and the parasympathetic nervous system.

Chapter 8
The Thymus Gland

When the human being passes beyond sexual maturity, the thymus gland enters into decrepitude. This has already been proven.

The thymus gland is located at the very base of the neck.

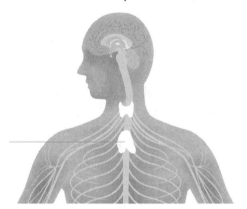

THYMUS GLAND

The thymus gland has a very irregular form and structure.

This gland is intimately related to the mammary glands. Now we can explain to ourselves why the maternal milk is totally irreplaceable.

The thymus gland regulates the vitality of the child.

The astrologists say that the Moon influences this gland. The Gnostic sages want to conserve this gland and not let it fall into decrepitude.

THE THYMUS GLAND

When this gland is active, the organism does not age.

The sage-doctors of antiquity said that when the vowel "A" is pronounced wisely, it has the power to make the thymus gland vibrate. The ancient sages utilize the wise mantra so vulgarized by people today: **Abracadabra**. This mantra is

said to keep the thymus gland active during life. They pronounced this word forty-nine times in the following way:

Abracadabra
Abracadabr
Abracadab
Abracada
Abracad
Abraca
Abrac
Abra
Abr
Ab
A

The word was pronounced so that the sound of the vowel
"A" was prolonged.

Even some doctors are beginning to cure by means of
musical sound. It is interesting to acknowledge that in the
voice of the doctor, in each of his words, there is a source of
life or death to his patients.

The endocrinological science should study the intimate
relationships between music and the endocrine glands. It is
better to investigate, analyze, and comprehend than to laugh
at what we do not know.

When a child is hungry, the mother must breast feed him.
The books on maternity that recommend a child go hungry
for so many hours are a crime against public health. This
matter of the human being wanting to correct nature is man-
ifestly absurd. When the infant cries in hunger, it is a crime
against nature to deny him food.

Chapter 9
The Heart

The heart is truly a double pump. One side of the heart pumps blood in one direction while the other pumps blood in the opposite direction. These two pumping directions complement and harmonize each other wonderfully. The most interesting thing about the two opposite blood streams pumped by the heart is that they do not collide but help each other to advance together.

The heart is truly the Sun of our organism. The heart is the greatest wonder of creation. Nevertheless, there are eminently cultured and educated people who do not know the physiology of the heart.

It is something to admire, to see the passage of blood through that swift river of the aorta. This artery is truly a mighty and beautiful river. We are filled with admiration and mystical beauty when contemplating that grand river full of life. This grand river ramifies into minor rivers, small arteries and then into small creeks that carry life to all parts, to nourish and give life to millions of small micro-organisms (cells, genes, etc.) All those organisms are triads of matter, energy, and consciousness. All those beings of the infinitely small adore us like a god. The smallest creeks of the blood are the capillary vessels. The cells of the diverse tissues and organs are found inside the weft of the capillary networks. Thus, the cells live from the blood streams pumped by the heart.

The cells are composed of molecules and atoms. Each atom is a true universe in miniature. Every atom is a triad of matter, energy, and consciousness.

The Nous atom,[16] which lives in the left ventricle of the heart, governs the atomic intelligences. The suction atoms of the heart obey orders of the Nous atom and transmit them to the engineer atoms that conduct the activity of each organ.

---

16 A term from *The Dayspring of Youth* by M. "The Master Builder [Nous atom] rests in the purest blood of the heart in absolute authority over the atoms that obey it."

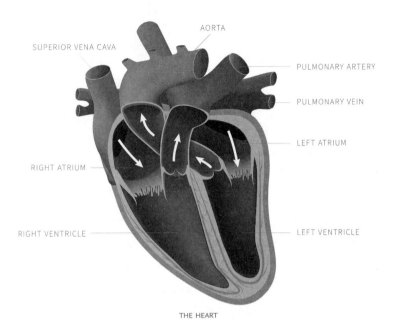

AORTA

SUPERIOR VENA CAVA

PULMONARY ARTERY

PULMONARY VEIN

LEFT ATRIUM

RIGHT ATRIUM

RIGHT VENTRICLE

LEFT VENTRICLE

THE HEART

The atomic workers of each organ obey orders from the engineer atoms and work according to those orders.

There are also a multitude of indolent atoms that cause diseases.

The Nous atom of the heart works under the direction of the Architect atom[17] and the latter under the orders of the Innermost.

The heart is a shallow muscle about the size of the fist, that looks more or less like a pear. The heart contracts, expands, and relaxes incessantly. This is the ebb and tide of the grand ocean of life. Every life has its systole and diastole. Everything pulses and repulses in the infinitely small, as well as in the infinitely grand. "As above, so below." This is the law of the grand life.

In the heart are two wonderful polarities: positive and negative. These are like two hearts incessantly pumping blood into two opposite directions.

---

17 "...the Nous atom knows best what is necessary for our development, as it works under the direction of a great atomic intelligence called the Architect, who places before it the plan it has to follow." —M, *The Dayspring of Youth*

The two compartments of the heart have two chambers, a superior and an inferior. The superior chambers are the atria. The inferior chambers are the ventricles.

The secret doctrine recognizes seven secret chambers in the heart and seven secret cavities in the brain.[18]

There is a right atrium and a right ventricle. There is a left atrium and a left ventricle. The superior chambers from right to left are the atria. The inferior chambers from right to left are the ventricles.

Meditating on the heart lotus, we control the tattva vayu (air principle), and the power over winds and hurricanes is granted. The Hindustani state that the lotus flower of the heart[19] has twelve wonderful petals. The whole intimate functionalism of the heart, its whole vital profoundness must be sought in the lotus flower of twelve petals whose subtle stem emanates from the heart temple.

THE HEART LOTUS
AND ITS SOUND

The vena cava, full of organic wastes, deposits blood into the heart. The right atrium receives the impure bloodstream and wisely passes it to the right ventricle that is beneath. A few instants later, the right ventricle pumps its blood charged with lymph and wastes through its valve to pass it to the interior of the lung by means of the pulmonary artery.

The cosmic intelligences have not neglected anything. It is interesting for the sage to contemplate this whole functionalism. It is wonderful to see the great pulmonary artery divide itself into the two smaller arteries, one for each lung. Inside the lungs, the pulmonary arteries ramify also, until they become minute capillary vessels. Each drop of blood has to pass inevitably through the capillary vessels of the lungs, where it delivers the excess anhydrous carbon and absorbs, in exchange, the exceeding oxygen. The rich oxygenated blood penetrates intelligently into the small veins and then to the larger veins. The two great pulmonary arteries deposit their

---

18 "As there are seven hearts in the brain so there are seven brains in the heart, but this is a matter of superphysics of which little can be said at the present time." —Manly P. Hall, *The Secret Teachings of All Ages*

19 Chakra Anahata

rich blood charged with oxygen into the left atrium of the heart. The blood has exchanged its excess of anhydrous carbon for oxygen. Now with life renewed from the left atrium, the blood passes to the left ventricle and then through the aorta under the rhythmic impulse of the heart and follows at last into all the arteries and sangineous vessels. In all this work we can see the intimate relationship between vayu (air principle) and the heart.

Therefore, the Hindustani are not too far off when they associate vayu (air principle) with the heart. This demonstrates to us the physiological-cosmic knowledge that the Asians possess concerning the heart organ.

Why do the Westerners not want to study the Asian Yoga? Why do the Westerners want to laugh at what they do not know? It would be wiser to study Sivananda, the great yogi. (The book entitled *Kundalini Yoga* is a prodigy of Asian wisdom.)

Those who wish to put their body in a Jinn state,[20] those who want to learn to put their physical body in the fourth dimension, must develop the lotus of the heart. A yogi with his body in a Jinn state can fly through the air, walk on water, as Jesus Christ did on the Sea of Galilee, or walk through fire without burning as many yogis of India do. A yogi with his body in a Jinn state can go through rocks as the disciples of Buddha did.

The lotus of the heart develops with meditation and prayer.

The Western doctors say that the heart produces two sounds, one low pitched and muted and the other loud and high pitched, "lub" and "dub." The physiologists assure us that the first sound is pronounced immediately after the contraction of the ventricles, and that the second is due to the closing of the valves that separate the ventricles of the aorta and the pulmonary artery. The Hindustani doctors go further because they have refined their senses. The yogis of India state that in the heart there are ten mystical sounds.

---

20   The condition that results from moving physical matter into the fourth dimension.

"The first is chini (like the sound of that word, like the voice of the Son of Man[21]); the second is chini-chini; the third is the sound of (the great cosmic) bell; the fourth is that of conch (the internal thundering of the Earth); the fifth is that of tantri (lute); the sixth is that sound of tala (cymbals of the gods); the seventh is that of (enchanted) flute; the eighth is that of bheri (big drum); the ninth is that of mrdanga (double drum); and the tenth is that of clouds (thunder, the sound of the seven thunders that in the apocalypse repeat the voices of the Eternal One)." —Hamsa-Upanishad

If the sounds heard by the Western doctors are true, why can the ten sounds of the Asian not be true? If the two sounds of the Western doctors have been demonstrated, why should the ten Asian sounds not be demonstrated?

Everything is a question of demonstrative scientific procedures. The Westerners have their demonstrative scientific procedures. The Asians also have their demonstrative scientific procedures.

The Asian concentrates mentally and meditates on the ten mystical sounds. The Asian mind absorbs itself in the ten mystical sounds. Hence, the yogi's "nissus formativus" or the [protoplasmic] astral body of the medieval doctors (within which there are all the psychic and spiritual principles of the human being), leaves the physical body in ecstasy within the ten mystical sounds of the heart. This is the Samadhi of the Hindustani yogis. Thus, this is how the yogi transports himself to the most distant worlds of the infinite.

Instead of laughing and criticizing these matters that they have neither studied nor experimented, the Western scientists should study yoga.[22]

21　The Son of Man is a symbol of how the force of the cosmic Christ expresses itself through Chokmah, the Second Logos, which is the Son, and becomes humanized in the initiate.

22　"The word YOGA comes from the root Yuj which means to join, and in its spiritual sense, it is that process by which the human spirit is brought into near and conscious communion with, or is merged in, the Divine Spirit, according as the nature of the human spirit is held to be separate from (Dvaita, Visishtadvaita) or one with (Advaita) the Divine Spirit." - Swami Sivananda, *Kundalini Yoga*

The Hindustani state that inside the chakra of the heart there is a hexagonal space of an ineffable black color. The ten mystical sounds are there.

Western minds laugh at all this. If the Western scientists would develop clairvoyance, they would see, and stop laughing.

Doctors are able to photograph the heartbeat. This is done with the instrument called the electrocardiograph. It is wonderful to see how they totally synchronize all the heartbeats, all the chambers, as if there were only two. This is only possible thanks to a handful of nerves. This handful of nerves, also called the ventricular atrium, automatically synchronize in a wonderful form the two atria in a single weak heartbeat contraction, and the two ventricles in a single strong heartbeat contraction. If the electrocardiograph is capable of photographing the heartbeats, how much more would he who develops clairvoyance see? A new world opens before the clairvoyant, an infinite world of immeasurable variety.

Within the heart is the internal Christ of any human being who comes to the world. He is our real Being.

Chapter 10
The Pancreatic Gland

The pancreas happens to be a gland partially without a tube. All the digestive juices of the human organism empty into the duodenum through the famous duct of Wirsung.

The famous Dr. Arnold Krumm-Heller, professor of medicine at the University of Berlin, stated in his *Zodiacal Course* that the constellation of Virgo has influence over the womb and especially over the barren islets of Langerhans.

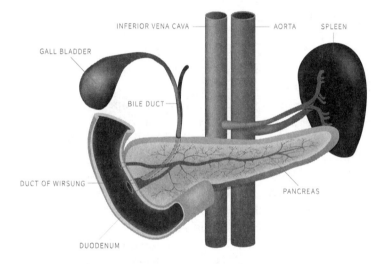

Insulin is important because it governs all the metabolism of the carbohydrates. The barren islets of the pancreas secrete insulin. When the barren islets of the pancreas do not function properly, diabetes develops. The principal work of the barren islets is to secrete insulin correctly, and the principal work of the pancreas is the transformation of sugars. When the sugars go directly to the blood steam, this is diabetes. With the treatments of insulin, medical science has achieved control of diabetes. However, it has not cured diabetes. We have known many diabetic patients that have been cured with the famous antibiotic tea. The formula of this tea is:

· 30 grams of avocado leaves

· 30 grams of eucalyptus tree leaves

· 30 grams of walnut tree leaves

Boil the three ingredients in a liter of water.

Dose 3 glasses daily, one before each meal.

Drink for six consecutive months.[23]

This harmless tea has no adverse effect on the insulin treatment.

The secretion of the islets of Langerhans passes directly to the blood. The Hindustani state that above the navel is found the lotus of ten petals. This chakra, situated in the region of the navel, controls the liver, stomach, and the pancreas. The yogis state that the color of this chakra is like clouds charged with lightning sparks and living fire.

THE NAVEL LOTUS AND ITS SOUND

The yogis of Hindustan that have developed this chakra of the navel can remain in fire without burning. The sages of Hindustan state that within the chakra of the navel sparkles the tejas tattva (igneous ether). The Western biologists state that this is impossible. The Western sages should travel to Hindustan and investigate this. Many skeptical Westerners that have traveled to India came back amazed to see these yogis remain in the fire without burning.

The Hindustani yogis develop this chakra of the navel with concentration and meditation. They concentrate full hours on the navel. When certain Western hypnotists traveled through those lands of Hindustan, Pakistan, the Great Tartary, Mongolia, China, and Tibet and witnessed these Asian sects and saw this meditation on the navel, they believed it to be self-hypnosis. Actually, it is quite the opposite. In truth, they put themselves through all these meditations and concentrations for hours in order to develop this chakra around the region of the navel.

---

23 For additional treatments, see *Esoteric Medicine and Practical Magic* by Samael Aun Weor.

Chapter 11
The Liver

The liver is the biggest gland of the organism. The liver is situated on the right side, exactly below the diaphragm. The liver has a dark red color. The liver weighs four pounds, more or less, and is a little less than nine inches long, seven inches wide, and four inches across through its thickest part.

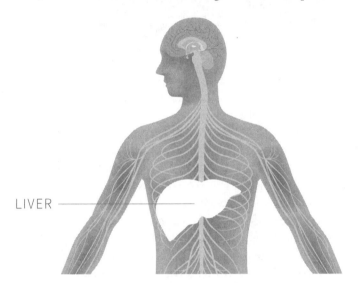

LIVER

Doctors call the liver "the organ of the five." The Kabbalists know that the five is the number of Geburah,[24] severity, the law.

Many mystics state that Christ is crucified in the liver. There is no doubt that the liver is the seat of appetites and desires. From that point of view, we can really state that we have Christ crucified in the liver.

The liver has five admirable lobes, five groups of wise harmonic tubes, five wonderful sanguineous vessels, and five basic functions.

---

24 In Kabbalah, the fifth sephirah from the top of the Tree of Life. Geburah גבורה means "power."

THE BRASS LIVER FOUND IN PIACENZA, ITALY

The number five of the liver reminds us of the law, the Nemesis[25] that weighs on all those actions that are the offspring of desire and of all evil.

On the brass liver found in the ruins of Piacenza were found the engravings of the twelve zodiacal signs. This invites us to think on the five of the liver. It is said that the ancient astrologists prognosticated by consulting the liver. They looked at the liver and forecasted.

The whole zodiac of the microcosmic human being has its own laws and its signs written in the liver.

The lobe of the liver unifies the whole structure of the liver. The lobe of the liver unifies the hepatic functions. When biologists study the hepatic gland, they are able to prove that the wonderful lobe of the liver is something like a small liver in miniature. This is admirable! Whosoever comes to totally know the whole lobe of the liver knows practically the whole liver. The lobe of the liver is a mass of admirable cells united by a wonderful adjoining tissue. Each lobe contains five of six beautiful and perfect sides; each lobe possesses its own set of minute and beautiful vessels, its own secreting cells and its own tubes. A group of small hepatic lobes of the liver construct the liver itself. This is the law of five.

---

25   From Νεμεσις, Greek goddess of equilibrium responsible for punishing evil deeds and rewarding good ones.

The cells of the liver secrete the bile so indispensable for the digestion of fats.

The liver produces the glucose so important for the tissues. This work of the transformation of sugar into glucose is an admirable work of alchemy. There are certain internal secretions of the liver that regulate the alchemical transmutation of glucose and of glycogen into sugar.

The liver controls the calories of the organism.

In its alchemical laboratory, the liver produces the substance called coagulase. Coagulase is an indispensable substance for coagulation.

All five functions of the liver are fundamental for the life of the organism. The liver is in charge of burning in its alchemical laboratory all the wasted and old cells, forming residues that are easily eliminated.

The hepatic artery gives the liver all the blood it needs. The adjoining tissue that enfolds the liver reaches to penetrate inside the organ itself and separate it into its five perfect divisions. Each small lobe of the liver is like an island surrounded by a multitude of sanguineous vessels.

The portal vein carries venous blood to the liver. This vein inside the liver ramifies into a multitude of vessels. Each small lobe of the liver has its own vein. Each cell of the small lobes of the liver is placed in a net of minute sanguineous vessels.

There are also small interlobular veins. Each cell of the small lobes of the liver receives the venous blood proceeding from the stomach, spleen, pancreas and intestines through the famous portal vein that, like a river of pure life, takes nourishment to the liver. The barren islets of the cells of the liver receive their sanguineous nourishment from the small interlobular veins. Nothing is left without life in the liver. Everything receives life.

Each cell of the liver is a true alchemical laboratory in charge of wisely transmuting the food into valuable substances for all the cells of the organism. All the transformed blood leaves through the small interlobular veins to pass to the interior of a vessel named the central vein.

The central vein drains off into that great abundant river known as the vena cava. The hepatic cells that live inside the liver like small conscious and intelligent workers have to transform many substances in the bile to help digestion. The bile remains in the bile duct until it is needed, then it is emptied into the duodenum.

The sages of Hindustan see clairvoyantly that from the hepatic gland emerges a lotus flower, the hepatic chakra.

Chapter 12
The Suprarenal (Adrenal) Glands

Adrenaline (epinephrine) is a very important hormone
in the human organism. It serves to maintain the tone of the
sanguineous vessel walls.

The cortex of the suprarenal is intimately related with the
development of the sexual glands. There is no doubt about
the influence so marked by the suprarenal cortex in relation
to sex. The suprarenal cortex influences the development of
the glands and above all the characteristics of sexuality. The
famous doctor of medicine Paracelsus stated in regards to the
kidneys the following:

> "The nature and the exaltation of Venus is found in the kidneys
> in the grade and predestination that correspond to the planet or
> the entrails. Well then, since the operation that Venus performs is
> directed toward the fruits of the Earth that must be engendered,
> the potency of the kidneys concentrates itself on the human
> fruit."

Undoubtedly, Paracelsus was referring to the sexual
organs with which Venus will never be able to exhaust the
body. He continues:

> "It is natural that the kidneys perform this function, and indeed,
> no other organ could accomplish it better. Thus, when Venus, for
> example, receives the Great Entity, the potency of the conception,
> the kidneys dry their power of sentiment (Sensus) and of the will
> of man."

The doctors of psychoanalysis can prove the former statement that Paracelsus affirmed. The psychoanalysis of Freud
has produced a true innovation in the field of medicine. The
croakers who have not wanted to accept psychoanalysis are
retarded and antiquated.

The Yogis see two chakras in the kidneys, one on each kidney. The sages of Hindustan state that the chastity or fornication of a human being is marked in these two chakras. This
brings to our attention that phrase in the Apocalypse of St.
John that states:

"I am he who searcheth the kidneys (reins) and hearts: and I will give unto every one of you according to your works." —Revelation 2:23

The great clairvoyants see two lotus flowers, one on each kidney. They state that when the human being is a fornicator these flowers are a bloody red color, and when he is chaste, they are a white color.

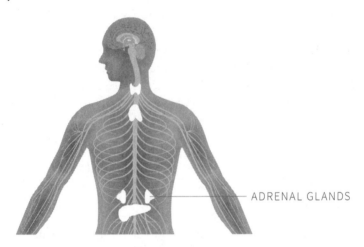

ADRENAL GLANDS

The adrenal glands are situated in the superior part of the kidneys. These small yellow glands resemble true pyramids. Each adrenal gland has its own cortex and medulla that differ from each other in their structure and function.

The hormone of the adrenal cortex controls the sodium and potassium of the blood and the cells.

Psychoanalysis has demonstrated that in those instances of fear, pain, anger, etc, the adrenal medulla secretes a larger quantity of adrenaline that prepares all the cells of the organism to face all kinds of emergencies.

The dog is an animal that has a very fine sense of smell. When someone is afraid of him, the dog perceives the smell of adrenaline from the adrenal glands of the frightened person, and the dog may try to bite the person. The dog, by his sense of smell, knows who is afraid of him.

Excess adrenaline interferes negatively in digestion. Very strong emotions can cause indigestion.

Chapter 13

The Spleen

The spleen is a very important organ in the human organism.

When the hour of sleep arrives, the soul wrapped in the astral body abandons the physical body and travels in the world of the fifth dimension. Meanwhile, something remains inside the physical body. This something is the ethereal double. The double is the lingam sarira of the sages of Hindustan. Dr. Paracelsus named that ethereal double the mumia.

This mumia is a double organism of ethereal matter. This mumia is the vital seat, the vital depth of the physical body, which is absolutely unknown to Western medicine. Yet it is known totally by Asian doctors.

The mumia of Paracelsus is a thermo-electromagnetic condensation.

The vital body has a fundamental chakra in the spleen. The lotus flower of the spleen specializes the vital currents of the Sun. The lotus flower of the spleen attracts the solar vital currents and absorbs them. We see then in the spleen that the white blood cells transmute into red blood cells.

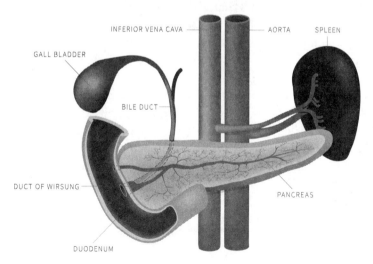

THE LOCATION OF THE SPLEEN

The vital energy collected by the spleenic chakra passes to the solar plexus and then spreads throughout all the nervous channels of the autonomic system, filling the whole human organism with life.

The thyroid gland collaborates in this job with its biological iodine, disinfecting all the channels of the autonomic nervous system.

When the soul wrapped in its astral body reenters the physical body, the body is already repaired. If the conscious being were not to leave the physical body, then his emotions and thoughts would interfere with the reconstruction of his human organism.

During the day, many organic refuses are being accumulated in the canals of the autonomic nervous system. This organic refuse impedes the circulation of the vital fluid. Slumber is the outcome of this interference. Thus, during the sleep process, the human organism is reconstructed.

A medium in a trance state can project the mumia through the spleen. This mumia is then utilized by some disincarnated entities who enter within it. Afterwards, these entities physically condense or materialize. This is how it has been possible to have seen and touched some people that have been dead. This is not a fantasy, because photographs have been taken of those persons that are already dead. The photographic plates cannot lie. Facts are facts.

The famous Dr. Louis Zea Uribe, professor of medicine in the National University of Bogota, was an atheist, materialist, and skeptic one hundred percent. When this man saw, touched, and felt those phantoms that materialized in a laboratory in Naples, he then was transformed radically and became a spiritualist one hundred percent. In a scientific laboratory in Naples the materializations that were made through the famous medium Eusapia Paladino were studied. Thus, the skeptic scientists saw, heard, photographed, experimented, and believed.

Chapter 14
The Vital Depth

The scientists that place doubt in the existence of ether have no scientific basis for their theories. Indeed, they just play with words, with terms, because instead of the term ether they use the term "radioactivity" or a "magnetic field," etc. So, these other terms neither take away from nor give to the reality of ether. In any case, their doubts, analysis, and change of terms will only serve them to study that which is called ether. Most of the time, people fight only for the question of terms of words, etc. Yet, in the final analysis, what counts are the facts, and the facts are facts.

With their powerful telescopes Russian astronomers have discovered worlds in a protoplasmic state. These protoplasmic worlds have come from the ether. We can accept, by simple logical induction, that there are ethereal worlds. Maybe some scientists will not be pleased with the term "ethereal." However, the term is of the least importance. The importance is the fact.

Before becoming protoplasmic, every world is in an ethereal state. The great Hindustani scientist Rama Prasad stated that everything comes from the ether, and everything returns to the ether. If protoplasm emerges from within the ether, then we have to accept that the ether is in the vital depth of everything that exists.

The Asian mystics consider that the ethereal body (vital depth) of the human body has four classes of ether. This does not appeal to the Western scientists. Nevertheless, when the Western scientists study the ether, no matter what name they give to it, they then will have to accept by simple analysis and by their own experience the reality of the four ethers of the Asian mystics.

Thus, the ethereal body of a human being has four ethers: chemical ether, ether of life, luminous ether, and reflecting ether. Each one of these ethers has its function in intimate relation with the whole organic economy.

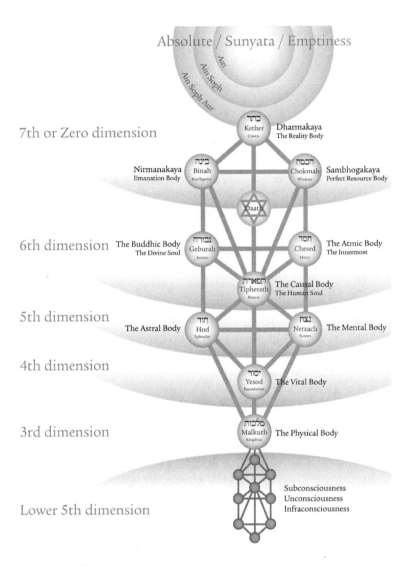

Absolute / Sunyata / Emptiness

Ain
Ain Soph
Ain Soph Aur

7th or Zero dimension

כתר
Kether
Crown
Dharmakaya
The Reality Body

Nirmanakaya
Emanation Body
בינה
Binah
Intelligence

חכמה
Chokmah
Wisdom
Sambhogakaya
Perfect Resource Body

Daath

6th dimension — The Buddhic Body
The Divine Soul
נבורה
Geburah
Justice

חסד
Chesed
Mercy
The Atmic Body
The Innermost

תפארת
Tiphereth
Beauty
The Causal Body
The Human Soul

5th dimension
The Astral Body
הוד
Hod
Splendor

נצח
Netzach
Victory
The Mental Body

4th dimension
יסוד
Yesod
Foundation
The Vital Body

3rd dimension
מלכות
Malkuth
Kingdom
The Physical Body

Lower 5th dimension
Subconsciousness
Unconsciousness
Infraconsciousness

"ETHER" CORRESPONDS TO THE FOURTH DIMENSION, THE SEPHIRAH
YESOD ("FOUNDATION") OF THE TREE OF LIFE (KABBALAH).

The chemical ether is related with all the processes of organic assimilation and nourishment.

The ether of life is related with the reproduction processes of the race.

The luminous ether is related with the processes of sensory perception.

The reflecting ether is intimately related with the faculties of memory, imagination, willpower, etc.

The vital body controls the whole motor vessel nervous system and is the seat of life. Each ethereal atom penetrates inside each physical atom and makes it vibrate. If we definitely extract the vital body from the physical body of a person, this person inevitably dies. It is totally absurd to suppose, even for a moment, that chemical-physical organisms can survive without the vital body.

The very atheistic, materialistic Russians, after having studied the matter profoundly, have become more prudent, acknowledging the vital depth of living matter.

The scientists who are exploring the human organism are getting closer to the ethereal body. They will detect it inevitably and soon they will be able to condense it with some kind of ectoplasm to study it in a laboratory.

All the functions of our organism, all the caloric activities, reproduction, combustion, metabolism, etc., have their base in the vital depth.

When the vital body weakens, then diseases of the physical body appear.

SPACE / AKASH

AIR / WIND

FIRE

WATER

EARTH

The primary elements (tattvas) are the basic
symbolism of temples and stupas.

Chapter 15

The Tattvas and Hormones

Ether exists in an igneous state (tejas).
Ether exists in a gaseous, fluidic state as the origin of air (vayu).
Ether exists in an aqueous state as the origin of water (apas).
Ether exists in a petreous state as the origin of minerals (prithvi).
These are the tattvas of the Hindustani.
When the tattvas tejas, vayu, apas, and prithvi materialize or condense, we have then the four physical elements, namely: fire, air, water, and earth.
Our ethereal [vital] body is formed by the tattvas.
The tattvas and the chakras are intimately related. The tattvas enter the chakras and then pass into the interior of the glands of internal secretion. When the tattvas are inside these minute endocrine laboratories (the glands), they intensify the glands' work by transforming themselves into hormones. Thus, the tattvas enter the organism but do not leave it.
The tattvas also transform themselves into genes and chromosomes that later on transform themselves into sper-matozoids.
Everything comes from ether. Everything returns into ether.
The ether is the condensation of a substance called aka-sha. This substance, akasha, is the first radiation of mul-aprakriti,[26] which is its root or insipid and undifferentiated primordial matter. This mulaprakriti is known among the alchemists as the ens seminis, the entity of semen.
Akasha is therefore the igneous radiation of the primor-dial matter. Akasha is contained within the semen. The alche-mists state that water (semen) is the habitat of fire (akasha). Akasha is therefore the Kundalini of the Hindustani.

---

26 "Root or origin of nature; primary cause or originant; original root or germ out of which matter or all apparent forms are evolved."

In the books of genesis (from all religious literature), the primordial matter (mulaprakriti) is represented by the waters. In the beginning, the protoplasm of any nebula is ethereal.

If we look further, we have to accept that behind each effect there is a cause. Therefore, the ether itself has to have a cause. We have learned from the yogis of Hindustan that the cause of ether is akasha.

The Asian sages state that akasha is a sea of fire. This super-astral fire is contained within the ens seminis (the mulaprakriti of the sages of India). The seed atoms of any known matter are the ens seminis.

Akasha is super-astral fire. Sounds condense through the mediation of akasha. The Kundalini serpent is fire and sound. Therefore, no one could incarnate the Word (Christ) without previously raising the sacred serpent, because it is impossible to concrete and materialize sound without akasha.

The prana vayus are sounding waves of akasha. These sounding waves condense themselves in the tattvas of the ether. The tattvas materialize themselves in the four elements of nature: fire, air, water, and earth. In conclusion, the chemical-physical world is the outcome of the materialization of sound. The chemical-physical world is condensed sound. We do not accept an anthropomorphic and dogmatic God, but scientifically, we accept sound as a causa causorum of the universe.

Furthermore, there has to be a cause for the precosmic sounds. The great Asian sages tell us of a Solar Logos. Dr. Krumm-Heller stated that "the Logos sounds." Indeed, the Logos is the Word.

"In the beginning was the Word, and the Word was with God and the Word was God. The same was in the beginning with God. All things were made by him; and without Him was not anything made that was made. In Him was life and the life was the light of men. And the light shineth in darkness; and the darkness comprehend it not." —John 1:1-5

The Logos is not an individual. The Logos is an army of ineffable beings.

Chapter 16

The Prostate

This very important gland, the prostrate, is very small.
Every man and male of the mammal species has one.
Examining very carefully, we can see that this wonderful
gland is situated exactly at the neck of the bladder.

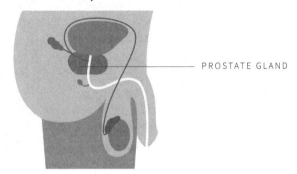

PROSTATE GLAND

Modern science still does not totally know all the functions of the prostate.

The prostate secretes a white and viscous liquid.

The sages of medicine know that in women, the urethra
measures only 35 millimeters and is very dilatable. In man, it
has been proven to be 20 to 27 centimeters in length.

The wizard-doctors from Egypt, Greece,
Samothrace, Troy, India, etc., always gave a lot
of importance to the prostate.

Swami Sivananda, great yogi doctor of
India, states that the lotus of the prostate[27] has
six petals.

The Prostate /
Uterus Lotus
and its Sound

Many beings live in the ultra of nature, in
the fourth dimension, with their solar astral
bodies. The Asian sages state that they have cognizance of
those beings thanks to their prostatic or uterine chakra. These
great Hindustani sages concentrate daily on their prostatic
chakra. They imagine that their chakra rotates from left to
right, like a magnetic wheel, while vocalizing the letter "M"

---

27 Chakra Svadhisthana. In women, it corresponds to the uterus.

Observed from within one's own body, the positive rotation of the chakras is clockwise. The same rotation, observed from afar by someone else, appears counter-clockwise.

Positive rotation looking from inside out at one's own chakras.

Positive rotation as seen by an outside observer.

with the lips closed. The letter "M" sounds as if imitating the bellowing of a bull, but without that deepness of voice. This is a profound and vibrating sound. This practice will awaken the prostatic / uterine chakra if it is practiced daily through many years.

When the prostatic / uterine chakra enters into activity, it grants us the power to leave the physical body, to move in the astral body. This is how we are able to move in the astral body independent of physical matter. In the astral body, the human being can investigate for himself the great mysteries of life and death. The prostatic / uterine chakra grants us the power of astrally projecting the personality.

The peyote is a Mexican cactus that produces the projection of the human personality. With the peyote, any human being can project himself in the astral body consciously.[28] This

---

28 "We do not recommend the use of this marvelous cactus, which makes the astral body separate itself from the physical body and preserves the lucidity of consciousness while acting in the astral world. Indeed, what we recommend is practice, much practice [of conscious astral projection], and soon you will act and travel within the astral body." —Samael Aun Weor, *Aztec Christic Magic*

cactus plant does not have thorns but flowers of a whitish, pink color, and its fruits of a light pink color. The ancient Aztecs worshipped the peyote as a sacred plant. The epidermis of this cactus is very smooth and it has from five to twelve sides that separate among themselves by beautiful lines of fine hairs.

The technical name of peyote is *anhalonium williamsil*. The peyote that is useful for the projection of the personality is not found in the capital of Mexico nor in the whole state of Mexico. Whosoever wants to find legitimate peyote would have to look for it in Chihuahua among the Taumara Indians or in San Luis Potosi in Northern Mexico.

The plant must be chewed. This plant must be ripe and fresh. It is useless if it is dried. In the moment of chewing the cactus, the disciple must be concentrated on his Innermost, that is to say, on his own internal Being. One must, in this moment, assume a mystical attitude. Let us remember that our internal Being is God himself. In those moments, while chewing the peyote, we must fall asleep concentrating on our internal God. The exact outcome will be astral projection. Then we will travel in the astral body. This is how we will be able to see, hear, and touch the things of the ultra of nature.

The things seen by the peyote are not hallucinations, as ignorant people believe. The intellectuals know that there is a fourth dimension. Any educated person knows this.

Science has demonstrated that the perception of our five senses is very limited. Beneath the color red is found the gamma of the infrared; above the color violet is found the gamma of the ultraviolet. Science does not ignore this.

The loss of elasticity in the crystalline (lens of the eye) prevents the image from forming in the retina. This is what is called bad focusing. In reality, no one perceives the object in itself, but merely the image of the object. Short-sightedness prevents us from seeing the image of a faraway object. There is also Daltonism. The inflammation of the retina causes Daltonism; this is the confusion of colors. In conclusion, the human eye only perceives sensory images. That is all.

However, there are ultra-sensory images in the ultra, and senses conditioned to receive those images. Those senses enter into activity with the peyote. This is how we can perceive the images of the ultra.

Therefore, if those images of the ultra were hallucinations, as the ignorant people say, then the sensory images that form in the retina would also be hallucinations.

We need to let go of eighteenth century materialism. We need to be more analytic, less dogmatic, and more didactic.

Matter is condensed energy. Energy condenses into different states. Factually, there are masses whose grade of energetic vibration is so fast that their sensory images escape the perception of our five senses. Likewise, there are masses whose grade of vibration is so slow that they submerge beneath the limits of our sensory perception. There are physical masses that the human being is normally incapable of perceiving above and below the limits of our external sensory perception.

Only with the powers of our astral body can we perceive other dimensions of the universe and life. The peyote has the power to put into activity, even if it is momentary, those wonderful faculties that allow us to investigate the fourth dimension of nature.

Many people might state that they do not believe. However, this is not a subject matter to believe or not to believe. These are scientific matters that need logical analysis and scientific investigation, free of prejudices and fanaticism. It needs experimentation.

One must profoundly explore all the recondite parts of the human being. We must not confine ourselves inside intransigent scientific dogmas. We need to be more liberal in our analysis. Materialism has already failed in Soviet Russia. The failure of materialism is proven by the fact that there are fifteen million Muslims in Russia.

The perceptions of the ultra are as natural as the perceptions of the five ordinary senses. They are not hallucinated deliriums, as ignorant people believe. This is not about convulsive pathologic suggestions from ignorant, fanatic, halluci-

nated people. We need more study and less pride. The perceptions of the ultra exist and must be studied.

The uncivilized natives in the Republic of Haiti who
practice voodoo can be criticized because of their practices of
black magic and because of their lack of intellectual culture.
Yet indeed, we do not have the scientific basis of any kind to
judge, with all logical preciseness, their hypersensory perceptions.

We do not deny that in many psychics there are psychic
paroxysms accompanied by convulsions, pythonism with all
its manifestations etc., etc. The pythonic crisis, the so-called
crisis of Loa of the Haitians, the ecstatic-convulsive crises
during which they have super-sensory perception, are in depth
absolutely unknown to science and forensic psychiatry.

If we put aside our intellectual pride, we will arrive at the
conclusion that we can analyze sensory phenomena, objective
states of the human organism. However, conventional science
still has no authority in order to judge, in a total form, the
perceptions of the ultra.

With no doubt, fanaticism is the worst enemy of reasoning and logic. However, people from universities also fall into
fanaticism. When people from universities laugh at clairvoyants and at convulsive-ecstatic crises, when we believe that all
the visions seen during one of those crises are hallucinations,
madness, etc., by dint of pride, we fall into the state of fanaticism and ignorance. Our fanaticism is hallucinated by the theories that we have read and by the intellectual principles with
which we mold our intellect.

If we believe that others are ignorant, likewise they may
categorize us as ignorant, even if we believe that we are very
cultured.

We are not the masters of knowledge. Therefore, convulsive and pathologic intellectual suggestion can convert an
intellectual into an intolerable fanatic.

Many natives of Haiti who practice voodoo perceive with
their clairvoyance tremendous realities of the ultra of nature.
In order to discuss something, it is necessary to know about
it. Therefore, the opinion of a critic has no value whatsoever if

he has not a complete knowledge of the subject matter. People from universities do not practice voodoo; they do not know it. Therefore, they do not have a complete knowledge of the subject matter.

People from universities see the natives of Haiti in their pythonismic crisis. Yet, they do not know anything about the things those natives see in their trances, because people from universities have not gone through those famous pythonic crises. The only thing they can do is to launch opinions without basis, because they have no complete knowledge of the case.

The prostatic / uterine chakra grants every human being the power to project himself into the astral body consciously. The important thing is to develop this chakra.

We repeat, this is not a subject matter to believe or not to believe. The important thing is to study, analyze, and experience.

When any intellectual person states, "I do not believe in that," they are demonstrating that they are superstitious. A cultured, studious, and investigative person states, "I will study it. I will experience it. I will analyze it."

Chapter 17
The Testicles and the Ovaries

The internal secretions of the testicles and the ovaries are definitive for the life of the human being on the earth. The fundamental differences between men and women are due to the secretions of the testicles and the ovaries.

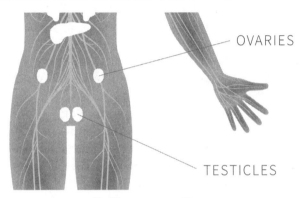

THE TESTICLES AND THE OVARIES

Only one spermatozoon and one ovum are necessary for the reproduction of the human species. That is all. Therefore, scientifically, we do not see the reason why the male enjoys spilling millions of spermatozoa, when indeed only one is needed to fecundate.

The egg is big, round, and possesses its own nucleus with a thick protoplasm that has an aspect of a yolk.

The spermatozoon is different; it is long and slim, has a pointed and oval body where the fundamental nucleus is found. The spermatozoon has a long tail resembling a tad-pole.

The movement of the feminine egg within the waters of life is slow. The feminine egg waits patiently for the masculine spermatozoon to find it. The male's spermatozoon, propelling itself with its fish tail within the waters of the sexual chaos, navigates very far in search of the egg that awaits it.

The biologists do not know with scientific exactitude the causa causorum that unites the spermatozoon to the egg. For science, this is an enigma. As in everything, scientists launch hypotheses which are more or less their scientific opinions. Thus, it is believed that the protoplasm of the egg possesses a great chemical attraction to the sperm, etc. All these are hypotheses but nothing more than hypotheses! Even if this hypothesis were to be true, it would still not resolve the enigma.

We cannot logically admit that a chemical reaction can be performed by itself without a conscious, controlling principle.

From the protoplasm of the egg, we will go on to the energetics of the egg.

Logic invites us to accept energy as a magnetic field of attraction to the egg. Logic invites us to accept electricity as a dynamic force impelling the spermatozoon to the egg.

In the final synthesis, the atom is an exponent of energies. The electromagnetic forces of every protoplasm are a tremendous reality. Everything radiates. We admit the mechanics of the phenomena, yet we need an explanation of the laws that regulate such mechanics.

Indeed, the cosmic consciousness is the primary intelligence that establishes the union of the spermatozoon with the ovum. We cannot accept an intelligent phenomenon without an intelligent cause. Facts are facts and before the facts we must surrender.

Gnostics talk about the Third Logos.[29] Science must know that the Third Logos is that primary intelligence. The Third Logos is not an individual. The Third Logos of the Gnostics is the primary intelligence of nature.

The creative energy of the Third Logos is that primary intelligence of nature that unites the spermatozoon with the ovum. The creative energy of the Third Logos bipolarizes itself into positive and negative.

The spermatozoon is the exponent of the positive forces of the Third Logos. The ovum is the exponent of the negative forces of the Third Logos. Both poles of the energies unite in order to create. The law is the law.

---

29 Greek λόγος, from λέγω lego "I say," means "word."

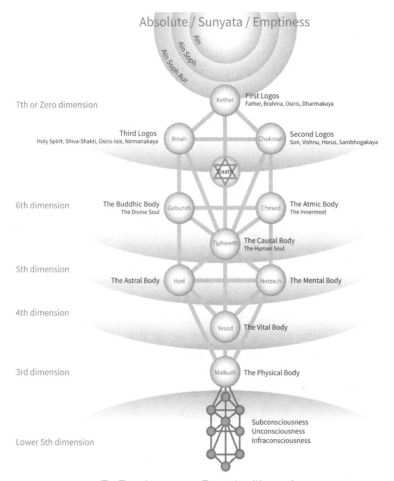

THE THIRD LOGOS ON THE TREE OF LIFE (KABBALAH)

The decapitation of John the Baptist occurs when the spermatozoon enters the ovum.

The materialist partisans of Darwinism point out the similarities of all animals in the embryonic state, including the human being. This they do in order to prove that the more complex and superior species have emerged by evolution and transformation from the more simple and inferior species. Nonetheless, we, the Gnostics, consider that the similarities of the animals in their embryonic state, including the human being, are revealing to satiety two things: first, the unity of life, second, an original genetic seed. The seed of all that exists sleeps as an original seed within the seminal atoms of the grand universal life.

The creative energy of the Third Logos makes the waters of life, the universal semen, become fecund. This is how the germs of every existence sprout.

Every species has a universal prototype within the original chaos. In the famous blastoderm,[30] there are three layers of absolutely different cells. The first one is the internal, the second one is middle, and the third one is the external. The spermatozoon united with the ovum multiplies by cellular division; this is how that cellular community called the blastoderm is created.

The gelatinous state of the spermatozoon and the ovum demonstrate that in the beginning of the universe, life was subtle, fluidic and gelatinous, and afterwards more gross and hard. This reminds us of the great turtle worshipped by the Mayan Indians. First, it is subtle and gelatinous, afterwards its hard shell full of constellations and worlds appears. As above so below... Fortunately, the scientists in Russia have discovered worlds in a protoplasmic state.

The spermatozoon and the ovum must pass through a process of evolution and development before becoming a new vehicle for the human soul.

The internal causes for the maturation of the ovum-sperm are very unknown to biology.

The intimate causes for the maturation of a universe in a protoplasmic state are an enigma to astronomy and astrophysics.

It would be very interesting if the scientists would resolve the enigma of the chromosomes. Why does the egg have only 48 chromosomes?[31] Why does the spermatozoon also have 48 chromosomes? Enigmas! Enigmas! Enigmas!

What is the intimate reason for the spermatozoon and the ovum losing, during their maturation, the same exact

30 "The layer of cells forming the wall of the blastocyst in mammals and the blastula in lower animals during the early stages of embryonic development." — Mosby's Medical Dictionary

31 Modern science has so far only found 46. There are two more related to the vital body, the subtle aspect of the physical body (fourth dimension).

mathematical number of 24 chromosomes each? Who is the one who endures the inconvenience of making such a perfect mathematical calculation?

When a spermatozoon unites with an ovum after their maturation, for what reasons do they together come to have the same original number of 48 chromosomes?

There are two mathematical operations in this, namely: subtraction and addition. The basic capital is 48. Can there be mathematical operations without a mathematical intelligence? All of this is showing us through simple logical deduction the reality of the primary intelligence of nature that we, the Gnostics, call the Third Logos.

After the human spermatozoon has fecundated the human ovum, the uterus gestates for nine months.

The cell of the ovum and sperm has two nuclei—one from the sperm and the other from the ovum. These two nuclei join themselves wisely. The protoplasm of these nuclei mix together.

There is a sphere of attraction inside the ovum-sperm cell. The great sphere of attraction also bipolarizes, obeying the primary intelligence. Each of the two polarities of that sphere of attraction contract and expand the nucleus, converting it into the mitotic spindle.

The chromosomes and genes are mixed in the center of the nuclei mitotic spindle. The genes are inside the chromosomes. The genes give us the heredity of our father and mother. Nevertheless, not everything that the human being receives is hereditary. Terrible murderers have been born from virtuous families, and great geniuses have been born from mediocre families.

If a clairvoyant examines an already mature spermatozoon when it directs itself into the ovum, then the clairvoyant will see in the superior vortex of the spermatozoon a very important atom. This is the seed atom. This atom is a trio of matter, energy, and consciousness. A very fine thread, united to a certain sum of energetic values of nature, comes from that atom. Those values are related to the soul, to the Being.

Within space, we are points who accede to serve as vehicles of determined sums of values from nature. Therefore, death is just a subtraction of fractions. Once the subtraction is done (death), only those values remain. Those values of nature are electromagnetic. Once the physical body is dead, those values rebuild another one through new biological processes, whose steps are followed very carefully by biology. This is the law of reincorporation. The law is the law, and the law is fulfilled.

There is energy inside the physical atoms of the ovum-sperm. This energy forms the mumia. The atoms of the astral body abide inside each atom of the mumia. (We know Theosophy's septuple constitution[32] of the human being; however, here we are just synthesizing).

We are not setting down dogmas. We are analyzing. Science has already been capable of the materialization of the astral body in some laboratories. Facts are facts, and before the facts we must surrender.

The virtues and defects of every human being depend upon the quality of values that reincarnate in them. For instance, a dervish Moor who lived in Spain during the era of the Moorish dominion over Spain studied the Qur'an. He read the Qur'an and studied the Bible. The outcome was that the knowledge ingested in him, and he became full of skepticism. That dervish Moor died full of doubts. At a later date, the values from that dervish Moor reincorporated and became a man named Voltaire.

Any human being can develop clairvoyance and see the values of the consciousness evolving throughout space-time.

The great American physiologist Brown-Séquard, mentioned by Dr. Krumm-Heller, invented a system of healing that was judged by many people as immoral. This system

32 The septenary constitution of the human being is:
1. Atman: the Innermost
2. Buddhi: the consciousness, the divine soul
3. Superior manas: the human soul, willpower, causal body
4. Inferior manas: the mind, mental body
5. Kama-rupa: the body of desires, the astral body
6. Linga-sarira: the vital (ethereal) body
7. Sthula-sarira: the physical body

consists of exciting the sexual organ without reaching the orgasm and the spilling of the semen [the seed, whether male or female]. In this case, the semen is cerebrated and the cerebrum is semenized. Thus the semen is assimilated inside the organism and the nervous system nourishes and fortifies itself totally. This system would not be an obstacle for the reproduction of the species. A spermatozoon can easily escape from the organism without the necessity of spilling the millions of spermatozoa that are lost in a seminal ejaculation.

The system of Brown-Séquard is known in Italy as Karezza. This is the Arcanum A.Z.F.[33]

Dr. Krumm-Heller stated that impotence can be cured with this system.

On page 174 of *Rosicrucian Novel,* Dr. Krumm-Heller states the following:

> "The Rosicrucian studies teach us that the semen is the astral liquid of the human being; it is life; it encloses power. Yet, it is so immense a power, that knowing how to drive it, one can achieve everything. This is why it is so important to know the Rosicrucian secrets, because one possesses a powerful weapon against the adversities of destiny."

On page 172 of the same novel, Dr. Krumm-Heller states the following:

> "The Rosicrucian magician feels the same nervous arousing as any human being full of desire. If men would know what they are capable of doing during this moment of nervousness, I am sure they would do anything but to follow the woman."

The Aztec sages of ancient Mexico knew very well what can be done in that moment of nervousness. Men and women were naked on the stone patios of the Aztec temples. For months they loved one other there, uniting sexually. Those couples knew how to withdraw from the sexual act before the orgasm. This is how they avoided the ejaculation of their semen. These couples did not allow the wonderful semen

---

33 The practice of sexual transmutation as couple (male-female), a technique known in Tantra and Alchemy. Arcanum refers to a hidden truth or law. A.Z.F. stands for A (agua, water), Z (azufre, sulfur), F (fuego, fire), and is thus: water + fire = consciousness. . Also, A (azoth = chemical element that refers to fire). A & Z are the first and last letters of the alphabet thus referring to the Alpha & Omega (beginning & end).

to escape out of their organism. This is the famous Italian Karezza, the system of the great American Brown-Séquard.

The awakening of the Kundalini is achieved with Brown-Séquard's system. Indeed, surgeons will not be able to find the Kundalini with the surgical scalpel. Yet, if they were to practice the Gnostic-Rosicrucian exercises, then they would become clairvoyant. Any clairvoyant doctor can see the Kundalini.

The Kundalini is the Aztec serpent Quetzacoatl; that is, the fire of the Holy Spirit, the igneous serpent of our magical powers.

The clairvoyant yogi sees a lotus flower with four wonderful petals situated exactly between the sexual organs and the anus.

This lotus flower with four wonderful petals is the church of Ephesus, the Muladhara chakra. The Kundalini is found inside this chakra. The Kundalini has the shape of a sacred serpent; it is a solar spiritual, fiery serpent that can only be seen with clairvoyance. It cannot be found with the surgical scalpel because it is not material.

The Kundalini is concentrated akasha. Akasha is the cause of ether and the agency of sound. Only those who raise the akashic serpent through the canalis centralis of the spinal medulla can incarnate the Word.

The Kundalini develops, evolves, and progresses inside the aura of the Solar Logos.

The chakra of the sexual organs is the center of the prithvi tattva (the petrous ether). Whosoever controls the prithvi tattva can control earthquakes.

There are seven magnetic centers within the spinal medulla. These seven centers of the spinal medulla are connected with the seven important plexuses of the autonomic nervous system. All the tattvic powers are within those seven centers. The flaming akasha opens those seven tattvic centers of the spinal medulla. This is how we become masters of the tattvas.

1. The first magnetic center of the spinal medulla is the abode of the tattva prithvi, the power of sex.

EPHESUS / MULADHARA AND ITS SOUND

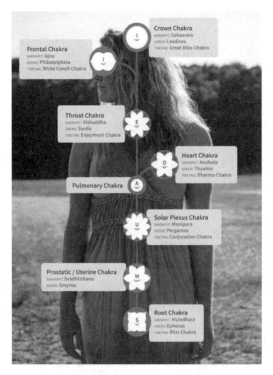

PRIMARY CHAKRAS RELATED TO SPIRITUAL DEVELOPMENT

2. The second one corresponds to the prostatic / uterine chakra. This is the church of the tattva apas (water), liquid ether.

3. The third chakra is at the height of the navel. It is related to the solar plexus. This is the church of the tattva tejas (igneous ether), universal fire.

4. The fourth center of the spinal medulla corresponds to the chakra of the heart. This is the sacred abode of the tattva vayu (gaseous ether).

These are the four inferior tattvic centers of the human temple.

The tower of the temple is the neck and the head. The following three superior tattvic centers are in this human tower.

5. The fifth center is the larynx. This is the church of the Word. Sound cannot exist without akasha. The Kundalini becomes creative with the Word.

6. The sixth magnetic center is related with the frontal chakra. This is the center of clairvoyance. When the Kundalini opens this center the human being becomes clairvoyant. This is how one can see the ultra.

7. The seventh tattvic center is the chakra of the thousand petals situated in the pineal gland. When the Kundalini opens this chakra we receive polyvoyance, omniscience, etc.

We receive all these powers with the system of Brown-Séquard. The only requisite is never to spill the semen during our whole life. Brown-Séquard's system is the Arcanum A.Z.F.

The famous North American Kabbalist Manly P. Hall, mentioned by the Dr. Francis A. Propato, states in his book *Occult Anatomy* the following,

"Those who are incapable of raising the fire of the spinal medulla through their sushumna channel will be cast down into a lateral kingdom similar to that of today's apes (monkeys, gorillas, etc.)."

The sushumna channel runs lengthwise and inwards within the medullar canal.

The Arcanum A.Z.F. must only be practiced between husband and wife in legitimately constituted homes.

Those men who practice the Arcanum A.Z.F. with many women commit the serious crime of adultery. The adulterous man will never achieve the awakening of the Kundalini and the tattvic powers. Likewise the same will happen with women; the adulterous woman who practices the Arcanum A.Z.F. with many men will never awaken the Kundalini or the tattvic powers.

The Gnostic initiates who adulterate lose their powers.

God is the Innermost. God is the inner Being of each human being who comes to the world. God is a divine hermaphrodite, male-female. God does not need a spouse to light the fire. Yet, the human being is not God. Human beings cannot light their fires without a spouse. The human being needs a spouse to enlighten the fires, because the human being is not God.

The human being must put aside the pride of believing that he is a god, because the human being is nothing more than a miserable slug that wallows in the mud of the earth. The great female yogi Helena Petrovna Blavatsky, after becoming the widow of the Count Blavatsky, had to remarry with Colonel Olcott in order to awaken her Kundalini and achieve the tattvic powers.

The Sacred Order of Tibet teaches their disciples the Arcanum A.Z.F.

In the mysteries of Egypt, the Arcanum A.Z.F. was taught to the initiates, and those who would divulge this great Arcanum were condemned to death. They were taken to a patio, and there, against a wall, they were decapitated. Their hearts were stripped away and their ashes were thrown to the four winds.

On the patios of the temple of the Aztecs, naked men and women participated in the Arcanum A.Z.F. for entire months. Whosoever ejaculated the semen, by any chance, was condemed to death for profaning the temple. Afterwards, he was decapitated.

The initiates from the schools of mystery of all times received initiations with the great arcanum. There was never known within any school of mysteries someone who had achieved initiation without the great Arcanum A.Z.F. This is the great arcanum.

Once on a given occasion, after having dictated a lecture, we were asked by a bachelor disciple if it were possible to practice the great arcanum with a woman of the astral world. We answered him that only with a woman of flesh and blood is it possible to awaken Kundalini.

Another brother who was also a bachelor wanted to practice with imaginary women! This is very ominous! When the mind creates a mental effigy, this effigy acquires consciousness and converts itself into a tempting demon of the mental world. During sleep, this effigy sexually discharges us through nocturnal pollutions (wet dreams).

It is very difficult for a student to disintegrate those mental effigies. Commonly, the students become victims of those mental effigies that their own mind invented. The best is to find a spouse that will really cooperate in the grand opus.

Those who do not have a spouse must raise their creative energy with sports in the open air, like hiking excursions and swimming. They must raise their creative energy when listening to good music and when admiring the great works of art: sculpture, painting, classical music, etc. In this way, the unmarried ones can raise their sexual energies and bring them up toward their hearts. There in that center of life those creative forces mix themselves with the luminous waves of the internal Christ and are taken toward the ineffable regions of the great light. We also elevate the sexual energies with the aesthetic sense, with charity, and love.

Nevertheless, in the name of truth, we must affirm the following: if you want higher initiation, if you long for the awakening of the Kundalini and the tattvic powers, you need to find a spouse, because the initiate without a spouse is like a garden without water.

Many mystical initiates believe that they are chaste because they do not have a spouse. Nevertheless, they have nocturnal pollutions. This is how they miserably lose their Christic semen, within which is found the genesis of the great life.

The sacred fire of the Solar Logos (Christ) is found within every seed, whether it is vegetable, animal, or human seed. This is why the seed has the power to reproduce itself.

Human beings must take care of their semen, their seed, as if it was potable gold.

We heroically extract the sacred fire of the Kundalini from our seed through the Arcanum A.Z.F.

Nocturnal pollutions are radically healed with the Arcanum A.Z.F.

We are children of a man and a woman. We are not children of any theory. The Word, the Son of Man, is the child of a man and a woman. The Son of Man is the child of immaculate conceptions. We need to lift up the Son of Man inside us, and in order to lift up the Son of Man inside us we need a spouse.

Part Three
Perception

Rabbi Isaac said, "Man's evil
inclination renews itself daily against
him, as it is said, 'Every imagination
of the thoughts of his heart was only
evil every day.' [Genesis 6.5]." And
Rabbi Simeon ben Levi said, "Man's
evil inclination gathers strength
against him daily and seeks to slay
him... and were not the Holy One,
blessed be He, to help him, he could
not prevail against it."

—Talmud, Kiddushin 30b

Chapter 18
The Perception of Reality

We are gathered this evening in order to really understand these minds of ours. It is clear that your minds are present here to listen to mine, and I am here to speak to you. However, we need our consciousness to be in true communion with the purpose of inquiring, investigating, seeking, in order to know the path ourselves, with the evident objective of attaining orientation on the inner self-realization of our Being...

To know how to listen is very difficult. To know how to speak is easier. It happens that when we are listening, it is necessary to be open to the new, with a spontaneous mind, a mind free of preconceptions, prejudices, etc. However it so happens that our mind—the ego, the I, the myself—does not know not how to listen, since it translates everything based on its prejudices. It interprets everything according to what it has stored in the formative center.

What is the formative center? It is memory. Why is it called the formative center? It is because within it is processed the intellectual formation of concepts.

Having understood this, it becomes urgent to learn how to listen with a new mind, and not repeat with what we have already stored in our memory.

After this preamble, we will try to agree upon concepts, ideas, etc.

First of all, it is urgent to know if the intellect by itself can lead us to the experience of the reality. There are bright intellects, we cannot deny that, but they have never experienced that which is the truth.

The Three Minds

It is worth knowing that there are three minds within us, namely, the sensual mind, the intermediate mind, and the inner mind.

· The sensual mind develops its basic concepts from the data provided by the five senses, and those basic concepts back up its reasoning.

· The intermediate mind is based on all kinds of beliefs, and cannot go beyond its canons.

· The inner mind is objective reasoning. Those who have climbed the steps of inspiration and intuition have undoubtedly opened the wonderful doors of the inner mind. Intuition express itself through the inner mind, meaning the person perceives and expresses the superlative consciousness of their own profound inner Being.

The Sensual Mind

Now, let us think a little about this sensual mind that we all use daily. There is no doubt that it elaborates its basic concepts with the data provided by the five senses, and those basic concepts support its reasoning.

Observing things from this angle, it is obvious that the subjective or sensual reasoning has as a foundation the external sensory perceptions. If the sole spring of its functionalism is based exclusively on the data provided by the five senses, undoubtedly it will not have access to something that escapes the vicious circle of external sensory perceptions; this is obvious. The sensual mind cannot know about the reality regarding the mysteries of life and death, concerning the truth about God, etc. From where could the sensual mind take such information if its sole source of nourishment it has is the data provided by the five senses? Obviously, the intellect does not have the means in order to know about reality...

In this moment something very interesting comes to my mind. There was once a great congress in Babylon at the time of the Egyptian splendors. That congress was attended by people from Assyria, Egypt, Phoenicia, etc. It is clear that the theme was intriguing: they wanted to know based on purely sensory analytical discussions if the human being has a soul or not. Obviously, at that time, that debate was based on their fives senses, since they were already substantially degenerated;

only in this way we can explain why those people selected that theme as the reason for their congress. In other times, a congress like that would have been ridiculous. For instance, the Lemurians never would have had the idea of celebrating that kind of congress, since for the people of the continent Mu, it was enough to detach as souls from their human body and get out in order to know whether their physicalities had a soul or not, and they did this with surprising ease since their souls were not permanently trapped like us within their physical bodies. So the idea of a theme like that only could have come from an already devolving, decadent, degenerated humanity...

In that congress there were many discussions for and against the soul. Finally, a great, wise Assyrian ascended to the tribunal of eloquence (that man had been educated in Egypt, he had entered in the mysteries) and in a very loud voice he said, "Reasoning cannot know anything about the truth, about reality, about immortality, about the soul. Reason can be useful to defend a spiritualist or materialist theory. Reason could elaborate a spiritualist thesis with a formidable logic, and also by opposition create a materialist thesis with a similar logic. So, therefore, the subjective, sensual reasoning nourished with the data brought by the five senses supports a diversity of minds. It can create spiritualist or materialist theses; therefore, sensual reasoning is not something on which we can rely. Yet, there is a different sense, which is the instinctive sense that perceives cosmic truths; this is a faculty of the Being. Subjective reasoning by itself cannot truly give us any data about the truth, about reality; sensory reasoning cannot perceptibly know about the mysteries of life and death." Thus, this is how that sage spoke, and he even said to the crowd, "You all know me, I have prestige among you and you know very well that I come from Egypt. You do not ignore that I dedicated my whole life to study. Yet, my sensual mind cannot provide data about reality." Then he concluded by saying, "You cannot know anything about the truth, the soul, or the Spirit with your reasoning, because the rational mind cannot know anything about these matters."

Well, this is how that man spoke with great eloquence, and thereafter he withdrew. He distanced himself from any scholasticism. He preferred to abandon subjective reasoning to instead develop in himself the aforementioned faculty that is known as the instinctive sense that perceives cosmic truths, a faculty that humanity in general once had, but it became atrophied as the psychological "I," the myself, the sensual mind-self developed.

It is stated that this great Assyrian sage, educated in Egypt, detached himself from every school and went to cultivate the land and to trust exclusively in that prodigious faculty of the Being known as the instinctive sense that perceives cosmic truths.

However, let us delve a bit further. There is a mind that differs from the sensual mind. I am talking emphatically about the intermediate mind. In the intermediate mind, we find all types of religious beliefs. Obviously, the data brought by all religions have their final journey in the intermediate mind.

Now, the inner mind is something that we must differentiate and clarify. The inner mind in itself and by itself, works exclusively with the data provided by the superlative consciousness of the Being. The inner mind could never function without the data provided by the inner consciousness of our Being.

Behold the three minds!

All of the theories and concepts of the sensual minds are known in the Christian Gospel as the "leaven of the Sadducees." Jesus Christ warns us, saying,

"Take heed and beware of the leaven of the Sadducees..."

...meaning, take heed and beware of the materialistic and atheist doctrines like the Marxist dialectic. Those kinds of doctrines correspond exactly to the doctrine of the Sadducees spoken to us by Christ.

However, the Lord of Perfection also warns us against "the doctrine of the Pharisees." That doctrine of the Pharisees corresponds to the intermediate mind... Who are the "Pharisees"? They are those who attend their temples, or their schools or religions or sects, etc., so everybody can see them. They are hearers of the word, but not doers of the word within themselves.

"But be ye doers of the word, and not hearers only, deceiving your own selves. For if any be a hearer of the word, and not a doer, he is like unto a man beholding his natural face in a glass: For he beholdeth himself, and goeth his way, and straightway forgetteth what manner of man he was." —James 1:22-24

So, Pharisees only attend their gathering so everybody can see them, but they never apply the word to themselves, and that is very serious. Such people are content with mere beliefs. They are not interested in intimate transformation. To that end, they waste their time and fail miserably...

So, let us take heed and beware of the leaven of the Sadducees and the doctrines of the Pharisees, and let us consider how to open the inner mind. How can we open it? We open it by knowing how to think psychologically.

Gnosis teaches us techniques in order to learn how to think psychologically.[1] If we learn how to think psychologically, we will finally manage to open the inner mind.

The inner mind, I repeat, works with data granted by the superlative consciousness of the Being. Then, thanks to that, the inner mind experiences the truth of the diverse phenomena of nature. For example, with the inner mind opened, we can talk about the law of karma not from what others say or do not say, but from direct experience. Also, with the inner mind opened, we become sufficiently prepared in order to discuss reincarnation, or the law of eternal return of all things, or the law of transmigration of souls, etc., but again, I repeat, no longer based on what we read or what we heard from some authors, but by what we experience ourselves in a real, direct manner; this is obvious...

Emmanuel Kant, the philosopher of Königsberg, makes a clear distinction between "The Critique of Practical Reasoning" and "Critique of Pure Reasoning." There is no doubt that rationalist subjective reasoning can never give us

---

1   Read the books *Fundamentals of Gnostic Education, The Great Rebellion, Treatise of Revolutionary Psychology,* and *The Revolution of the Dialectic.*

anything that did not belong to the world of the five senses. Intellect, by itself, is rationalistic and subjective...

If a sensory, intellectual minded person hears about a topic about reincarnation or karma, he will demand proofs, demonstrations, as if the truths that can only be perceived by the inner mind could be demonstrated to the sensualist mind. To demand evidence about that which is beyond the external sensory world is equivalent as to demand a bacteriologist to study microbes with a telescope, or to demand an astronomer to study astronomy with a microscope... They demand proofs, but these evidences cannot be given to the subjective reasoning, because subjective or sensualist reasoning has nothing to do with what does not belong to the world of the five senses. And themes such as reincarnation, karma, life postmortem, etc., are in fact exclusive to the inner mind, never of the sensual mind.

Reincarnation, karma, life after death, etc., can be demonstrated to the inner mind, but first of all that demonstration demands from the candidates to have opened their inner mind. Thus, if they did not open it yet, how can we make a demonstration like that? Obviously, this would be impossible, right?

Having comprehended this clearly, it is now convenient for us to delve a little into the subject of faculties. Understand that the intellect by itself is one of the most crudest faculties in the levels of Being. If we want to comprehend everything with the intellect, then we will never attain apprehension of cosmic truths.

Indubitably, beyond the intellect there is another cognitive faculty; I want now to emphatically refer to **imagination**.

Imagination

Many are those who have underestimated that faculty; some even disparagingly call it with the title of "the mad one of the house," an unjust title, because if not for the imagination, we would not have recorded this lecture, the car would not exist, there would be no trains either, etc. The sage who wants to make an invention must first imagine it, and thereafter make a drawing of their invention on paper. The architect who wants to build a house, must have first imagined it, and thereafter made blueprints of it on sheets of paper. So imagination has permitted the creation of every invention. Imagination is not therefore something to be despised... That there are several types of Imagination, we cannot deny it.

The first type we can denominate mechanical imagination; that type of imagination is also called fantasy. Obviously, it is constituted by the scraps of memory. It is useless and even harmful.

But, indeed, there is another type of imagination: this is intentional imagination, in other words, cognizant imagination. Obviously, when this type of imagination is splendidly developed, it can give us access to the ultra of all things.

Nature itself has imagination, this is obvious. If it were not for imagination, all creatures of Nature would be blind, but thanks to this powerful faculty there is perception. Perceptive images are formed within the perceptive center of the brain or perceptive center of sensations, and this is how we can perceive.

The creative imagination of Nature has given rise to the multiple forms of everything that is, everything that has been, and everything that will be...

In the Hyperborean or Pre-Lemurian epochs, the intellect was not in use, but imagination. At the time, the human being was innocent, and the marvelous spectacle of the cosmos was reflected upon their imagination as if in a crystalline lake. That was another type of humanity. Today it is painful to see how many people have already lost the power of imagination. In other words, humanity has frightfully degenerated this precious faculty.

It is possible to develop imagination, and its development would lead us beyond the sensual mind; this would teach us how to think psychologically. We already said, and we repeat, that only psychological thinking could open the doors of the inner mind. Thus, if we develop imagination, we can learn how to think psychologically...

Imagination, inspiration, and intuition are the three obligatory steps of initiation. But if we were left bottled up exclusively within the physical, sensory functionalism of the intellectual device, then in no way is it possible to climb the steps of imagination, inspiration, and intuition...

Comprehend, I am not stating that the intellect is useless. I am far from saying such an extremely imprecise affirmation. What I am doing is clarifying concepts.

Every faculty is useful within its orbit; yet outside its orbit it is useless. Any given planet within its orbit is useful; yet outside its orbit is useless and catastrophic. Likewise are the faculties of the human being: they have their orbit. To want to bring sensory reasoning out of its orbit is absurd.

Why do many people fall into materialistic skepticism? What is the reason that even pseudo-esoteric and pseudo-occult students, so in vogue these days, are always fighting against doubts? Why are they like many butterflies flitting from one school to another school, and finally reach old age without having done anything?

Through experience I have observed that those who remain bottled up within the intellect fail. Yes, those who want to verify with their intellect the truths that cannot be proven with the intellect, fail. Symbolically speaking, they make the mistake of wanting to study astronomy with a microscope or trying to study bacteriology with a telescope.

Let each leave each faculty in its place, in its orbit; let us not get it out of its orbit.

We need to think psychologically, and it is obvious that we must completely reject the leaven of the Sadducees and Pharisees, and to learn how to think psychologically. This would not be possible if we continue bottled up within the intellect. Then, it is better to start climbing the ladder of imagination, thereafter we will pass to the second step which is inspiration, and finally we will reach intuition...

An Exercise to Develop Imagination

But let us see how imagination can be developed. We can start with a simple exercise. I have spoken many times about the exercise of the glass of water, an easy exercise. If we put a glass of water a short distance from us, and if we place a little mirror at the bottom of that glass, and if we add few drops of quicksilver [mercury][2] to the water, and if thereafter we concentrate our sight to the center of the glass itself, meaning to the whole center, over the surface of the water, but in such a way that our sight passes through the glass, then obviously, we will have a splendid exercise for the development of imagination. In that water, we will try to see the astral light; yes, we will make a great effort to see it. In the beginning obviously we will see nothing, yet after some time of performing this exercise we will see colors in the water; this is how we then begin to perceive the Astral Light.[3] This is how the sense of self-psychological observation becomes active.

For example, much later in time, if a car passes on the street, we will see in the water a ribbon of light and will see the car running down the ribbon of light. This indicates that we are beginning to perceive with the transcendental faculty of imagination.

Finally, the day will arrive in which we will no longer need a glass with water in order to see, instead we will see the air with different colors; we will see the aura of people. We will know that each person carries an aura of light around. That aura has different colors. The skeptical person always carries a green-colored aura, a dirty green. The devotee wears a blue-colored aura. Yellow reveals much intellect. The dirty green, skepticism. Gray, sadness. Lead gray, a lot of selfishness. The black represents hatred. The dirty red, lust, fornication. The bright, sparkling red, anger, etc.

---

2   Mercury is a highly toxic heavy metal that is banned in some countries, yet in others can be bought at the corner store. Since mercury poisoning is a very serious concern, use of this exercise requires great caution in handling and disposing of the material. Do not drink the mercury or get it on your skin. Note also that there are other exercises one can safely use for the development of imagination (clairvoyance). Study *The Divine Science* for more practices.

3   "There is one vital substance in Nature upon which all things subsist. It is called archæus, or vital life force, and is synonymous with the astral light or spiritual air of the ancients." —Manly P. Hall

Obviously, in order to see the aura of people we have to work hard with this exercise. We have to work with it at least three years, ten minutes every day, without missing a single day to work with it. Obviously, if we have the strength in order to practice this exercise ten minutes a day, then the time will arrive in which the faculty of imagination or clairvoyance, which is another term given to imagination, will have to function in us...

Nonetheless, that is not be the only exercise for the development of this precious faculty. Something else is needed: we need meditation...

Meditation to Develop Imagination

Seated on a comfortable chair with the body perfectly relaxed, or lying down on the bed, but with the relaxed body and the head towards the north, we must imagine something: for example, the growth of a plant, a rosebush. Imagine that it has been carefully planted in black and fertile ground. And by continuing with this visionary, transcendental, and transcendent process, we also imagine that we water it with pure waters of life... we visualize its growth process: how the stem finally emerges; how it marvelously unfolds; how thorns arise from within that stem, and finally how various branches sprout from that stem. Imagine how those branches are also covered with leaves until finally a bud appears that delectably opens and becomes a rose. Thus, in that state of "manteia" as the initiates of Eleusis stated, speaking in the Greek and maybe even the Orphic manner, we would say it is even convenient to feel by ourselves the delectable aroma rising from the red or white petals of that beautiful rose.

The second part of this imaginative work would be to display with full clarity the process of dying of all things. It would be enough to imagine how those scented petals are gradually falling withered and lifeless; how those branches, once strong, become, after some time, a pile of sticks, and finally, the wind, the hurricane comes, and blows all of the leaves and sticks.

This is an in-depth meditation about the process of birth and death of all things. It is clear that this exercise practiced assiduously, daily, eventually will grant us profound insight into what we could call the astral world.

First of all, it is good to warn every candidate that any esoteric exercise, including this one, requires continuity of purpose from the disciple, because if we practice it every other day, we make a very serious mistake. This precious faculty of imagination can only be developed by having real dedication in the esoteric work.

When from within our imagination in meditation something new, something different from the rose arises, it is a clear sign that we are progressing. In the beginning, the images lack color, but as we work, they will be replete with multiple charms and colors; thus, this is how we will progress in deep inner development.

A step forward in this matter will take us to the remembrance of our life and our past lives. Unquestionably, those who had developed this imaginative faculty in themselves may well try to capture or apprehend by means of this transparency or translucence the last moment of his past existence; then, in that lucidity or mirror of imagination, a deathbed would be reflected — if in bed is where we were dying, because someone could have died on a battlefield or in an accident... It would be interesting to see our former loved ones, those who in the past existence accompanied us in the last moments, those who heard our cries of pain in the last hour.

Continuing with this wonderful process related with imagination, we could try to know not only the last moment of our previous life, but the moment prior to that one, and thereafter prior to that one, then the prior last years, the penultimate, then youth, adolescence, childhood, and thus to meticulously recapitulate the whole of our former lifetime.

Similarly, this exercise will take us further: it will also allow us to capture each one of our previous lives. Thus we will recollect and verify by direct vivid experience the reality of the law of the eternal return of all things.

Thus, it is not the intellect that can precisely verify these realities. With intellect we can discuss this topic, to affirm or deny it, but that is not verification.

So, therefore, I invite you to comprehension. Imagination will open for you the doors of the elemental paradises of nature.

If with the imagination we try to perceive a tree, if we meditate on it, we will see that is composed of many small celluloses. We perceive its physiology, its roots, its fruits, but also we will accomplish delving a little deeper and see, directly, the inner life of the tree. There is no doubt that this tree has what we might call "essence" or "soul." When in a state of manteia, samadhi, ecstasy, rapture, we perceive the consciousness of a plant, we discover with perfect clarity that this consciousness is certainly an elemental creature, a creature that has life, and which is not perceptible to the five senses, not perceptible to the intellectual capacity that is completely excluded from the mystical-sensory field, but indeed perfectly perceptible to the translucent. It is indeed intriguing that in the next steps, we can even talk, converse with that Elemental.

Obviously, the fourth vertical has unusual surprises. Indubitably, this is the Eden that the Bible talks about to us. Eden is the fourth dimension of nature. The earthly paradise is located in the fourth coordinate. The Elysian Fields, the Promised Land where the rivers of pure water of life flow with milk and honey is precisely the fourth dimension of our planet Earth.

Therefore, the creative imagination, the translucent wonderful mirror of the soul, well developed with ideal efficiency by means of exact esoteric rules, undoubtedly allows us to verify what I am emphatically affirming here.

So, therefore, I clearly invite you to a superlative analysis of all of this. I invite you to the development of that cognitive faculty always known as "imagination." It is an extraordinary faculty...

In the fourth vertical we will discover extraordinary temples, and it is because the elemental life is classified by the Logos — one is the family, for example, of the orange groves and another the family of eucalyptus trees — for there are temples in Nature for each plant family. The devas cited in the pseudo-esoteric Theosophist or occult texts govern elemental life. These devas are perfect human beings in the most complete sense of the word; they are initiates who know how to manipulate the laws of nature.

Creative imagination allows us to verify for ourselves that the Earth is not a dead body, or something rigid, a lifeless physical crust. Creative imagination allows us to know for ourselves that the Earth is a living organism.

It comes to memory at this time the Neoplatonic assertion which affirms that "the world-soul is crucified on the Earth"... That soul of the world is a conjunction of souls, a conjunction of lives that palpitate and have reality.

For the Hyperborean people, the volcanoes, the deep seas, the veins of metals, the gorges of the mountains, the hurricane winds, the flaming fire, the roaring beasts or birds, were nothing else than the body of the gods... Hyperborean people did not see the Earth as something dead. For them the world was something alive, an organism that has life, and which has it in abundance. Then they spoke in the pure rising of the divine language that as a river of gold runs under the thick jungle as the golden light of the sun... Those who knew how to play the lyre played the strangest primeval symphonies on it... at that time, the lyre of Orpheus had not yet fallen to the floor of the temple to be smashed into pieces... Those were different times. Those were the times of ancient Arcadia, when humans rendered worship to the gods of the aurora, and when each birth was celebrated with transcendental mystical festivities...

Therefore, if you develop efficiently the faculty of imagination, you will not only remember your past lives, but verify in an specific way what I am didactically expressing here with complete clarity.

Inspiration

Imagination is only the first step. A higher, second step leads us to inspiration.

The faculty of inspiration allows us to talk face to face with every particle of elemental life. The faculty of inspiration allows us to feel within ourselves the heartbeat of every heart...

Let us again imagine for a moment the exercise of the rosebush. If after the whole process, if once we completed meditating on the birth and the death of it, and sticks and flower petals have gone with the wind, and if we want to know more, we then need inspiration... The plant was born, has borne fruit, has died, and after all that, what? We need then inspiration in order to know the meaning of the birth and the death of all things.

The faculty of inspiration is even more transcendental, and needs a higher expenditure of energy. It is about leaving aside the symbol upon which we had meditated. It is about capturing the inner meaning of it. For this we need the faculty of emotion, the emotional center. The emotional center comes to enhance this esoteric work of meditation. The emotional center allows us to feel inspired, and then, inspired, we come to know the meaning of the birth and death of all things...

With imagination we could verify the reality of our previous existence. With inspiration we could capture the meaning of that existence: its reason, its cause, its why...

Inspiration is a step beyond the faculty of creative imagination. With imagination we can verify the reality of the fourth vertical, but inspiration will allow us to capture its deep significance...

Intuition

Finally, beyond the faculty of imagination and inspiration, we need to reach the heights of intuition. So, imagination, inspiration, intuition are the three steps of initiation...

Intuition is something different. Let us go back now to our rosebush example. Undoubtedly, by means of the process of imagination, during the transcendental and transcendent esoteric exercise, we have seen the process, we have seen how the rose bush grew, how it developed, and finally, how it died, how it became a pile of sticks... And how inspiration allowed us to know the meaning of all of the previous processes. But intuition will now lead us to the spiritual reality of them.

With intuition, with that precious, superlative faculty, we enter an exquisitely spiritual world; we will meet face to face, not only the elemental that we have seen with our imagination, meaning the elemental of the rosebush, but moreover we will meet the virginal spark or divine Monad, or the supreme igneous particle of the rosebush. We will enter a world where we will find the creator Elohim, cited by the Mosaic or Hebrew Bible; we will see the entire creator host of the Army of the Word — in other words, we shall meet the Demiurge Creator of the universe...

Intuition is the faculty that will allow us to talk face to face with the "archangels," with the "Thrones," and they will no longer be for us mere speculation or belief, but a palpable, manifested reality.

Intuition will grant us access to the upper regions of the universe and cosmos. Then by means of intuition we can study cosmogenesis, anthropogenesis, etc.

Intuition will allows us to enter the temples of the White Universal Fraternity, into the temples of the Elohim or Prajapatis, or Kumaras, or Thrones...

Intuition will allow us to know the genesis of our world. With intuition we can even attend the very dawn of creation, to know — not because someone has said it, but by direct perception — how this world emerged from the Chaos, how was it created, in what manner it appeared in the concert of the worlds...

Intuition will allow us to know in a specific and direct manner what the brilliant intellects of present times do not know...

There are many theories about the world, the universe, the cosmos, and they constantly go out of fashion, like the pharmaceutical remedies, like the fashions of the ladies or gentlemen. One theory follows another, and this other by another. To that end, the intellect does nothing but speculate. The intellect fantasizes a great deal of the time, without ever being able to experience reality, but intuition allows us to know reality. Yes, intuition is a transcendental cognitive faculty.

It is grandiose to be capable of attending the spectacle of the universe, to feel oneself for a moment apart from creation, to look at the world as if it were a theater, and oneself a spectator, to evidence how a comet or any cosmic unity, etc., comes from the Chaos, how it arises from the Not-Being (that is, the real Being).

Intuition is the faculty that allows us to know that the Earth exists because of the karma of the gods, otherwise it would not exist. Intuition is the faculty that allows us to verify the crude reality of that karma. Indeed those Elohim, Prajapatis, or parents, which in their conjunction constitute that which is divine, acted in a past cycle of manifestation long before the Earth and the solar system had emerged into existence...

The Moon

Let us see a very peculiar case. Much has been discussed about the Moon. Many people think that the Moon is a piece of Earth launched into space by centrifugal force, something like when someone fires a rocket, but intuition allows us to verify things in a completely different manner. Intuition allows us to know that the Moon is much more ancient than the Earth. There was a reason why our ancestors of Anahuac said, "Grandmother Moon." Obviously they perceived that the Moon is our "grandmother." She is the mother of the Earth, and the Earth is the mother of us all; to that end, the Moon is our grandmother. Wise concepts of Anahuac!...

In the past cosmic day, the Moon was a world rich in minerals, plants, animals, and human life. It had deep seas, volcanoes that erupted, etc. The very modern scientists have had to surrender to the concrete evidence that the Moon is more ancient than the Earth. The Earth indeed came much later, over the course of the centuries.

Those who made the mistake of affirming that "the moon was a detached piece of the Earth" now have to admit they were wrong, since it was verified with special devices — by means of the study of the pebbles brought from the Moon — that it is more ancient than the Earth. And this is how it is: the Moon had humanity, had plant life, was a fecund world...

But why did that world become a moon? Intuition allows us to know that everything that is born must die, and every world of the starry space eventually will become a new moon. This Earth which we inhabit, one day will grow old and will die, and will become a new moon.

Thus, there are very heavy moons, for example, the moon that revolves around the sun Sirius, which has a density five thousand times greater than the density of lead...

So, concerning our Moon, we say that it is the mother of the Earth. But why do I make this very strong statement? Because by means of intuition we see how after that old Moon, our grandmother, died, the Anima Mundi of the Moon, crucified on that satellite, was submerged within the bosom of the Eternal Cosmic Common Father, the Absolute; thus, when a new epoch of manifestation arrived, after a long interval, when, we would say, a new great cosmic day of activity began, then the Mother-Moon, that Anima Mundi, constructed a new body, it reincarnated. It formed a new body, which is this Earth. All the creatures that once existed on the Moon died, but the same germs, the living germs of all plants animals and all human life did not die; those germs, projected by cosmic rays, were deposited here in this new planet, even the seed-germs of our physical bodies! For this reason we state that we are descendants of the Moon.

Yes, the Moon is the mother of all living beings, the Moon is the mother of the Earth... when one makes a statement like this before a group of educated people, before the erudites of the intellect, before those who are used to juggling with the mind, before the fans of syllogisms and pro-syllogisms and episyllogisms of subjectivist rationalism, well, obviously one is exposed to mockery, sarcasm, irony, derision, scoffing, because the former affirmation can never be admitted by the subjectivist rationalism of the intellect; this which I am stating can only be verified by intuition.

The Inner Mind

If you want someday to truly attain enlightenment, the perception of reality, the complete knowledge of the mysteries of life and death, unquestionably you will then need to climb the marvelous steps of imagination, inspiration, and intuition, since mere rationalism will never bring you to these inner profound experiences...

We will never pronounce ourselves against the intellect; what we are doing is just specifying functions, and this is not a crime. Indubitably, the intellect is useful within its orbit; yet, out of its orbit, I repeat what I already stated at the beginning and during this lecture, it is useless. Thus, if we become fanatics of the intellect, and we definitively refuse to climb the steps of imagination, then undoubtedly we will never learn to think psychologically.

The minds of those who do not know how to think psychologically remain trapped, with absolute exclusivity, within the physical-sensory, and may even become in fact a fanatic of Marxist dialectics...

Only psychological thinking can open the inner mind; this is obvious. Those who have climbed up the steps of inspiration and intuition, undoubtedly, in fact, have opened the wonderful doors of the inner mind; "intuitions" arise from within. They express themselves through the inner mind. In other words, the inner mind serves as the vehicle for intuitions.

This inner mind is the same objective reasoning, clearly specified by Gurdjieff, Ouspensky, Collins, or Nicoll. To possess objective reasoning is to have opened the inner mind, which works exclusively with intuitions, with the data of the Being, of the consciousness, of what is superlative, of that which is transcendental and transcendent in us, and not otherwise...

Part Four
Criminology

"Between the acting of a dreadful
thing and the first motion, all
the interim is like a phantasma,
or a hideous dream."

—William Shakespeare, *Julius Cæsar*

"Clairvoyance" by Rene Magritte

Chapter 19

Different Types of
Clairvoyant Perception

Clairvoyance: perception of non-physical
imagery. Inferior forms include hallucinations,
dreams, daydreaming, fantasy, memory, etc.
Superior forms provide perception of other
dimensions, free of the limitations of physical
spacetime. Another word for clairvoyance is
imagination.

There are five fundamental types of clairvoyant perceptions.

1. Conscious clairvoyance

2. Unconscious clairvoyance

3. Infraconscious clairvoyance

4. Subconscious clairvoyance

5. Supraconscious clairvoyance

These five types of clairvoyant perceptions produce different forms of mental reactions.

In forensic psychiatry,[1] there are different biotypological
characters. Diagnostically speaking, when impacted by clairvoyant perceptions, each personality reacts in accordance to
their particular, individual psycho-pathology. There is the
apparently "normal" paranoid, and the sick paranoid.[2] There

---

1   A sub-speciality of psychiatry related to criminology, in which doctors
    study the relationship between mental illness and criminality.

2   Paranoid personality disorder: "Pervasive distrust and suspicion of
    others and their motives; unjustified belief that others are trying to
    harm or deceive you; unjustified suspicion of the loyalty or trustwor-
    thiness of others; hesitant to confide in others due to unreasonable fear
    that others will use the information against you; perception of innocent
    remarks or nonthreatening situations as personal insults or attacks;
    angry or hostile reaction to perceived slights or insults; tendency to hold
    grudges; unjustified, recurrent suspicion that spouse or sexual partner is
    unfaithful" — Mayo Clinic

also is the schizophrenic[3] with violent, instantaneous, and terrible reactions. There also is the neurasthenic[4] with an sick, double personality, the assassin and vulgar oligophrenic,[5] the epileptic, the hypersensory type of schizoid[6] or hyper-aesthetic with epileptic genotype, etc.

During the moment of a conditional reaction, every clair-voyant speaks and acts conditioned by the type of psycho-pathological personality that characterizes him as a human entity.

For the development of clairvoyance, it is necessary to possess an intellectual culture.[7] To have an intellectual disci-pline is necessary for the development of the latent powers, chakras, discs, magnetic wheels of the astral body.

A clairvoyant without any intellectual culture and without any intellectual discipline degenerates into a delinquent and vulgar person. A clairvoyant without any intellectual culture can fall into the following crimes: calumny, public or private slander, defamation of honor, threats, uxoricide, homicide, suicide, patricide, fratricide, incest, theft, matricide, kidnap-ping, ambush, sexual seduction, violence and force, infanti-cide, etc., and many other cases of crime studied by psychiatry and psychology.

The pathogenic role of superstitious fear induced by the infraconscious, subconscious, or unconscious clairvoyant per-ceptions give origin to murder, calumny, and public slander, and in general to all kinds of common crimes. The infracon-scious, subconscious, or unconscious clairvoyant perceptions

---

3   "Schizophrenia is a severe brain disorder in which people interpret reality abnormally. Schizophrenia may result in some combination of hallucinations, delusions, and extremely disordered thinking and behav-ior." — Mayo Clinic. Read chapter 18.

4   The term neurasthenia has a highly variable history and questionable value, but was generally used to refer to a condition of nervous weakness or exhaustion. Read chapter 18.

5   Inferior mental development or retardation

6   Schizoid personality disorder: "Lack of interest in social or personal rela-tionships, preferring to be alone; limited range of emotional expression; inability to take pleasure in most activities; inability to pick up normal social cues; appearance of being cold or indifferent to others; little or no interest in having sex with another person" — Mayo Clinic

7   To be well-educated and well-read in matters of the consciousness.

produce different situational reactions in accordance with the biotypological type of clairvoyant.

The different types of clairvoyants — namely the neurasthenic, schizophrenic, oligophrenic, epileptic, and hypersensory class of schizoid — fall into states of psychopathic consternation, compulsive and pathological suggestion, superstitious delirium of persecution, etc. All of these take them into the abyss of delinquency.

Therefore, before delivering ourselves to the development of esoteric powers, we need to study ourselves and make a personological, psychopathological diagnosis of our personality.[8] After discovering our own particular psychobiotypological "I," we need to reform ourselves with an intellectual culture. We need an educational psychotherapy[9] in order to reform ourselves.

Indeed, the four gospels of Jesus Christ are the best educational psychotherapy. It is necessary to totally study and practice all the teachings contained in the four gospels of Jesus Christ.

Therefore, only after reforming ourselves morally can we deliver ourselves to the development of the chakra discs, magnetic wheels, of the astral body. It is also urgent to study the best authors of Theosophy,[10] Rosicrucianism,[11] psychology, yoga, etc.

---

8 The "mask" (persona) that covers our mind. See the glossary entry.

9 To investigate our psyche and educate ourselves about our true state. For more on this, study *The Revolution of the Dialectic* by Samael Aun Weor.

10 Theosophy originated in the United States in 1875, founded by H.P. Blavatsky.

11 The Rosicrucian school was known primarily as a secret society in Europe from the sixteenth century onward. However, "Trustworthy information is unavailable concerning the actual philosophical beliefs, political aspirations, and humanitarian activities of the Rosicrucian Fraternity. Today, as of old, the mysteries of the Society are preserved inviolate by virtue of their essential nature; and attempts to interpret Rosicrucian philosophy are but speculations, anything to the contrary notwithstanding." —Manly P. Hall. "At this present time there is not a Rosicrucian school in this physical world. The only and unique Rosicrucian order is in the internal worlds." —Samael Aun Weor, *Tarot and Kabbalah*

SPIRITUALISM, MEDIUMISM, CHANNELLING

Mediumism is a technique of black magic that is more
commonly known now as channelling. Channellers
are either cunning hoaxes or outright states of
possession by demons. No genuine spiritual master
needs to communicate through the body of another
person. See glossary for more information.

Chapter 20

Positive and Negative Clairvoyance

The Rosicrucian initiate Max Heindel states in his book *The Rosicrucian Cosmoconception* that when the chakras of the astral body rotate from left to right (clockwise), then clairvoyance becomes positive. Max Heindel asseverates that when the chakras rotate from right to left (counterclockwise), then clairvoyance becomes negative.[12]

The exerted clairvoyants are positive. The mediums and seers of spiritism or spiritualism are negative. The positive clairvoyant knows how to drive his faculty by will. The negative clairvoyant sees without wanting to see. The negative clairvoyant always becomes cheated by the tenebrous entities.

The crime of "Mama Coleta" that occurred on February 6, 1944 in the San Francisco Farm, Rodrigo neighborhood, close to Cifuentes, Province Las Villas, Cuba, is a concrete example of negative clairvoyance, as well as spiritist or spiritualist mediumism. The neighborhood of "Mama Coleta" was indeed the scenario for mediumism, spiritualism, negative clairvoyance, incest, and crime.

The female medium Francisca, with her psychopathic and nervous personality, was indeed victim of the tenebrous entities that wander in the astral plane. The medium Francisca's fear contaminated her sister Candida. The two sisters sheltered themselves in the bed of their brother Candido. This is how both sisters fell into the crime of incest. There was a double incest.

Their brother Candido had lived with a concubine; thus, when he saw the nervous state of his clairvoyant sister, he distrusted the woman with whom he had lived. He supposed that his ex-concubine had cast a spell on their home. The panic reached the maximum when his younger brother brought him a doll that the ex-concubine had given him as a gift.

Afterwards came the second part of this drama that culminated with the crime of "Mama Coleta." Candido consult-

---

12 See illustration page 102.

ed a "santero"[13] who, in spite of the opposition of "Mama
Coleta," performed some ceremonies and a cleanse onto the
medium-seer Francisca. Thereafter, he declared that the one
responsible for his disgrace was the soul of a warlock named
Barrueta. Afterwards, the "santero" granted the medium-seer
Francisca the power of rejecting spells. Indeed, the female
medium Francisca, with her negative clairvoyance, was seeing
tenebrous entities. She was seeing against her will. She was
seeing demons everywhere. She could not control her sixth
sense.

When "Mama Coleta" discovered the incest, the negative
clairvoyant Francisca defended herself by stating that she did
not have carnal relations with her brother. She was instead
having intercourse with the soul of the warlock Barrueta, who
was inserting himself within the body of her brother. To that
end, in accordance with her, she was not perpetrating the
crime of incest.

The night of the events was terrible. The medium
Francisca seemed a lunatic. She violently ejected the food that
was cooked for her, believing it to be poisoned. She ripped at
the furniture of her home. She threw the clothes of her family
outside their house. She was in a state of delirium: shouting,
dancing, and clairvoyantly seeing the warlock Barrueta.

Her whole family kneeled with their faces towards a wall
with their arms opened in the shape of the cross. Soon, all of
them fell into a mass suggestion. All of her brothers struck
the father of that family, because they stated that the warlock
Barrueta was inserted within the body of their father.

Afterwards, they killed "Mama Coleta" by punching her
horribly, because the seer Francisca saw demons going inside
the body of the wretched old woman.

The last victim of that medium's negative clairvoyance
was her brother. The seer Francisca saw her brother transforming himself into the warlock Barrueta. Thus, she struck
her brother's head with a big, heavy rock that fractured the
bones of his cranium and tossed out from it pieces of his
encephalic mass.

---

13 a priest of Santería

The last thing this female seer did, naked and armed with a stick, was ride a horse outside in the streets. Screaming, she rode the horse around the streets while beating demons with the stick. Moments after, she was stopped by the police and everything ended when all of them were imprisoned.

The former narrative is a concrete case of negative clairvoyance. The seer Francisca had a "mental deficit, together with transitory amnesia and absolutely negative clairvoyant visions of a mediumistic character."

Commonly, these types of seers are oligophrenics who exhibit the same credibility as a weak and thoughtless being.

These negative seers fall into compulsive suggestion. These negative seers, while under their compulsive or pathologic suggestion, reach the horrible abyss of delinquency.

Indeed, these negative clairvoyants see forms that exist within the infraconsciousness of this great nature.

A true scientist cannot accept the visions of a negative clairvoyant as infallible. Only true, positive clairvoyance is infallible.

In order to develop positive clairvoyance, it is required to practice the necessary esoteric exercises and to study the best authors of Theosophy, Rosicrucianism, yoga, psychology, etc. Our worst enemy is ignorance, therefore we recommend our readers study the great works of the female Master Helena Petrovna Blavatsky, entitled *The Secret Doctrine*. We also recommend *Kundalini Yoga* by Sivananda, the books of Dr. Arnold Krumm-Heller, the books of Dr. Adoum, the books of Rudolf Steiner, etc.

Positive clairvoyance is achieved only with great intellectual culture and great esoteric discipline. The truly positive clairvoyance is only achieved by the highest cultured people who are submitted to the most rigorous intellectual disciplines. The illuminated intellect is the outcome of positive clairvoyance.

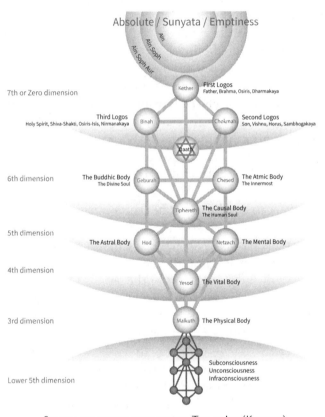

Absolute / Sunyata / Emptiness

Ain
Ain Soph
Ain Soph Aur

7th or Zero dimension — Kether — First Logos
Father, Brahma, Osiris, Dharmakaya

Third Logos
Holy Spirit, Shiva-Shakti, Osiris-Isis, Nirmanakaya — Binah — Chokmah — Second Logos
Son, Vishnu, Horus, Sambhogakaya

Daath

6th dimension — The Buddhic Body
The Divine Soul — Geburah — Chesed — The Atmic Body
The Innermost

Tiphereth — The Causal Body
The Human Soul

5th dimension — The Astral Body — Hod — Netzach — The Mental Body

4th dimension — Yesod — The Vital Body

3rd dimension — Malkuth — The Physical Body

Lower 5th dimension — Subconsciousness
Unconsciousness
Infraconsciousness

SUPERIOR AND INFERIOR WORLDS ON THE TREE OF LIFE (KABBALAH)

Chapter 21
The Consciousness

Only those who have achieved awakening in the superior worlds possess conscious clairvoyance.

During the normal hours of sleep, all human beings live in the suprasensory worlds wrapped in their astral bodies. During sleep and after death humanity lives in the suprasensory regions of the great mother nature. Unfortunately, while in the suprasensory worlds people act with their consciousness asleep.

Positive clairvoyance is possessed only by souls who live awakened in the suprasensory worlds. Indeed, those who possess continuous consciousness, whether out of their body when it is asleep or inside it when it is awake, are always in the state of watchfulness. They are positive clairvoyants. They possess continuous consciousness.

Every authentic extrasensory or esoteric investigation begins from that perfect state of surveillance.

It is necessary for the dreamer to awaken within the internal worlds before converting himself into a competent investigator in the superior worlds.

The mediums of spiritism or spiritualism are incompetent to investigate in the superior worlds, because they have their mental body dislocated. The mediums of spiritualism are mentally unbalanced; therefore, any investigation they attempt to do in the superior worlds results in failure.

The psychopathic states of the mediums of spiritualism, the compulsive and pathologic suggestions, the paroxysmal epileptic states during their trance, and the psychic obsession to which they are exposed, convert them into fallacious, abnormal, and mentally unbalanced individuals.

Logical thought and exact concepts are necessary in order to investigate in the superior worlds.

Every true, positive vision must be totally supported by concrete facts of the physical world.

JESUS AND THE WOMAN ACCUSED OF ADULTERY

"He that is without sin among you, let
him first cast a stone at her." —John 8:7

The truth does not diverge from human nature. Therefore, if what we consider true diverges from human nature, then it cannot be true.

If the clairvoyant is not a saint, then at least one must be a perfect gentleman or lady. We know of the case of a paranoid clairvoyant who slandered a virtuous mother, accusing her publicly and pointing her out as an adulterer and a witch, etc. This poor innocent and virtuous woman was mocked publicly by the paranoid clairvoyant.

We also know another case where the clairvoyant was a neurasthenic; he slandered and threatened a virtuous and honorable citizen to death, accusing him of being a warlock and asseverating that he was endowed with diabolic powers.

We know about a schizophrenic clairvoyant who reacted instantaneously against an honorable citizen. The schizophrenic clairvoyant accused that man of having an affair with the clairvoyant's wife. The schizophrenic clairvoyant said that he saw this with the use of his clairvoyance. If this clairvoyant had been a neurasthenic, he would have murdered that gentleman. If he had been paranoid, he would have studied and planned a perfect murder. If he had been an oligophrenic, he would have killed the man by starving him or by shooting him, even though the victim had never thought of having an affair with the clairvoyant's wife. If the clairvoyant had declared his accusation in front of the judges, they would have declared the other man innocent because of the lack of evidence, since in order to sentence someone it is necessary to prove the "corpus delicti,"[14] the responsibility of the accused.

The majority of clairvoyants could be prosecuted for slander, threats, and defamation of character.

Another aspect that one must take into account is the evidence of the "corpus delicti." If the "corpus delicti" is not demonstrated in any of the established forms and penal code proceedings, then the accused is innocent.

---

14 Latin for "body of the crime," indicating the principle that before a person can be convicted of committing a crime, that crime must be proven to have occurred.

"Therefore all things whatsoever ye would that men should do to you, do ye even so to them." —Matthew 7:12

The truth does not diverge from human nature. Therefore, if what we consider true diverges from human nature, then it cannot be true.

Christ said:

"Judge not, that ye be not judged. For with what judgment ye judge, ye shall be judged and with what measure ye mete, it shall be measured to you again." —Matthew 7:1, 2

The clairvoyant must be rigorously analytic, highly intellectual, and strictly scientific.

The clairvoyant's worst enemy is ignorance. The clairvoyant must learn to see in the absence of the "I," the myself. The clairvoyant must see without judging.

Chapter 22
The Psycho-bio-typic "I"

The mind is bottled up within the "I." Every conditional reaction of the mind is the outcome of the psycho-bio-typic "I."

Every perception passes from the senses into the mind. The "I" translates all the information collected by the mind in accordance with its prejudices, desires, fears, remembrances, preconceptions, maliciousness of a certain type, fanaticism, hatred, envy, jealousy, passion, etc.

The clairvoyant always has a "bad secretary" from whom he needs to liberate himself. This secretary is the "I," the myself, the ego.

The "I" of the clairvoyant traps all suprasensory representations that arrive into his mind, then he interprets them in accordance with his prejudices, hatreds, jealousies, mistrusts, maliciousness of a certain type, passions, remembrances, pride, envy, arrogance, etc. The subsequent reactions of the clairvoyant are the outcome of his own psycho-bio-typic "I."

The paranoid clairvoyant is full of pride. He likes to keep himself isolated from the world. He prefers to deal only with very few people. He is a very intelligent person, yet he is sly and distrustful. He tends to believe himself to be infallible. He believes himself to be a great master. He believes that he can dominate the world. He does not accept opinions from anyone, since he believes that only he is truly wise, great, and powerful. When this type of paranoid clairvoyant reacts with hatred, malice, distrust, etc., he can even, in cold blood, plan an intellectual assassination.

The neurasthenic clairvoyant has a double personality. Just as he prays and preaches ineffable things, he also speaks of pistols, daggers, war, violence, etc. When facing an unpleasant representation, this type of clairvoyant reacts with calumnies, insults, homicides, etc. When one of his two personalities becomes full of complexes or humiliation, he then asks for forgiveness and speaks with devotion in order to make amends. Once he attains his purposes, his other personality reacts with pride, anger, arrogance, violence, treason, etc.

An in-depth analysis upon this double personality type takes us to the conclusion that Judas Iscariot represents a type of neurasthenic clairvoyant. Judas represents a double personality, since in one moment he was following the master and in another he was against the master. He kissed the master, and thereafter betrayed him. He repented of his act, and thereafter committed suicide. This is how the neurasthenic type is.

The "I," the myself, does not exist within Christ.[15] Christ does not react against calumnies, slaps, mockeries, threats, whippings, etc. Christ overwhelms because of his terrific serenity. When crucified Christ said only, "Father, forgive them, for they know not what they do." The "I" does not exist inside the Christ; this is why he neither reacts nor judges anybody. Christ is a perfect clairvoyant who knows how to see with comprehension, without judging, without translating, because he does not have the "I." Christ is the clairvoyant who sees, comprehends, and knows. Christ is the universal spirit of life incarnated inside Jesus of Nazareth.

The clairvoyant needs to learn how to contemplate internal representations in the absence of the "I." The clairvoyant needs to see without judging, without translating, without pre-concepts, without fanaticism, without passion, etc. The clairvoyant needs to be highly comprehensive.

When a schizophrenic clairvoyant reacts against an unpleasant representation, he can fall into the worst crimes because of his violent, instantaneous and terrible reactions.

Commonly, a schizoaffective clairvoyant is woeful, melancholic, auto-concentrated, and introspective. He possesses melancholic ideas; he gets weary with any intellectual work, etc.

---

15 The word Christ is a title, not a personal name. "The Gnostic Church adores the saviour of the world, Jesus. The Gnostic Church knows that Jesus incarnated Christ, and that is why they adore him. Christ is not a human nor a divine individual. Christ is a title given to all fully self-realized masters." —Samael Aun Weor, The Perfect Matrimony

The schizoid clairvoyant, when facing an unpleasant representation, if he is not rigorously analytic, can react by murdering others and thereafter committing suicide.

A masochist clairvoyant enjoys whipping himself while in the presence of his mystical representations or performing terrible penances to the death.

Clairvoyance demands logical thought and an exact concept. One needs to have perfect mental equilibrium in order to be an exerted clairvoyant.

A clairvoyant with some psychic trauma can suffer serious mental disorders and can unconsciously create fatal images in the mental world.

When a mentally disordered clairvoyant contemplates his own suprasensory creations, he can then receive a nervous, emotional shock. He can also receive a vertiginous impetus, or an unexpected and acute emotional rapture. All of these can certainly take this clairvoyant into the abyss of crime. Psychic trauma is the outcome of great moral pain, or a great frightening experience, or the loss of a beloved one, etc.

The sadomasochist clairvoyant has reached such a state of sexual perversion that he is easily converted into a mystic-erotic assassin. The sadomasochist clairvoyant loves sweet evilness and falls into the bloodiest phallic cults. The black masses of the Middle Ages with their naked women upon the altar and the assassination of innocent children are living examples of this tenebrous and fatal kind of clairvoyance. The human sacrifices of all times and of all religions are the outcome of the sadomasochist clairvoyance. Those human sacrifices are living examples that show us what this type of sadomasochist clairvoyance is. So, the assassination of people on the altar for liturgical ritual purposes is nothing else than a barbaric sadomasochist clairvoyant custom.

The black mass with human sacrifices was celebrated in many medieval castles during the fifteenth century. Marshal Gilles de Rais in Tiffanges, France, had in his castle a church whose priest celebrated the black mass. Retz was accused of having assassinated two hundred children in his black masses.

Catherine de' Medici also celebrated black masses with the sacrifice of innocent children.

The Witches' Sabbath with its black masses and its witchcraft were in rivalry with the priests of the "holy office" of the Catholic Inquisition in regards to the assassination of innocent children. This is what sadomasochist clairvoyance is, a criminal and terribly perverse type of clairvoyance.

Therefore, we can become perfect clairvoyants only by dissolving the psycho-bio-typic "I," which everybody carries inside.

Chapter 23
The Human Mind

The brain has five fundamental parts:
1. The encephalon
2. The cerebrum
3. The midbrain [mesencephalon]
4. The medulla oblongata or hindbrain
5. The pons or breach

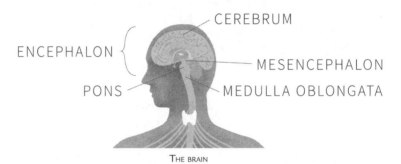

THE BRAIN

Indeed, those who state that the encephalon governs the intelligence, memory, willpower, etc., ignore the existence of the mental body. Those people should study all the volumes of *The Secret Doctrine* written by Helena Petrovna Blavatsky.

The brain is made in order to elaborate thought, yet it is not the thought. The brain is an instrument of the mind, yet it is not the mind. We must distinguish between the brain and the mind. We must study the intimate relations of the brain with the mind.

In our former chapters we spoke about the astral body. In those chapters we stated that the mind, the psychic and spiritual principles of the human being are within the astral body.

The mind is a marvelous subtle body that has its own ultra-biology and ultra-pathology that is in intimate relation with the central nervous system and the brain.

Thought is a function of the mental body. The human being can think without the physical brain; he can think inde-

PHOTOGRAPHS OF KATIE KING TAKEN BY SIR WILLIAM CROOKES

pendently without the aid of cerebral matter. This has already been demonstrated in scientific laboratories where some disincarnated entities were materialized.

We are stating concrete facts that are already demonstrated. If the reader still has not read anything about the materializations of Katie King in the laboratory of Sir William Crookes with the help of the Fox sisters, the mediums for materialization, then we recommend to do it. The concrete fact is that the astral body of the defunct Katie King materialized over three consecutive years in the already mentioned scientific laboratory. Then, the scientists saw, heard, touched, etc. the entity. Katie King allowed herself to be submitted to all types of experiments. There were no frauds there, because the scientists controlled the experiments to prevent even the slightest possibility of fraud.

After three years of experimentation, Katie King, before many photographic cameras, slowly dematerialized. She left for the scientists a materialized lock of her hair as final proof of the reality of her materialization. We are, therefore, stating facts that have already been demonstrated.

The encephalon is governed by the mind, yet the mind is not governed by the encephalon. The encephalon is the instrument of emotions and of the consciousness, yet the encephalon neither produces emotions nor consciousness. What is logical cannot be refuted by ignorance. Logic is logic. The people who affirm that the brain produces thought, emotion, and consciousness are ignorant, because they have not studied the mental body. So, we cannot, based on our ignorance, refute what is factual. It is necessary for the ignorant to study.

The twelve pairs of cranial nerves demonstrate to us the hermetic principle that states, "As above, so below." If above there is a zodiac with twelve constellations, also here below there is a zodiacal human being with twelve pairs of cranial nerves. Each pair of nerves controls some region of the physical body. The twelve pairs of nerves control all the twelve parts of the zodiac human being. Those nerves are:

1. Olfactory nerves.

2. Optic nerves.

3. Oculomotor nerves.

4. Trochlear nerves.

5. Trigeminal nerves.

6. Abducens nerves.

7. Facial nerves.

8. Vestibulocochlear nerves.

9. Glossopharyngeal nerves.

10. Vagus nerves.

11. Spinal nerves.

12. Hypoglossal nerves.

These twelve pairs of nerves inform the mind of all that happens in the human zodiac. The office that collects that information is the brain, and the office worker is the mind.

Thus, the organs of the senses of external perception collect the information that comes from the exterior world. Then, the information passes into the cerebral office where the office worker (the mind) analyzes and studies it. Unfortunately, the office worker has always a bad secretary who betrays him. That bad secretary is the "I," the myself, the ego.

For instance, we go to the movie theater where we watch an erotic movie; there, the office worker within his cerebral suite collects all the perceptions. The office worker studies the movie; he contemplates it; he enjoys himself with it. Thereafter, the secretary, by his own whim, on the sly and in secrecy, plunders the erotic images and reproduces them in nature's mental plane. This is how these images convert themselves into living effigies of the mental plane.

Later on, during our normal sleep, the mind, bottled up with the "I," fornicates with those mental effigies. This is why nocturnal pollutions occur.

The dreamer fornicates with the mental images that he, himself, created. The dreamer clairvoyantly sees those images. This is what is called unconscious clairvoyance.

Someone is jealous and supposes that a friend of his is having an affair with his spouse. Thus, his "jealous I," with those fantasy pictures he created, elaborates a drama in secrecy. Then, nocturnal dreams occur, and he sees horrible dramas where his spouse is committing adultery with his friend and many other terrible things. This is what is called unconscious clairvoyance.

If the clairvoyant is an oligophrenic, then he will vilely assassinate his friend. If he is neurasthenic, he then will insult, calumniate and finally assassinate him. If he is paranoid, he then will intellectually plan a technical and perfect assassination. If he is schizophrenic, he will violently break that friendship. If he is a sadomasochist, he will assassinate his spouse in the most horrible way. If he is a very cultured schizoid with a genotypic epileptic base, he then can receive a very intense emotional shock that will make him commit the crime of homicide and will afterwards fall into a complete psychic state of collapse.

The majority of clairvoyants fall into the abyss of delinquency because of their lack of culture and intellectual discipline.

Let us suppose that a clairvoyant distrusts a friend because he assumes that he is a black magician. For that reason, within his unconsciousness he elaborates the most terrible forms; thereafter, these forms appear in his dreams. This is unconscious clairvoyance. This is why he can suffer a tremendous situational reaction that will take him into crime, calumny, public slander, defamation of character, assassination, etc.

All unconscious clairvoyant perceptions enter the cerebellum. Thereafter, the cerebellum transfers those perceptions through the cell groups of the pons or breach into the cerebrum. So, when they enter the cerebrum the unconscious perceptions become conscious.

The pons connects the midbrain with the medulla and with the two famous cerebral hemispheres.

In ancient times, the medulla oblongata constituted the whole brain, which could perfectly control all the cells of the human organism. The medulla contains seven functional centers that govern sneezing, coughing, suction, mastication, deglutition, regurgitation, the functions of the salivary and gastric glands, and the closing of the eyelids.

The midbrain is also very interesting. Part of it joins the two cerebral hemispheres with the cerebellum and the pons or breach. Clairvoyant perceptions pass through the pons. All the centers that govern the human organism are located within the functional areas of the brain.

Oftentimes a clairvoyant perception is recorded in a fixed way within one cerebral cell. This is similar to an image that is recorded on photographic film. In this case, the mind perceives that unconscious clairvoyant image at all hours. Surgeons have resolved that problem by extirpating the cell where the image is recorded.

A concrete case of unconscious clairvoyance and homicide was the assassination of the great Colombian politician Jorge Eliecer Gaitan. The authorities' investigation had shown that the assassin was an active member of the school A.M.O.R.C. from San Jose, California. It was also stated that he was expelled from that school because they considered him a mentally unbalanced individual. That personage was an unconscious clairvoyant. He lit a pair of candles in front of his altar, in accordance with an A.M.O.R.C.-Rosicrucian ritual. Thus, in the mirror he saw two images, Simon Bolivar and Francisco de Paula Santander, who was Simon Bolivar's enemy. Therefore, the assassin told himself, if Santander tried to kill me in my past reincarnation, now in my present existence I will take revenge on him and I will kill him. Thus, the 9th of April, the day of the events, he treacherously killed Jorge Elicer Gaitan when this politician was leaving the government palace of Bogota.

The experts on ballistics considered that before that homicide the assassin had to have practiced a lot at the target range, since the three shots in the victim's back were well aimed, exact, and precise.

What happened afterwards was frightful. This Bogotanian assassin astonished the whole world. The excited crowds launched themselves to battle against the government. If, in the middle of such a situation, the cunning of a very fox-like liberal politician had not been present, the populace would have taken the presidential palace.

The former narrative is a concrete example of homicide and unconscious clairvoyance. There is no doubt that the vision in the mirror was the secret source of that crime. The political enemies of Gaitan made the rest. Possibly, they financed that crime; they bought the assassin, etc. The secret source of this crime was unconscious clairvoyance. The unbalanced mind of the assassin created the images that were projected into the mirror. This is all.

Unconscious clairvoyance is the secret cause of one hundred percent of homicides.

Forensic psychiatry needs to expand itself a little more.

Oftentimes, the perceptions from unconscious clairvoyance remain deposited within the unconscious depths of the human mind. Those perceptions convert themselves into secret temptation, which is the cause of many crimes.

In the depths of every human being there are many unconscious factors that can cause one to commit homicide. The secret sources of any crime are unconscious. Many saints had unconsciousness filled with carnal passion, sadism, robbery, crime, violence, jealousy, hatred, resentments, etc. During the dream state those saints suffered horribly. During their dreams, those saints fell into the most frightful crimes. Within their unconsciousness, those saints were great evil doers. When they awakened from their dreams, they understood their frightful moral misery. Thus, this is why they were performing terrible penances and "covering themselves with sackcloth."

Those who achieve making a moral defect into awakened consciousness will attain the total disintegration of that defect.

When a human being disintegrates all of his defects, then his "I" is dissolved.

The truth comes into us when the "I" is dissolved. This is how we become perfect clairvoyants.

The truth is born from creative comprehension. The truth is non-temporal, eternal, and divine. The "I" cannot know the truth, because the "I" is just a bunch of memories. The "I" is of time. The "I" is born in time and dies in time.

Death is just a subtraction of fractions. After finishing the mathematical operation (death), only the values remain. Later on, those values return into newborn physical bodies. Those values are the "I," the myself, the returning ego. Therefore, the "I" is just an illusion.

Any crime, any felony, and any vice are the fatal outcome of the affirmation of the "I," of the myself.

The origin of pain is within the "I."

The "I" is dissolved when we annihilate desire.

Where the truth abides, the "I" cannot abide, because the truth and the "I" are incompatible.

The "I" is a transitory error of the wheel of samsara (the wheel of reincarnation and karma). The "I" is the heresy of separatism.[16]

The "I" is the origin of egotism, hatred, fornication, adultery, envy, anger, etc. The "I" is the thirst of pleasures and the source of pride and vanity. Therefore, in order to incarnate the

16 The "I" is the cause of the illusion of being separate from the Being, the Innermost, divinity, etc.

truth one needs to dissolve the "I." In order to attain internal peace, one needs to dissolve the "I," the myself. In order to acquire perfect clairvoyance and supreme illumination, one needs to dissolve the "I."

The truth is the internal Christ of every human being.

The "I" is the Satan that we carry inside.

Where the "I" is the truth cannot be.

Those who divide themselves into two "I's," one superior and another inferior, walk upon the path of error.

Those who affirm the existence of a divine "I" are making Satan godly.

There is no such thing as a separated individual spirit. There is only the universal spirit of life.

Therefore, the immortal spark (spirit) of every human being is the Being that is one with the universal spirit filled with supreme happiness.

Chapter 24
The Infraconsciousness

Infraconscious clairvoyance is commonly qualified and known by the name "nightmares." Also, there are "sleep drunkenness"[17] and the hypnic "twilight state."[18]

Sleep drunkenness has a longer duration than the hypnic twilight state.

In sleep drunkenness, the cerebral cortex is involved not as a cause but as vehicle called dream consciousness, reflected as distinct variations of sleepwalking.

In the hypnic twilight state there is intense action of the mesencephalon [midbrain]. This intense action is not the cause but the effect of certain short circuits from psycho-infraconscious currents. These originate psychic effects and automatic acts that are sometimes criminal.

In sleep drunkenness there is subsequent lacunar amnesia[19] with distinct degrees and traces. In the hypnic twilight state the sensation of amnesia caused by definitively automatic action does not exist. The common factor of both phenomena of psychic origin is the inhibition of normal consciousness by the natural process of the dream state.

Now, we mention a case of infraconscious clairvoyance cited by Swartzer:

> "A woman from Pesth dreamed that a dog chased her and she was trying to reject it by stoning it. She, awakened by that nightmare, took her little girl who was sleeping by her side and threw her with violence, as if she was a stone, against the wall in order to scare the vicious dog."

---

17 "A half-waking condition in which the faculty of orientation is in abeyance, and under the influence of nightmarelike ideas the person may become actively excited and violent." —Farlex Partner Medical Dictionary

18 "A state of clouded awareness wherein the person is transiently not aware of their current environment, experiences fleeting auditory or visual hallucinations, and reacts to them by engaging in irrational acts, like public nudity, fleeing, or committing acts of violence." —Psychology Dictionary

19 Memory loss of certain isolated experiences.

Let us see another case of infraconscious clairvoyance cited by Krafft-Ebing:

> Sargant Simmonds said, "At half-past one o'clock this morning... I heard a female voice—"Oh my children! save my children!' I went to the house...[and found a mother] who was in her night-dress [and in an extremely excited and perturbed state]. Everything in the place was in great confusion. She kept on crying out, 'Where's my baby? Have they caught it? I must have thrown it out of the window!' ...She told me that she had been dreaming that her little boy had said that the house was on fire, and that what she had done was with the view of preserving her children from being burnt to death... The window had not been thown up. The child was thrust through a pane of glass..." —J.C. Bucknill and D.H. Tuke, A Manual of Psychological Medicine

We have found another case of infraconscious clairvoyance on page 203 in a book written by Drs. Diaz Padron and E. C. Henriquez:

> "Very late one night, a man who was alone in his apartment was dreaming that bandits were assaulting his home. Very strong knocks were heard from the door that was next to the stairs. The tenant awoke and rose holding a gun in his hand. He opened the door and shot the gun without seeing or aiming at anyone.

> "The bullet shot a young boy who carried an urgent telegram. When the homicidal one saw the deliverer of the telegram falling, he then became aware that he had just wounded an innocent person. In that moment, he completely awoke."

Those nightmares and evil dreams are phenomena of infraconscious clairvoyance that can originate false conclusions, resulting in crime.

When the clairvoyant is an neurasthenic occultist or esotericist, he can then become a premeditator and perfidious assassin.

A neurasthenic-type occultist student was dreaming of a citizen. With his infraconscious clairvoyance he saw that citizen tormenting him with witchcraft and black magic. A few days later, the neurasthenic insulted and threatened to death the perplexed and astonished citizen. This type of infraconscious vision with premeditation, calumny, and perfidy is very common in some occultist and spiritual students, etc.

The lack of mental appreciation of the infraconsciousness by esotericist or spiritual clairvoyants is due to fanaticism and ignorance.

The mental disorder of ignorant fanatics is due to superstitious fear, to suggestion, and also to the lower aggressive instincts of their psycho-typic "I."

As the infraconsciousness is within the human being, likewise it is within nature. The tenebrous memories of the whole history of the Earth and of its root races are deposited within the infraconsciousness of nature. Antediluvian monsters live within the infraconsciousness of nature. These are the specters of the past, the nightmare phantoms.

The infraconscious clairvoyant only perceives the cavernous memories of the past and the tenebrous creations from the infraconscious lower depths of the human beings and beasts.

In the infraconsciousness of nature there is only fatality.

Every human being has a double, an opposite, who lives within the infraconsciousness of nature. Facing Buddha, we find his brother and enemy Devadatta, the king of hell. Facing Anael, the angel of love, we find Lilith,[20] the antithesis of love.

An infraconscious clairvoyant may see the double of someone and thereafter deduce erroneous conclusions whose final outcome is calumny, homicide, etc.

The infraconsciousness is the tenebrous remnant from a remote past.

A sadomasochist is a sexual pervert that can assassinate his spouse just for pure sexual pleasure. This sexual perversion is infraconscious. The infraconscious values of the psychological "I" constitute the lowest animal depths of the human being.

The tyrannical, obsessive, sexual perversion of the sado-masochist is the concrete manifestation of his infraconscious values.

---

20 An ancient symbol appearing in Sumerian mythology (4000 BC), later known in Kabbalah as the feminine half or the first "wife" of Adam. After the division, she became the source of many demonic spirits who continue to plague mankind, including the sucubi and incubi generated by masturbation and sexual fantasy.

When this genre of infraconscious values flourishes in his
mind, the human being falls into
crimes like homosexuality, stupor, force, violence, corruption of
minors, etc. Sometimes, such a
sexual pervert becomes a mystic,
an ignoramus, a sanctimonious
one, etc.

We knew the case of a mystical sexual pervert who gave coins
to six and seven year old girls "for
their candies." This is how he was
cultivating them while they were
growing up. Later, he seduced
them sexually, and finally, in
order to avoid conflicts and problems, he engaged them with other
men. Nonetheless, that satyr[21]
was a mystic spiritualist who,
filled with sweetness, was always
smiling. He was a hierarch from a
spiritual society.

SATYR

Oftentimes, the sexual perversion of the infraconsciousness places its satyrs in the arena of compulsive psychoneuro-
sis that causes them to commit the most terrible crimes regis-
tered by the police news chronicles.

---

21 Satyrs are a type of creature described in Greek mythology with animal
features who are only interested in pleasure. Satyrs have levels of symbolic meaning, but here the word is used to refer to a man who is ruled
by lust. "Men with excessive sexual needs, who indulge in one erotic
adventure after another and even commit sexual crimes, are said to
suffer from "satyriasis." This, incidentally, is a more frequent affliction
than nymphomania. Such a state may be permanent and may occur
periodically. It is almost invariably caused by **lascivious imagination**,
which engenders an abnormally increased desire and a corresponding
reaction on the part of the sexual organ. It may reach such a degree of
sexual hyperaesthesia that the man literally goes "sexually mad". In such
a state of bestial sexuality he may indulge in pederasty, intercourse with
animals, or rape." —Waldemar

Sexual infraconscious perversion has two very well defined poles: the brain and sexuality. Thieves are positive (+); prostitutes are negative (-). These are the two poles of the human infraconsciousness. Observe the intimate psychic affinity that exists between prostitutes and thieves.

These two poles of the human infraconsciousness live in an eternal struggle within each individual. We clearly see in the example of the spiritual satyr cited in this present chapter the struggle of the infraconsciousness.

The satyr's brain cultivates the girls with coins for their candies and waits a little while for their maturity. Then, the satyr's sexuality possesses and consummates the crime of seduction. The satyr's brain projects and plans; afterwards, he engages the girls with other men in order to avoid conflicts. Behold here the struggle between brain and sexuality.

Many times the infraconsciousness betrays a virtuous spouse and carries her towards adultery. Many prostitutes, who in their past were magnificent spouses, live in brothels. When the sexual perversion of these harlots polarizes itself in their brain, drained by pleasure, they then commit terrible crimes that take them to jail.

These incarcerated, unhappy women feel themselves victims of human injustice; they consider themselves innocent. Indeed, those women are victims of an energy that they ignore. No one has cured such unhappy women; not a single psychiatrist has taught them how to use and drive their sexual energy. They do not know the great mysteries of sex. They are victims of a society that, after perverting them, despises and miserably humiliates them. Society corrupts these unhappy women, daughters of pain, in order to confine them within horrible panopticons and jails where they only end up perverting themselves still more.

The infraconsciousness cannot be confined within jails.

The delinquent does not reform himself in jails. The jail system is a complete failure. Inside jails, the delinquents multiply their hatred and rancor against society.

The sexual problems in jails, the homosexuality and all kinds of filthy vices against nature, are showing us until satiation that the infraconsciousness cannot be confined within jails.

The biggest sin is ignorance.

Only with a wise educational psychotherapy can the reform of delinquents be achieved. The corrective educational treatment within jails can transform them into true reformatory schools. Jails should not exist. There shoud be only reformatory schools, etc. In these schools, the delinquents can be cured with educational psychotherapy.

Convicts must be treated with infinite love and mercy.

Chapter 25
The Subconsciousness

When a criminal is psychogenically analyzed, subconscious factors have to be taken into account.
These types of factors are reduced into three, namely:
- genotype (inheritance / genetics)
- phenotype (education)
- paratype (circumstances)

The upright social conduct of any individual is the outcome of perfect equilibrium among these three factors.

When there is disequilibrium among these three factors, the outcome is crime.

These three factors can be positive or negative. They are positive when they manifest as upright thoughts, upright feelings, and upright actions. They are negative when they manifest as criminal thoughts, criminal feelings, and criminal actions.

Let us study these three factors separately.

Inheritance / Genetics

Inheritance is the vehicle of karma, nemesis, or law of destiny. Here, we are not asking you to believe; you may not believe in it. However, what we need is to analyze and to profoundly delve into the distinct inner depths of the mind.

Concerning beliefs, to say, "I believe or I do not believe," is proper for ignorant people. We are mathematicians in our scientific investigations and very demanding in our analysis and our expression.

Death is a subtraction operation. When that arithmetic operation is finished, only the values remain. These values are what continue. These values constitute the psychological "I," the myself, the ego, that reincarnates in order to satisfy its frustrated desires and in order to continue existing though a new personality.

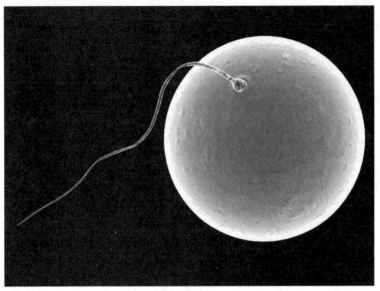

SPERM AND OVUM MEET

The "I" is a bunch of memories, passions, desires, hatreds, violence, lust, greed, etc. The "I" constitutes those values. Those energetic values are anterior to the seminal germinal cell.

If we investigate all the intra-atomic and inter-atomic states of the seminal germinal cell, we only find electricity and magnetism.

We are not establishing dogmas. Let us perform the test. Let us take the seminal germinal cell into an atomic physics laboratory. Thus, if we split the atom of the seminal germinal cell, we will liberate energy, because according to atomic physics any atom is an exponent of energies.

If a scientific clairvoyant analyzes those liberated energies of the atom from the seminal germinal cell, he then will find the reincarnating ego (the values).

Existence begins with the cell that is elaborated within the man's testicles and prostate. This cell (sperm) is decapitated when entering within the maternal ovum.

The factors of inheritance are deposited in the genes. The word gene comes from the same Greek root that originates the words genesis, generation, genre, etc.

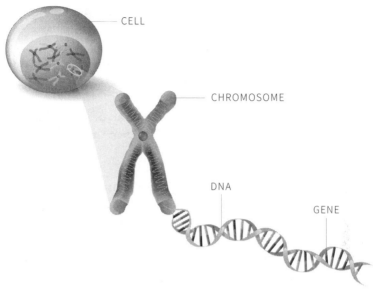

CELL

CHROMOSOME

DNA

GENE

GENES ARE IN OUR DNA, WHICH IS WITHIN THE CHROMOSOMES

The genes are within small bar forms that are named chromosomes. Paternal and maternal inheritance is in within the genes.

Inheritance is the vehicle of the cruel nemesis of life.

Inheritance is the outcome of karma (the law of action and consequence, nemesis).

"For with what measure ye mete, it shall be measured to you again." —Matthew 7:2

As the action is, so will the consequence be. This is the law.

We carry the outcome of our past evil deeds within our inheritance. Axiomatically speaking, we state the following: evil actions are the causa causorum of inheritance.

This axiom is comprehensible when we understand the law of reincarnation and of nemesis (karma).

The values of a man who was an artist will reincarnate in a family of artists who will provide the necessary genetic inheritance for him.

A sum of mystical values will reincarnate among compassionate people.

The values of a libertine person will reincarnate among libertine people. The values of an assassin will reincarnate among assassins and thieves.

It has happened many times: cases of saints reincarnating among bandits and vice versa. When this happens, it is the law of destiny adjusting accounts.

We carry within our subconsciousness all of that inheritance. The factors of our inheritance betray us many times.

Education

Now, let us analyze education. This second factor of the subconsciousness is very important. Education begins at home. The child learns more through example than from precept.

In modern homes the child witnesses the adultery of his parents.

The child is an eyewitness of the anger, greed, and lust of those who gave him life.

The child sees with astonishment in his home the revolver or the rifle of his father and the magazines or tales of assassins and thieves, etc.

The child goes to the movies where he enjoys watching scenarios of detectives against thieves who assault people in the roads or who assault banks. When the night of Christmas or any other holiday arrives, the child receives cannons, revolvers, and pistol toys. So, the child can then play as a bandit or a thief who assaults people in the roads, etc.

All of these are stored in the subconsciousness of the child.

The child's parents are the ones who poison him little by little with the fatal venom of delinquency.

Time passes, the child grows, and the ideas of crime that were deposited within his subconsciousness develop, evolve, and progress. This subconsciously occurs even when the child's vital conscious part ignores everything that happens within the profound regions of his subconsciousness. Any given day the fruit (ideas of crime) ripens and the harvest is crime.

Everything that is sown within the subconsciousness flourishes in the mind over time. The situational reaction of a homicidal one who never wanted to kill is the fatal outcome what he learned as a child. The new gangster, the street-smart thief, the new burgler who was a good citizen, is the outcome of a false education. Pornographic, erotic novels and movies engender prostitution, seduction, and abduction with force and violence, etc. The pornographic movie actors and writers are teaching perversities to the subconsciousness of children and adults. Therefore, the time has arrived to fight against moral corruption from the prostitutes of intelligence.

The child learns in school bloody histories of slyness, maliciousness, distrust, etc., that are recorded within the subconsciousness. With all of this recorded within the subconsciousness, the fatal outcome is crime.

Circumstances

Now, let us study circumstances, certain critical circumstances that irritate the subconsciousness and provoke criminal reactions.

Objective circumstances combine themselves with similar subconscious circumstances within the subconsciousness in order to provoke crime.

Objective and subjective images combine themselves in order to provoke crime. Example: an unemployed man, hungry and miserable, remembers having seen in his infancy his father in the same crisis. Then, he remembers that in order to solve the problem his father assaulted a person in the streets and robbed him. Then he remembers the good food that was served at the table of his home after the robbery, etc. Therefore, the critical circumstance of the unemployed man together with the circumstance of his subconscious remembrance combine and provoke the crime.

Synthesis

The three factors genotype, phenotype, and paratype are the psychogenesis of every criminal act.

Crime can be extirpated from its most intimate roots only with an integral culture.

Crime can be extirpated from the mind only with an integral culture.

The subconscious clairvoyant perceives the history of the human race through the centuries. The memories of all our past reincarnations live within our subconsciousness.

Oftentimes when seeing a remembrance a subconscious clairvoyant falls into crime. For example, it can happen that a subconscious clairvoyant may clairvoyantly see his loyal spouse committing adultery. The clairvoyant is sure of his vision; he knows the word hallucination has been invented by ignoramuses in order to disguise their ignorance. He knows that the vision exists.

If the clairvoyant is a non-cultured individual without intellectual discipline of any kind, then he will react in accordance to his bio-psychological "I."

If he is a neurasthenic clairvoyant he will treacherously assassinate his spouse after having vilely slandered her as an adulterer.

The paranoid clairvoyant will intellectually plan a very intelligent crime.

The epileptic type of clairvoyant will momentarily react with an explosive outburst of brutal anger. Then, after having broken through his explosive anger, his phenotypic super-structure of personal control created by his social habits and his education, he will madly drag himself to assassinate his virtuous and loyal spouse.

The oligophrenic clairvoyant would commit a filthy and horrifying crime. This is how he would assassinate his loyal spouse.

The schizophrenic clairvoyant would abandon her immediately.

The sadomasochist clairvoyant would assassinate her during the very sexual act or after it.

These are the dangers of subconscious clairvoyance. The clairvoyant does not doubt his vision. He thinks that his vision is not a hallucination.

If the subconscious clairvoyant does not study psychiatry, Theosophy, psychology, Rosicrucianism, etc., he can then fall into the most horrifying crimes.

The loyal spouse of our example could have been an adulterer in her past reincarnation. Therefore, the clairvoyant without discipline and intellectual culture will ignore what the past and the subconsciousness are. The outcome of his ignorance and his lack of culture is crime, public slander, etc.

In many spiritual schools, the subconscious clairvoyants may skin their neighbors alive. They calumniate the innocent; they accuse them of witchcraft, sorcery, black magic, adultery, robbery, extortion, etc. Nobody escapes them; they slander everyone.

It is peculiar to see those subconscious clairvoyants as proud ignoramuses who boast of being wise. They foretell infamies. They torment their neighbors by accusing good citizens. They base their actions on their subconscious clairvoyance. They clairvoyantly see people in the old past of their ancient lives, committing errors that in their present life they are incapable of committing.

The penal code should also punish the calumniator clairvoyants.

Constantly, we hear those subconscious calumniator clairvoyants utter phrases such as the following: "That fellow is a black magician and he is putting a spell on me," or "The lady 'X' is committing adultery with the gentleman 'Y.'"

They affirm it, even when the slandered woman may be a saint. Those clairvoyant ignoramuses lack respect for others.

Nevertheless, we cannot blame their clairvoyance. Indeed, the sixth sense is as natural and normal as the eyes, the ears, the olfactory sense, the mouth, and the sense of touch.

The clairvoyant is not to blame for those errors. The cause of all of those errors is the lack of intellectual culture and the lack of respect towards our neighbor.

The memories of all of those errors that we committed in our past reincarnations live within our subconsciousness. The clairvoyant without intellectual culture sees all of those errors from the past, then he gets confused, and the outcome is calumny against just and honorable people.

The cultured clairvoyant, the intellectual clairvoyant, who has studied psychiatry, Theosophy, psychology, Rosicrucianism, etc., does not fall into such errors, because he has intellectual discipline. The cultured, educated, respectful, and intellectually disciplined clairvoyant enjoys illuminated intellection; he knows how to read the subconsciousness of nature with complete cognizance.

The cultured, educated, respectful, and intellectually disciplined clairvoyant is capable of retrospectively studying the whole history of the Earth and its root races. He is an illuminated clairvoyant.

Chapter 26

The Supraconsciousness

The most elevated kind of clairvoyance in the universe is supraconsciousness. All of the avatars or messengers from the superior worlds have been supracognizant clairvoyants. Hermes Trismegistus, Rama, Krishna, Buddha, Jesus Christ, etc., were supracognizant beings, messengers from the superior worlds, initiators of new eras of historic evolution.

Imagination, inspiration, and intuition are the three obligatory ways of initiation. We are going to examine each one of the three steps seperately.

Let us begin with:

Imagination

For the wise, to imagine is to see. Imagination is the translucence of the soul.

What is important is to learn to concentrate thought on one thing only.

Whosoever learns to think on only one thing makes marvels and prodigies.

The disciple that wants to reach imaginative knowledge must learn to concentrate himself and know how to profoundly meditate.

The best exercise in order to attain imaginative knowledge is the following. While seated in front of a plant, we concentrate on it until forgetting everything that is not related with it. Then by closing the eyes we become drowsy, and we keep in our imagination the form and figure of the plant, its structure, perfume, and color.

The disciple will imagine the living cells of the plant. The disciple must provoke drowsiness during these practices. The disciple, while in drowsiness, will profoundly meditate on the internal constitution of the plant. It possesses protoplasm, membrane, and nucleus. The protoplasm is a viscous, elastic and transparent substance, similar to the egg white (albuminoid matter). The disciple, while in drowsiness, must reflect upon the four fundamental elements in the protoplasm of the cell of the plant. These four elements are carbon, oxygen, hydrogen, and nitrogen. The membrane is a marvellous substance without color, a substance within which the water becomes totally insoluble. This substance is the well-known cellulose.

The disciple, while concentrated, will imagine the nucleus of the cell as a small corpuscule, where the great universal life palpitates. The nuclear filament is within the nucleus, as well as the nuclear juice and the nucleolus which are all covered by the nuclear membrane. The nucleolus is formed by corpuscules infinitely full of shining beauty. These are residual products of the incessant reactions of the plant organism.

The disciple, while well-concentrated, must imagine with complete logical precision all of those mineral substances and organic combinations that are harmoniously unfolding within the cellular protoplasm of the plant. Let us think on the grains of starch and on the portentous chlorophyll, without which it is impossible to reach perfect organic synthesis. The chlorophyll is presented in granulated form (chloro-leucite) as a very beautiful yellow color (santofilia) that becomes that precious green color of the plant while under the solar rays.

Every plant is a perfect cellular community with incalculable perfections. The student, filled with a mystical attitude and enchanted by the exuberant beauty of the plant, must meditate on the perfection of the plant and in all of its scientific processes.

The mystic is in rapture when remembering all of the phenomena of nutrition, relation, and reproduction of each cell of the plant.

Let us see the chalice of the flower. Here are its sexual organs, here is the pollen, the masculine reproductive element. Here is the pistil or gynecium, a very precious feminine organ, with its ovary, stylus, and stigma. The ovary is a sack full of marvellous ova. The stamen can occupy different positions in relation with the pistil, for instance insertion beneath the ovary, insertion around the ovary, or above it.

Fecundation is verified with the function of the feminine germs and masculine gametes. After exiting the anther, the pollen, the masculine gamete, reaches the ovary of the plant where the ovum, the feminine gamete, is anxiously waiting. The seed is the precious and enchanted ovum that after being fecundated is transformed and grows.

Now the student should remember the step on which he is meditating. A sprout will emerge as a delicate bud; imagine it growing slowly, until seeing it with your imagination spreading branches, leaves, and flowers. Remember that everything that is born must die. Imagine the plant's process of dying. Its flowers wither its leaves dry and the wind blows them away. Finally, only a few twigs remain.

This process of birth and death is marvellous. By meditating on the whole process of birth and death of a plant, by meditating on its marvellous life, if the concentration is perfect and drowsiness achieves a profound level, then the chakras of the astral body will spin, develop, and unfold.

Meditation must be correct. The mind must be exact. Logical thought and exact concept is needed for the purpose of developing the internal senses absolutely perfectly.

Every incoherence, every lack of logical and moral equilibrium obstructs and damages the evolution and progress of the chakras, disks, or lotus flowers of the astral body. The student needs a lot of patience, willpower, tenacity, and absolute conscious faith. On any given day, within dreams, while in meditation, emerges a distant picture, a landscape of nature, a feature, etc. This is a sign that there is progress. The student elevates himself little by little into imaginative knowledge. Little by little the student is removing the veil of Isis. On any given day, the plant on which he was meditating disappears. Then, a beautiful child who replaces the plant is seen. That child is the elemental of the plant, the soul of the plant.

Later, during a dream, he awakens his consciousness; then he can say, "I am in the astral body." The consciousness awak-

ens little by little. In this way, the moment arrives in which the
disciple will acquire continuous consciousness.

When the student enjoys continuous consciousness he
no longer dreams; he can no longer dream, because his consciousness is awakened. Then, even when the physical body is
sleeping, he moves himself consciously in the superior worlds.

Exact meditation awakens the internal senses and performs a complete transformation of the internal bodies.

Whosoever awakens consciousness has reached imaginative knowledge. He moves in the world of symbolic images.

The symbols that one saw while he was dreaming are now
seen without dreaming; before, he was seeing them with a
sleeping consciousness. Now he moves himself among them
with a vigilant consciousness, even when his physical body is
profoundly asleep.

When the student reaches imaginative knowledge, he sees
the symbols but he does not understand them. He comprehends that all of Nature is a living scripture that he does not
know. In order to interpret the sacred symbols of great nature
the student needs to elevate himself into inspired knowledge.

Inspiration

Let us now study inspiration.

Inspired knowledge grants us the power of interpreting
the symbols of great Nature. The interpretation of symbols
is very delicate. Many clairvoyants have become homicidal or
have fallen into the crime of public slander because of not
knowing how to interpret symbols.

Symbols must be analyzed coldly without superstition,
maliciousness, mistrust, pride, vanity, fanaticism, prejudg-
ment, preconceptions, hatred, envy, greed, jealousy, etc. All
defects belong to the "I," to the "myself," to the reincarnating
ego.

When the "I" interferes by translating and interpreting
symbols, then it alters the meaning of the secret scriptures
and the clairvoyant falls into a crime which can conduct him
to jail.

Interpretation must be tremendously analytical, highly scientific, and essentially mystical. One has to learn how to see and how to interpret in the absence of the "I," of the "myself." It seems very strange to many mystics that we the brothers and sisters of the international Gnostic movement speak of divine clairvoyance with the penal code in hand. Those that think in this way consider spirituality as something that has nothing to do with our relationship to daily life. These people act wrongly; they are mistaken. They ignore that what each soul is in the superior worlds is the exact result of the daily life that everyone of us lives in this valley of tears.

If our words, thoughts, and actions are not just, then the result appears in the internal worlds and the law falls upon us.

The law is the law; to be ignorant of the law does not mean the exclusion of its fulfilment.

The worst sin is ignorance. To teach the one that does not know is a work of mercy.

The whole tremendous responsibility of the law falls upon the clairvoyant.

One has to interpret symbols of the great nature in the absolute absence of the "I." Nonetheless, self-criticism must be multiplied, because when the "I" of the clairvoyant believes he knows a lot, then he feels himself infallible, omniscient, wise, and even supposes that he sees and interprets with the absence of the "I." These types of clairvoyants fortify the "I" so much that they end up converting themselves into terribly perverse demons. When a clairvoyant of this type sees his inner god, then he interprets the vision in accordance with his tenebrous criteria, and exclaims, "I am doing well."

We have to know how to interpret by basing ourselves on the law of philosophical analogies, on the law of correspondences, and on the numerical Kabbalah.

We recommend *The Mystical Kabbalah* by Dion Fortune. This book is marvellous, study it.

One that has hatred, resentment, jealousy, envy, pride, etc., does not achieve elevation of himself to the second step called inspired knowledge.

When we elevate ourselves to inspired knowledge, we understand and comprehend that the accidental accumulation of objects does not exist. Really, all phenomena of nature and all objects are found intimately and organically joined together, internally dependent upon each other and mutually conditioning each other. Really, no phenomena of nature can be integrally comprehended if we consider it isolated[22].

Everything is in incessant movement. Everything changes, nothing is quiet. In every object there is internal struggle. An object is positive and negative at the same time. Quantitative transforms itself into qualitative. Evolution is a process of the complication of energy.

Inspired knowledge permits us to know the inner relationship between everything which is, has been, and will be.

Matter is nothing but condensed energy. The infinite modifications of energy are absolutely unknown, as much as for historical materialism[23] as for dialectical materialism[24].

Energy is equal to mass by the velocity of the light squared. We the Gnostics separate ourselves from the two antithesis of ignorance, and we integrally study man and nature.

Life is every determined and determinant energy. Life is object and subject at the same time.

The disciple that wants to reach the inspired knowledge must concentrate profoundly on music. *The Magic Flute* of Mozart reminds us of an Egyptian initiation. The nine symphonies of Beethoven and many other great classical compositions elevate us to the superior worlds.

The disciple, profoundly concentrated in the music, must observe himself within it, as the bee within the honey, which is the product of his whole labor.

---

22 This is studied as "interdependence."

23 "A major tenet in the Marxist theory of history that regards material economic forces as the base on which sociopolitical institutions and ideas are built." — American Heritage® Dictionary of the English Language

24 The philosophical theory developed by Karl Marx and Friedrich Engels that posits that matter is the only reality.

When the disciple has already reached inspired knowledge, he must then prepare himself for intuitive knowledge.

Intuition

The world of intuition is the world of mathematics. The student that wants to elevate himself to the world of intuition must be a mathematician, or at least must have notions of arithmetic.

Mathematical formulas grant us intuitive knowledge.

The student must concentrate himself on a mathematical formula and profoundly meditate on it. Afterwards, he must empty the mind and make it completely blank, then simply wait for the Inner Being to teach the contained concept which is enclosed in the mathematical formula. For example, before Kepler publicly announced his famous principle that "the square of the period of revolution of a planet varies directly as the distance from the sun cubed," that formula already existed; it was contained in the solar system, even when the wise did not know it.

The student can mentally concentrate himself on that formula. He must empty his mind, become drowsy with his mind completely blank, and wait for his own inner Being to reveal to him all of the marvellous secrets which are contained in the formula of Kepler.

The formula of Newton concerning universal gravity can also serve us in order to exercise ourselves in initiation. This formula is the following. "The force between two objects varies directly with each of the masses and inversely with the square of the distance between them."

If the student practices with tenacity and supreme patience, his own inner Being will teach or instruct him in the Great Work. Then he will study at the feet of the master and he will elevate himself to intuitive knowledge. Imagination, inspiration, and intuition are obligatory steps of initiation. Whosoever has raised the three steps of direct knowledge has reached supraconsciousness.

In the world of intuition, we find only omniscience; the world of intuition is the world of the Being, it is the world of the Innermost.

In this world the "I," the "myself," the ego, cannot enter.

The world of intuition is the universal spirit of life.

The world of imaginative knowledge is a world of symbolic images.

Inspiration grants us the power of interpreting symbols.

In the world of intuition, we see the great cosmic theater and we are the spectators. We assist in the great drama of life. In the world of intuition, the whole drama, which is represented in cosmic scenes, is reduced to terrific arithmetical operations. This is the amphitheatrum of cosmic science.

From that region of mathematics we see that there are physical masses above and below all of the limits of external sensory perceptions. Those masses are invisible. We can perceive them only with clairvoyance.

Matter is condensed energy. When its vibration is very slow, its mass is beneath the limits of external sensory perceptions. When its vibratory movement is very fast, then the mass is above the limits of external sensory perceptions. With the telescope, we can only see worlds whose degree of vibration is active within the limits of external sensory perception.

Above and below the limits of external sensory perceptions there are worlds, solar systems, and constellations populated by many types of living beings.

So-called "matter" is only energy that condenses into infinite masses.

The senses of external perception only reach a fraction of what is perceivable.

Dialectical materialism and metaphysics are untimely and antiquated.

We the brothers and sisters of the Gnostic movement go in a distinct way.

It is urgent that scientists study *The Treatise of Occult Science* by Dr. Rudolf Steiner, great Hungarian medic, born in 1861, friend and disciple of Nietzsche and Ernest Hegel, and the founder of the Anthroposophical Society.

It is indispensable that those who are lovers of science investigate in depth the whole portentous Asian wisdom, poured as a river of gold in the immortal pages of *The Secret Doctrine*. This work consists of six volumes and is a monument of the archaic wisdom. The great master H.P.B. is the genius author of this precious treasury of the ancient wisdom.

Those who reach supraconsciousness convert themselves into true illuminated clairvoyants. No authentic clairvoyant boasts about his faculties.

No legitimate clairvoyant says that he is a clairvoyant.

When a true clairvoyant sees something important, he gives his concepts in a very cultured way and with supreme respect for others. He never says, "I am seeing." He always says. "We understand, we have learned." This is how all of those that have reached the ineffable summits of supraconsciousness distinguish themselves by their gentility, humility, and modesty.

You should read *Kundalini Yoga* by Sivananda. Meditate on the blessed White Lodge. Inquire within the Gnostic treasuries. Meditate on the profound symbolism contained in each one of the arcana of the Tarot.

Those who reach the heights of supraconsciousness enter into the amphitheater of cosmic science.

The triple way of science, philosophy, and revolutionary cosmic mysticism conducts us into the ineffable regions of the great light.

Gnosis is highly scientific, highly philosophical, and transcendentally mystical.

KRISHNAMURTI

Chapter 27

The Krishnamurti Case

A great conflict occurred inside the Theosophical Society during those times when Annie Besant was occupying the presidency of this marvelous organization, whose founder was the great initiate Helena Petrovna Blavatsky. The problem that presented itself was the Krishnamurti case. Lady Besant lifted her finger aloft in order to asseverate to the four winds that the Hindu boy Krishnamurti was the living reincarnation of Jesus Christ. The great clairvoyant Leadbeater and other eminent Theosophists totally agreed with Lady Besant. All of them were asserting that the Hindustani boy was Jesus Christ newly reincarnated.

We still remember that foundation of that order named "The Star of the East" whose unique purpose was to welcome the Messiah. Later on, Krishnamurti himself dissolved it.

In that epoch a division occurred in the heart of the Theosophical Society. Some asserted that Krishnamurti was the Messiah. Others did not accept that concept, thus they withdrew from the Theosophical Society.

Among those who withdrew was Dr. Rudolf Steiner, the powerful illuminated clairvoyant, eminent intellectual, founder of the Anthroposophic Society. The work of Rudolf Steiner is grandiose. His books are wells of profound wisdom.

The Spanish group Marco Aurelio also withdrew from the Theosophical Society.

The split that occurred in the heart of the famous Theosophical Society was a true tragedy.

We need to analyze the Krishnamurti case.

While some Theosophists were convinced that Krishnamurti was the reincarnation of Jesus Christ, others stated that he was just an ignorant boy. They stated that the only thing he knew was how to drive an automobile and play tennis, etc. So, what was the matter? Why did they not agree? What is most intriguing is that the greatest clairvoyants of the Theosophical Society were divided into two opposite camps.

Absolutely logical questions emerge: why did the clairvoyants split apart?

These clairvoyants saw the internal Being of the Hindu boy. Then why did they not agree? Is it perhaps because some clairvoyants see in one way and other clairvoyants in another distinct way? Is it possible that the clairvoyants contradict each other? If the clairvoyants saw the inner Being of Jiddu Krishnamurti, what was the cause of their disagreement?

When a thousand people see an object with their physical sight, they say, "This is a table, a chair, a rock, etc." When they see a person, they say, "This is a man or a woman or a child, etc." Then, what is going on with clairvoyance? What is the reason in the concrete case of this Hindu boy in which the clairvoyants could not agree on their concepts? There is no doubt that Krishnamurti was a true puzzle for the Theosophical Society.

The most critical thing was to see those clairvoyants fighting amongst themselves.

This is something that confuses the minds of those that are starting in these studies.

Krishnamurti fell into skepticism. He remained skeptical for many years. Yet, finally he responded and started his mission.

All of us, the endoteric Gnostic brothers and sisters, proposed ourselves to investigate the Krishnamurti case in the superior worlds.

After many patient works, we arrived at the following conclusions:

First: Every human being is a trio of body, soul, and spirit.

Second: When the spirit [Chesed / Atman] defeats matter, it becomes a buddha[25].

---

25 The term "buddha" is a title. There are a vast number of buddhas, each at different levels of attainment. At the ultimate level, a buddha is a being who has become totally free of suffering. The inner Being (Hebrew: Chesed; Sanskrit: Atman) first becomes a Buddha when the Human Soul [Tiphereth] completes the work of the Fourth Initiation of Fire (related to Netzach, the mental body).

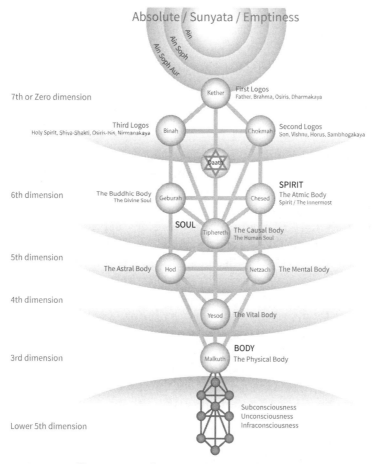

Absolute / Sunyata / Emptiness

Ain
Ain Soph
Ain Soph Aur

7th or Zero dimension

First Logos
Father, Brahma, Osiris, Dharmakaya
Kether

Third Logos
Holy Spirit, Shiva-Shakti, Osiris-Isis, Nirmanakaya
Binah

Chokmah
Second Logos
Son, Vishnu, Horus, Sambhogakaya

Daath

6th dimension

The Buddhic Body
The Divine Soul
Geburah

Chesed
SPIRIT
The Atmic Body
Spirit / The Innermost

SOUL
Tiphereth
The Causal Body
The Human Soul

5th dimension

The Astral Body
Hod

Netzach
The Mental Body

4th dimension

Yesod
The Vital Body

3rd dimension

Malkuth
BODY
The Physical Body

Lower 5th dimension

Subconsciousness
Unconsciousness
Infraconsciousness

THE BODIES OF THE BEING ON THE TREE OF LIFE (KABBALAH).

Third: When the soul [Tiphereth / Manas] purifies and
sanctifies itself, then it is called a bodhisattva.

Fourth: The spirit of Krishnamurti is a buddha.

Fifth: The soul of Krishnamurti is a bodhisattva.

There are many buddhas in Asia who have not incarnated
the Christ yet[26].

---

26 The incarnation of Christ is the basis of the straight path, also called the
path of the bodhisattva. Read *The Three Mountains* by Samael Aun Weor.

There is a ray within every human being that unites us to the Absolute. That ray is our resplendent dragon of wisdom, the internal Christ, the sephirotic crown[27].

The buddhas who have not incarnated the internal Christ have not Christified themselves yet.

Krishnamurti's buddha has already incarnated his resplendent dragon of wisdom, his particular ray, his own internal Christ.

When Lady Besant, Leadbeater, and other Theosophists studied the Krishnamurti case, they became astonished with the splendid light of that Christified buddha. However, since they did not know the Christic esotericism, they completely believed that Krishnamurti was the reincarnation of Jesus Christ. The mistake was not in their clairvoyance. The mistake was in their lack of intellectual culture. They only knew about the Theosophical septenary[28]. They only knew about the body, soul, and spirit. Yet, they ignored that beyond these three aspects (body, soul, and spirit) every human being has a ray (the internal Christ) that unites us to the Absolute.

They saw the internal god of Krishnamurti and believed that he was Jesus of Nazareth; that was their mistake. What is most critical is the damage that they perpetrated upon the Hindu boy. When a bodhisattva is told that his internal god is a master, he becomes confused; he is damaged; he develops a complex.

The Hindu boy saw those instructors arguing among themselves because of him. Thus, the outcome was a psychological trauma for his human personality. Krishnamurti had a psychological trauma.

There is no doubt that the Theosophist clairvoyants did great damage to the Hindu boy. The Theosophist hierarchs should have left the Hindu boy in peace. He would have developed himself freely in India. Then, his work would have been marvelous.

The great buddha of Krishnamurti did not give his whole message, because his bodhisattva had a psychological trauma.

---

27 The top three sephiroth on the Tree of Life: Kether, Chokmah, Binah.
28 See page

If we examine the doctrine of Krishnamurti, we see that the best of it is Buddhism. Unfortunately, he did not know the Christic esotericism. The Hindu body drank from the fountain of the Buddhist gospel. It is a pity that he did not know the Christic esotericism. Later on, he mixed the Buddhist philosophy with the conventional philosophy from the Western world. Thus, the doctrine of Krishnamurti is the outcome of that mixture. The doctrine of Krishnamurti is Buddhism. However, the doctrine of Aquarius is the outcome of the mixture of Buddhist esotericism with Christic esotericism. The doctrine of Krishnamurti is free Buddhism. However, the living fountain of that doctrine is the marvelous gospel of the Lord Buddha.

We are not against Krishnamurti; we only regret the fact that the internal buddha of that Hindu philosopher could not give the whole message. That is all.

When a clairvoyant discovers that the Innermost (the spirit) of someone is a master, then it is best for that clairvoyant to be silent, in order not to damage that person.

When somebody knows that his inner being is a master, he becomes filled with pride and arrogance. Fortunately, Krishnamurti learned how to be humble.

There are also fallen bodhisattvas. They are worse than demons.

No one has to be told that his inner Being is a master. The clairvoyant must be prudent. The clairvoyant must learn how to be silent.

The spirit of someone could have achieved the degree of master in some ancient reincarnation. The bodhisattva (human soul of the master) could have fallen later on, thus now that soul can live upon the path of evil.

The master never falls. The one who falls is the bodhisattva (human soul) of the master.

The clairvoyant must be prudent; thus, before announcing a new master, he must wait with patience many years, in order to see how the person of flesh and bones, the terrestrial bodhisattva, behaves. The master could be very great above;

yet, the person of flesh and bones (bodhisattva) here below is dangerous.

In any case, "By their fruits you will know them." [Matthew 7:15-20]

Madame Blavatsky stated that one of the greatest mysteries of esotericism is the mystery of the double personality.

All the fights and errors of the Theosophical Society were the cause of the trauma of Krishnamurti.

The Krishnamurti case is very important.

Dr. Steiner knew the Christic mysteries. This is why he did not allow himself to be confused. Steiner was Gnostic.

Steiner did not accept that Krishnamurti was the reincarnation of Jesus Christ.

Many followed Steiner and many others Lady Besant.

The clairvoyant Steiner had a vast intellectual culture; this is why he did not fall into that mistake. Steiner was a true Rosicrucian Gnostic.

Chapter 28

The Mentally Obsessed, the Client, the Succubus

Many cases of witchcraft are frequently presented before the tribunals. Regarding witchcraft cases, the authorities laugh about them. They concretely judge common crimes. They completely exclude stories regarding warlocks, santeros, sorcerers, or whatever they want to call them.

The warlocks or black magicians, etc., already know that the authorities do not believe in their tenebrous science. When the mentally obsessed, the clients, the sorcerers, etc., have to answer in front of the authorities, they prefer to talk concretely about the exterior aspect of the crime, since they know by their own experience that the authorities do not believe in witchcraft, sorcery, etc.

Internally, the warlocks consider the authorities as people who know very much. Yet, the warlocks know that regarding witchcraft or matters of sorcery, the authorities are absolutely ignorant. This is the concept that the honest sorcerers have about the authorities, sorcerers who sincerely believe in their religion and in the power and efficacy of their rites.

There are also false sorcerers who only live by extortion; they exploit their neighbors' credulity. These false sorcerers are extortionists.

We are going to study the honest sorcerers.

We do not deny that the mentalists, the ones who perform obsession, the godfather, the incubus, etc., are ignorant people. It is logical that ignorance is the mother of all crimes. Yet, this problem cannot be resolved with corrective educational treatments that are based on strictly conventional culture. Neither are these problems resolved with loss of liberty nor with forced labor.

The sorcerer continues to be a sorcerer in jail or in exile, with conventional culture or without it. The sorcerer states,

"These people know a lot, yet regarding my science, they do not know anything. My science is superior."

To that end, the instructive and corrective conventional systems, as well as the systems of penalization, are useless in order to reform sorcerers. Those ignorant people can only be reformed with a superior spiritual culture. Those cases can only be treated with corrective educational treatments based on Theosophy, Rosicrucianism, yogic philosophy, etc. Professors on these matters should be available with special reformatories in order to treat these cases.

Witchcraft is behind thirty percent of common crimes. However, the delinquents keep silence, because they know that the judges are skeptical and totally ignorant about matters of witchcraft.

Indeed, the judges have a conventional intellectual culture. Yet, they do not know anything about the science of sorcerers. Only the study of Gnosis, Theosophy, Rosicrucianism, yogic philosophy, etc., can change the skepticism of the judges. This way, they will move more towards the populace's soul.

Forensic psychiatry can tremendously expand with these studies in order to profoundly explore the causa causorum of any crime.

The responsibility of the criminal facing the tribunals has extremely deep roots, so deep that not even the psychoanalysis of Freud suspects it.

We must leave aside mental laziness and those prejudices that make us utter phrases like, "Oh but what would people say if I study this?" or "What would people say if I educate myself in this?" We must study Gnosis, Theosophy, Rosicrucianism, yogic philosophy, etc.

Occult wisdom is the fundamental depth of any science.

The great German doctor Arnold Krumm-Heller narrates in his *Rosicrucian Novel* the case of a warlock who was performing sorcery on a wretched woman. He was performing his sorcery through the medium of a used piece of cloth from his victim. The unhappy woman became deranged—or better said, the warlock made her insane. When Dr. Krumm-Heller described the case to the authorities, they mocked him. Of course, this is why, based on this type of authoritative skepticism, the delinquents from sorcery can commit the most horrible crimes. The terrestrial law does not affect the warlocks, since they always shelter themselves under the skepticism of the judges. Warlocks are pleased with the skepticism of the judges, since their skepticism is convenient for them. Yet, woe to them if the judges were to know about witchcraft.

A Russian scientist invented an electronic brain that is capable of registering the mental force of a human being. If someone gives a command to that electronic device, then the apparatus collects his cerebral radiations. Then, that device places in movement other different machines through its very complicated and difficult mechanism. This is how the reality of the force of thought has already been demonstrated. Once, scientists laughed at statements about mental force; yet now, in Russia, instead of pressing automatic buttons to move machines, they are starting to utilize mental force.

We do not deny that the mentalist, the one who obsesses, the obsessed one, the client, and the succubus are oligophrenic. They are ignorant fanatics who, while in their state of delirium, commit horrendous crimes. Yet, the reality is that such people are utilizing mental force that is already demonstrated by that scientific Russian device.

Mental waves travel throughout space. Shortly, the scientists will invent antennas that will be capable of capturing mental waves using apparatuses similar to the radio that will translate mental waves into sound. At that time, no one will conceal his thoughts anymore. Nevertheless, in this day and age there are already apparatuses capable of measuring mental waves. Scientists measure mental waves based on micro-voltage.

Therefore, the hour has arrived in which the judges have to stop laughing and start studying.

Victor Hugo said:

> "The one who laughs at what he does not know is an ignoramus who walks the path of idiocy."

Let us look at hypnotism, for instance. Until a relatively short time ago, it seemed to everyone that hypnotism was related with sorcerers and skulls amidst foggy nights. In this day and age, hypnotism is already officially accepted by medical science in order to heal the sick. There are clinics with scientific devices for hypnotism.

There are also sorcerers who utilize hypnotism in order to perform their criminal deeds. This is already established in the penal code of many countries. A sorcerer can give a person a mental suggestion during a hypnotic trance. The sorcerer can mentally suggest to a passive person and command him to execute a crime. Later on, that person, without knowing where or why, goes and executes the command given by the sorcerer. This is how horrendous and frightful crimes have been committed.

The sorcerers also use distinct "voodoo dolls" that they place at the doors of their victims. When the authorities get their hands on one of those famous "voodoo dolls," then the proverbial skeptical laugh of the judges is provoked. People already know the skepticism of the judges. This is why the accused ones prefer to hide those famous "voodoo dolls." The "voodoo dolls" can be made with special powders, water, toasted corn, feathers, dolls, pieces of cloth with menstrual blood, etc.

The force of thought lies in the depth of these famous "voodoo dolls." The imagination of the sorcerer is exalted with the "voodoo dolls." This is how he projects cerebral waves that are capable of damaging and killing his hated victims.

It so happens that many of those victims of witchcraft and "voodoo dolls" fall into deliriums of persecution; they feel threatened by the paranormal forces of the sorcerer. If the victim is hysteric and impulsive, he can then commit a hysterical homicide, an act of hysteria.

Oftentimes, these types of criminals (who in their depth are victims) suffer "hysterical epileptic" attacks.

Huxley, the materialistic scientist, accepted that many types of living beings populate the ether (the ultra). The dialectic materialists reject the ether; they state that there are only electromagnetic energies; however, this is only a new name that is given to the ether.

Within a drop of water there are millions of microbes; for them, the drop is infinite.

There are beasts and monsters within the "ultra-special" that the human being cannot perceive. People cannot perceive them due to the distinct modifications of matter. Metaphysics and dialectical materialism know nothing about this. As the ultra-micrometer can register up to the ten thousandth part of a millimeter, the clairvoyant can perceive these types and forms of life (even if the materialists laugh about it).

An English doctor invented a lens with which the aura, the irradiation of the astral body, can be seen.

Soon, there will be lenses that will see the fourth dimension. Then scholastic metaphysics and dialectical materialism will be ludicrous before the solemn verdict of public consciousness.

At that time through those lenses we will see the monsters and larvae that obsess the minds of delinquents.

If the judges laugh about it, then they also have to laugh at microbes, and renounce the microscope and vaccinations.

Logic invites us to consider that if there are physical microbes that damage the physical body, there must also be mental microbes—larvae, incubae, succubae, basilisks, dragons, etc.—that damage the mind.

In a short time these types of mental microbes will be visible to the whole world. Yesterday, the microscope was invented in order to see physical microbes. Tomorrow, the ultra-microscope will be invented in order to see microbes from the ultra-world.

If there are physical epidemics, there are also moral epidemics, that is to say, immoral waves of suicide, thievery, violence, etc.. This can be confirmed in cities.

Microbes are the agents of those epidemics, in both cases. Logic is logic.

The demon-possessed ones from Jatibonico in which a whole family suffered the most strange and diverse mental disturbances, and the case of "Mama Coleta" mentioned in chapter sixteen of this book, are concrete cases of psychic obsession. These are cases of moral epidemics.

The active agents of those epidemics are from the ultra, namely "trolls, larvae, incubae, evil spirits," etc. These types of names stir resistance in the skeptical materialist. Let us not argue about terminology. If you like, baptize these living things from the ultra with the name "ultra-sensory microbes." I think this name will satisfy the skeptical materialists. Most of the time, we human beings argue over terminology. So let us agree on the former term, and thereafter let us continue analyzing the subject.

In their psychological depth, the skeptical materialists have a trauma. The cause of that trauma is Roman Catholic dogma. They were disappointed by the Roman sect; thus, the outcome of their disappointment was a psychological trauma. They are enemies of Hegel. Now, anything that smells of spirituality, unconsciously seems to these skeptical materialists as being from the Roman Catholic Church. This is their psychological trauma.

So, you skeptical materialists, let us inform you (in order for you to hear to us aside from your traumatic and sick "I") that we are neither Catholics nor materialists. Yes, listen, we are neither Catholics nor materialists, we are Gnostics. Gnosis signifies knowledge, wisdom.

Then let us study the ultra-sensory microbes.

The sorcerer Barrueta mentally obsessed the unhappy clairvoyant medium woman of chapter sixteen. What? Does the term "sorcerer" bother you? Are you afraid to believe in sorcerers? Well then, be afraid also of microbes. What if we named the sorcerers microbes and the microbes sorcerers? It is just a matter of terminology, right? Then, why do we have to argue?

Let us analyze without preconceptions. The medium and the whole family of the "Mama Coleta" case were obsessed by "evil spirits, trolls, sorcerers," etc., ultra-sensory microbes that will become visible within a short time, when optics advance towards the ultra.

As a leper's body is invaded by the bacterium of Hansen, and a person with tuberculosis has his lungs invaded by the bacterium of Kock, likewise ultra-sensory microbes can obsess the mind and direct a human being to commit a crime.

There are two types of epidemics and two types of sicknesses, namely the physical and the psychic.

Everything is reduced to the atom. The atom is a trio of matter, energy, and consciousness. We need to investigate how the atomic intelligences behave.

If no one in the epoch of Pasteur accepted microbes, if they laughed at that sage because he was disinfecting surgical instruments, why is it so strange then that they laugh about us, the Gnostics, because we accept the existence of ultra-sensory microbes? These are just things of this epoch! Yet, when the science of optics advances, then they will be our best defenders. This is how the course of history has always been.

The famous "voodoo dolls" from sorcerers are contaminated poisonous substances. Those substances are true ultra-microbe-carriers that can sensibly infect the organism of their victims and can lead them towards dementia and death. Even if the medical science of this century ignores this, later it will know it.

The sorcerers' "voodoo dolls" are very dangerous, bacterium-carrier substances.

A psychic epidemic was the causa causorum of the "Mama Coleta" case.

Jails are filled with delinquents who are mentally sick. The ultra-sensory microbes make the mind sick and conduce the human being to crime.

Millions of delinquents feel themselves to be innocent, and there is still no mental prophylactic for them, or offices for mental health.

In this day and age, people speak abundantly about physical culture, yet institutes for psychic culture are more necessary now than ever.

We admit to the existence of air currents that are truly carriers of infectious bacteria, yet we ignore the existence of mental currents that are transmitters of ultra-sensory microbes, capable of damaging, causing illness, and even killing their victims.

The "Mama Coleta" case is related with a mental infection transmitted by the mental currents of a sorcerer. His victims fell into jail and death; yet he, the secret assassin, remained immune. He was not caught; he saved himself by hiding behind the skepticism of the judges.

Cases of psychic obsession must be studied by forensic psychiatry.

Jails are filled with mentally sick people. There is no doctor for those wretched ones. Thousand of delinquents are innocent.

Forensic psychiatry needs to be expanded.

There is a specific antidote for each sickness.

Sorcerers are not reformed with external culture. No sick person is cured with an incompatible remedy. We cannot cure typhus with remedies for measles. Each sickness needs its special antidote. Sorcerers are reformed with their special antidote. The antidote for sorcerers is the esoteric wisdom, namely: Gnosis, Theosophy, Rosicrucianism, yogic philosophy, etc.

It is obvious that when a delinquent is condemned, the evidence of the "corpus delicti" is required. It is also necessary to justify the "corpus delicti" in accordance with all the legal forms established by the codex of penal processes.

A human being cannot be condemned for the crime of black magic if the evidence of the "corpus delicti" is not known. Neither can he be condemned if the "corpus delicti" has not been justified in accordance with all the legal forms established by the codex of penal processes.

When a citizen is accused of the crime of black magic, when a citizen is accused as being a black magician, the "corpus delicti" must exist, and that "corpus delicti" must have been rightly justified in accordance with the penal processes.

When a citizen is accused, when a citizen is designated a black magician without the "corpus delicti," without criminal antecedents, without judicial evidences, then the accuser falls into the crime of calumny and defamation of character.

People who dedicate themselves to the studies of esotericism, Theosophy, Rosicrucianism, Gnosis, yogic philosophy, etc., constantly fall into the crimes of calumny, public slander, defamation of character, etc. Those people must take care of their tongue, because frequently they fall into the crimes of calumny, public slander, defamation of character, etc. To asseverate that such a fellow or such a lady is a black magician is a crime of calumny, public slander, and defamation of character. The spiritual brothers and sisters should learn how to control their tongues.

For "by their fruits you will know them." Each person is known through his deeds. A citizen cannot be a black magician without criminal antecedents.

A lady and a gentleman who accomplish their duties as mother or father and pay their debts, have never killed, stolen, slandered, etc., cannot be black magicians.

The skeptics of materialism laugh about all of these things. Therefore, leaving aside the fanaticism of the materialistic sect, we, the Gnostics, say the following: "The one who laughs at what he does not know is an ignoramus who walks the path of idiocy." Therefore, when a scientist mocks Asian yoga and esoteric Buddhism, he becomes an ignoramus who walks the path of idiocy.

Thanks to the practical science of the West, technical advancement has been achieved as well as a revolution in forensic psychiatry. The practical, experimental, and demonstrative science of the West allows us to place physical matter at our service.

The practical, experimental, and demonstrative science of Asian yoga allows us to awaken the senses of internal perception. We can see, hear, touch, and feel the fourth dimension. When a human being expands his senses of perception, he then receives new scientific information that increases his wisdom. The esoteric science is the fundamental basis of nature.

When Western and Asian science are completely joined, then the human being will reach a new integral and total culture, free of fanatical sectarianism.

The science of criminology is stagnant in this day and age because of the superstitions of the fanatical materialistic sect.

Chapter 29
The Alienated

It is impossible to know the fundamental cause of any mental disequilibrium without expanding psychiatry with Theosophy, Rosicrucianism, Hermeticism, yogic philosophy, and high Gnostic esotericism. This is how expanded psychiatry can discover and cure the alienated.

We knew the case of a young woman who fell into a state of furious madness. This young lady was interned for six months in a mental health center. There, she was submitted to the classic medical treatments with the famous electric shocks, diet, etc. Nonetheless, everything was a complete and absolute failure.

That lady, when in shock, was writhing like a serpent; she was foaming through her mouth while pronouncing incoherent words, etc.

We, the students of expanded psychiatry, purposed ourselves to profoundly study this case. Thus, we found the following symptoms:

Indeed, she had abnormal ideas related with strange psychopathic deliriums. She had deliriums of persecution. She believed herself to be wanted by the police and condemned to death. She felt herself accused and wanted for robbery, etc.

When exploring the psyche of this sick woman, we found anguish during her delirium and a choleric physiognomy. Sometimes she was filled with terror and, at other times, melancholy.

It appears among the antecedents of her social evolution that during her infancy, adolescence, and youth she developed normally in her home and in school without anything strange having occurred to her.

She did not present symptoms of bruises, wounds, or anything of the sort.

Her psychopathic personality was of a totally schizoid type and she was introverted in an abnormal way.

The great sages are introverted; yet, they are not schizoids. They are normally introverted individuals.

The schizoid attitude of this sick lady belonged to the hyper-sensory and hyper-emotive type.

The type of schizoid personality described by Kretschmer is a difficult exploration for psychoanalysis. The interior life of those subjects is a constant mystery.

The schizoid type is hermetic, contradictory, sometimes very sensible, charitable, and tender, yet other times, very cold, cruel, and indifferent.

This sick lady had a certain aggressiveness with a suicidal complex.

The schizoid constitution, the depressive tendency, the suicidal complex with deliriums of persecution and anguish presented a very complicated diagnostic.

Thus, before this case, medical science capitulated, and the sages with all of their science failed. Nevertheless, we, the students of expanded psychiatry, did not surrender. We proposed to study her case. We investigated her hereditary antecedents, and we did not find any insane or schizoid person among her ancestors.

The study of her brain and the general clinical analysis did not present any strange anomaly.

This problem was very difficult. Everything was enigmatic. The family of the sick woman had to take her out of the mental health center. Medical science had failed with this case.

What is most intriguing about this sick woman is that during her deliriums in which she felt to be condemned to death, she was trying to free herself from some imaginary ropes. She believed herself to be tied with ropes. She was holding the imaginary ropes and struggling to liberate herself from them in order to escape death. Materialistic science could not cure that case. The sick woman was an enigma for the doctors.

The scientific investigations of the erudite—the materialistic studies, the rigorous corroborations of the different chemical, physical, biochemical, physiological, etc. phenomena—are incomplete, because the erudite have not studied Gnosis. They do not know about *Kundalini Yoga* by Sivananda. They do not know about *Jnana Yoga* by Vivekananda. They have not studied *The Subtle Laws of Nature* by the famous Hindustani sage Rama Prasad. They have not exercised themselves with the Tattvic powers. They do not know about the esoteric and endoteric anthropogenesis and cosmogenesis. They do not know anything about esoteric anatomy nor about the law of karma, etc. To that end, materialistic science is incomplete and is a failure. It is only a building without a foundation. It is enough to push that building a little in order to convert it into minute sediment!

The most critical aspect of this matter is not the materialistic science but the fanaticism of the partisans of dialectical materialism. The fanatic partisans of dialectical materialism do not accept anything that disagrees with their materialistic pontificates and priests (the tricksters of science). Those sectarian fanatics do not want to recognize other methods for investigation and scientific corroboration. They want to recognize only their authoritative pontificates and priests. They believe themselves to have the last word of knowledge; they are convinced that no one knows more than they do.

To that end, the geographic East and the cultural East—namely Tibet, Great Tartary, China, Siam, Mongolia, etc.—do not exist for the fanatic partisans of dialectical materialism, because they believe that they are the center of the universe and no one knows more than they do. They think that everything that does not belong to them is worthless, and only what belongs to them is of value, because they think themselves to be wise, powerful, omnipotent, etc.

What is most ludicrous about these sectarians of dialectical materialism is that they do not want to see beyond their noses. They put a limit to life based on their little intelligence. They seem to be like medieval people who believed that beyond the Cape of Finisterre there was no more land and this was the limit of the Earth. When Christopher Columbus talked about his projected adventure, they called him a madman. Thus, if the queen of Spain, Isabella the Catholic, had never helped Columbus in his intrepid enterprise, then the

Spaniards would never have discovered America. Another intrepid one would have arrived ahead of them.

The sectarian materialists, who do not see beyond dogmatic procedures, look like the caterpillar that believes the leaf where it lives is everything. The caterpillar ignores that above and below that leaf there are many other leaves on the tree where it lives. Likewise, the sectarian materialist ignores that there are other worlds above and below his external sensory perceptions. What is worse is that those sectarian materialists not only ignore, but moreover, they ignore that they ignore. They are doubly ignorant.

We, the Gnostics, do not reach the point of affirming that scientific materialistic investigation is useless. What we, the Gnostics, condemn is the fanaticism of the materialistic sect.

It is logical that the scientific investigation of the phenomena of matter is useful to the human being. Nevertheless, materialistic science is not the entirety of science. Neither are the rigorous procedures of investigation and scientific corroboration from the Western world and from the materialistic sages the only ones.

Everything must be in its own place. We cannot study astronomy with a microscope, nor can we study microbes with a telescope.

The Gnostic Rosicrucian sage knows the systems of investigation from the East and the West.

The worlds of ultra and of the astral body of the human being exist; they are a tremendous reality. The physical material world exists and it is also a tremendous reality.

We investigate the worlds of the ultra and of the astral body with the systems and methods of the yogis of Hindustan. We study the physical world with the methods of Western investigation.

These systems complement and harmonize each other. In the future, these systems will give us a new culture and a new civilization that is highly mystical, formidably technical, and scientific.

The human being of the future will place matter under his service. Machines will serve the community. The human being will not be a victim of any machine.

Medical science, astronomy, technology, aviation, industry, etc., will liberate the spirit from slavery, from material labor.

The human being of the future will be endowed with illuminated intellect. The human being of the future will be endowed with the powers of clairvoyance, and, nonetheless, he will have gigantic scientific and technical advancements. He will be highly spiritual and marvelously intellectual.

So, the fanatical secularism of the partisans of dialectical materialism is conservative, retarded, and anti-revolutionary.

The alienated ones increase in number every day, and doctors cannot cure them, because they do not know the mental body. If the materialistic sages would study the Asian yogic philosophy, then they would know the mental body. That way, they could cure thousands of mad people who live without hope.

A clairvoyant student of expanded psychiatry proposed to investigate the past reincarnation of the young alienated lady who was discarded by the materialists.

The outcome of the clairvoyant investigation gave us the clue. The "values" that were reincarnated in that young lady were incarnated in her past life as a thief, a highway robber. That thief, highway robber, bandit, was sought by the police and executed during the epoch of Don Porfirio Diaz (Mexico). The bandit was tied to a tree and thereafter shot.

Now, we had a clue about her sickness. Then, we could explain the imaginary ropes and the delirium of persecution. The anguish of the mad young lady concerning death was no longer an enigma for us. The whole problem was resolved.

Death's impressions had been engraved in the subconsciousness of her reincarnating ego. These were the same values of the executed bandit. The memories were deposited in the subconsciousness of the young lady. These values revived in her consciousness the whole terrible anguish of that horrible, tragic drama. The outcome was her madness that the materialistic sages could not cure.

The commotion was so terrible for this young lady that her mental body was fissured. Many malignant atoms entered through those gaps of her mental body and infected her brain, forcing this sick young lady to perform absurd things.

Even though the materialistic sages are bothered by our procedures, we cannot deny that we were obligated to utilize thaumaturgy[29] in order to heal the sick lady.

After six months of treatment with esoteric medicine[30], the sick young lady returned to her senses; she became radically cured.

This was a great victory for thaumaturgy and expanded psychiatry.

Mental health centers are filled with furious or passive maniacs.

The sicknesses of the alienated are in the mental body.

The mental body has its sicknesses and its symptoms.

It is necessary to study the mental body and its sicknesses.

The Third Logos closed the wounds of the mental body; this is how the sick lady was healed absolutely.

Jails are filled with alienated criminals.

Many normal delinquents have had a passing disturbing moment, thus they commit crimes in those instants of terrible over-excitement.

Sometimes, malaria fever produces furious deliriums whose final outcome is crime. The so-called hallucinations produced during fever states are legitimate perceptions of the ultra.

Commonly, delirium is observed during scarlet fever, small pox, malaria fever, typhus, etc.

Any alteration, any transitory mental disturbance, any perturbation of the psychic functions, even the ones that are the outcome of infected deliriums, can lead to crime.

The subjective sensory impressions that occur during somnolence or lethargy in the course of pathologic processes, are not illusions. Those impressions are legitimate ultra-sen-

29 Greek, "wonder works," also called magic, the work of a magi, priest.
30 See the book *Esoteric Medicine and Practical Magic* by Samael Aun Weor.

sory perceptions that enclose the clues of sickness. Expanded psychiatry studies these perceptions in order to find the clue that will allow us to cure a sick person.

In the course of a situational reaction with a transitory mental disturbance, a person can commit homicide, robbery, etc.

Anthropometry[31] cannot give us an explanation of intimate causes of a situational reaction with transitory mental disturbance and crime. Somatoscopic and somasometric attributes[32] cannot give with logical exactitude the most intimate clues of a situational reaction with a transitory mental disturbance and crime. Oftentimes, the somatoscopic and the somasometric characteristics of assassins and thieves are found in normal citizens who do not register judicial antecedents.

Only by profoundly exploring the depths of the mind can we discover the secret origins of a situational reaction, a transitory mental disturbance, and its related crime.

Secret factors from the infraconsciousness, subconsciousness, or unconsciousness can be the cause of those mental transitory disturbances and of those types of situational reactions that carry any man or any woman towards crime.

Ultra-sensory microbes invade the mind and produce those situational reactions, transitory mental disturbances, and common crimes.

Our affirmations might appear absurd to materialists. Yet, when did our affirmations not appear absurd to them? Were they perhaps the same ones who mocked about Pasteur and microbes? Is it then so strange now that they mock our ultra-sensory and hyper-sensory microbes? Those microbes are already classified, namely incubi, succubi, basilisks, dragons, elementals, larvae, tantric entities, etc. If you materialists want to see and analyze them, then get a special lens. This special lens is clairvoyance. Do the perceptions of clairvoyance bother you? Well then, it is very clear that you are fanaticized! A psychological trauma is what lies in the depths of the materi-

---

31 "The branch of anthropology concerned with comparative measurements of the human body." — Farlex Partner Medical Dictionary
32 Measurements from examination of the body

alists' fanaticism. So, in regards to this type of trauma within these types of minds, everything that relates to spirituality provokes a psychological resistance. Therefore, the materialists' minds have a psychopathic sickness, indeed.

With an in-depth, integral culture on a spiritual, social, and scientific basis we will radically change the present situation of the world.

AGLA[33] and the powerful Gnostic movement, as well as Sivananda Aryabarta Ashrama, are the powerful integral cultural lever with which we can revolutionize the world and give it a total change.

The Gnostic movements grant us the esoteric Christic wisdom. The Gnostic wisdom will grant us a powerful intellectual, social, and revolutionary culture.

Sivananda Aryabarta Ashrama teaches us a rigorously analytical and tremendously scientific yoga.

Our esoteric wisdom endures the most rigorous inductive and deductive analysis. In this day and age, the problem of the alienated ones is very critical. We can resolve this problem only with expanded psychiatry.

First of all, we need to free the mind from the conservative ideas of materialism and to enter deeply into the studies of AGLA.

---

33 American Gnostic Liberation Action, one of the groups formed by Samael Aun Weor.

Chapter 30

Total Revolution and Partial Revolution

The order of the factors does not alter the product[34].
Partial revolution is not total revolution.

The order of economical and political factors can be modified without the vital product suffering any change. Life continues with all of its pains. Partial revolution changes the order of the factors, yet it does not alter the vital product. Human beings continue to torment each other.

We Gnostics do not like partial revolution; we want total revolution. We can have total revolution only by dissolving the "I," the myself, the ego.

The "I" sabotages and damages the revolutionary order.

The "I" forms conflicts amidst the revolutionary orders.

The "I" wants to escalate, to rise, to show off, and to make itself noticed everywhere.

The "I" exploits. The "I" steals. The "I" cheats. The "I" slanders. The "I" calumniates and makes turbid the waters of revolution.

The "I" conflicts and forms problems in public education, in agrarian matters, in commercial transactions, in the public ministry, etc.

The truth comes to us when we dissolve the "I." When we dissolve the "I," we think with a consciousness of multitudes. We do not affirm the "I" when we dissolve the "I," instead we affirm the pronoun "we."

When we attain total revolution, each of us becomes a perfect government. Who wants to govern when each one of us is already a perfect government?

This is total, integral, absolute revolution.

When the "I" will be dissolved, all governments will disappear, because they will be useless.

The "I" is the origin of crime and pain.

---

34 Terms of mathematics, referring to the fact that whether the factors are written as 2x3 or 3x2, the result (the product) is the same.

The "I" created pain. The universal spirit of life did not create pain. The "I" is the author of pain. The "I" is Satan. Satan created pain. If what is divine did not create pain, if Satan created pain, then pain is useless, absurd, and stupid.

Those who affirm that through pain we reach perfection are deifying Satan (the "I"). Whosoever loves pain is masochistic and satanic.

We decapitate the "I" only with the Arcanum A.Z.F. We dissolve the "I" only with a profound creative comprehension.

Every human being has formed some opinion about the truth. Every religion of every school has its own opinion about the truth. Human beings search for the truth; they adore the truth.

We, the Gnostics, state: "Know the truth and the truth shall make you free[35]." This is how total revolution will exist. However, we warn you that no one can search for what he does not know. The truth is the unknowable from moment to moment. The truth comes to us without us searching for it. The truth comes to us when the "I" is dead.

Pain cannot lead us towards the truth, because pain belongs to Satan. Only the Arcanum A.Z.F. and profound creative comprehension can lead us towards the truth.

Every desire originates ideas. Every idea transforms itself into projects. Every project is desire. Projects conduce us towards crime. Projects are true monsters that devour the neighbor, and in the end, they swallow their progenitor. This is how we become victims of our own inventions.

Desire is the origin of crime. Desire is the origin of pain.

The delinquent enjoys when his desire is satisfied. The delinquent suffers when his desire is frustrated. Every human being is a delinquent even if he is not in jail.

If we comprehend the process of desire, we then dissolve the "I." When the "I" is dissolved, the origin of crime is finished. There is total revolution when the "I" is dissolved.

You must transmute desire into willpower. This is how you will finish with desire.

---

35 John 8:32

When sexual desire is transmuted into willpower, it becomes the flaming fire that victoriously ascends throughout the spinal medulla.

Every desire can be transmuted into light and fire. Transmute desire into light; thus, the "I" will dissolve as a fatuous diabolic flame. This is how there will be total revolution.

Desire is extinguished when we transmute it. We can transmute every desire based only on creative comprehension.

Desire is the fundamental matter of every crime. The three most dangerous crimes are anger, greed, and lust. Anger is the violent outcome of frustrated desire. Greed is desire of accumulating. Lust is sexual desire.

Anger can be transmuted into sweetness. Greed can be transmuted into charity. Lust can be transmuted into love.

When the human being does not respect the life of his neighbor, he overestimates his own desire very much; this is how he kills.

When the human being steals, it is because he has the desire of accumulation, or he desires what he does not have.

The impurity of the mind is the dog of desire.

To lie is the desire of falsifying the truth.

Gossip and slander are frustrated desire or overestimation of one's own desire. When someone feels himself frustrated in his own desires, he then gossips against his neighbor. When someone overestimates his own psychological "I," he then gossips against his neighbor.

The one who takes a false oath and the one who blasphemes against the divine overestimates his own desires too much.

Idle conversations are children of desire.

The one who envies, covets what he does not have. The one who covets is envious of his neighbor. When someone covets, he desires. When someone envies, he covets what he does not have and feels distress because of his neighbor's goods.

Malice is accumulated desire. Hatred and resentment are frustrated desire.

Ignorance is the mother of desire.

Desire of killing is transmuted into the science for healing and giving life. Desire of stealing is transmuted into altruism and charity.

Mental impurity is transmuted into chastity.

Desire of lying is transmuted into words of truth.

Desire of gossip and slander are transmuted into words of wisdom and love.

Desire of blasphemy and prejudice are transmuted into supreme veneration and adoration of the divine.

Desire for pleasure of idle conversations are transmuted into sublime silence and words of wisdom.

The frustrated desire of envy is transmuted into intimate happiness for our neighbor's goods.

The accumulative desire of greed is transmuted into the happiness of giving everything, even one's life, for the love of this suffering humanity.

The rottenness of malice is transmuted into the innocence of the child.

Anger, rancor, and hatred are distinct forms of desire that are transmuted into supreme sweetness, infinite pardon, and supreme love.

We must transmute all thoughts, words, and actions of desire into wisdom and love. This is how we annihilate the "I."

That which is non-temporal, the eternal one, the truth, the inner Christ, comes to us when we annihilate the "I."

The only way to dissolve the "I" is by annihilating desire.

The only way to annihilate desire is by transmuting it. When a superior law transcends an inferior law, the superior law washes away the inferior law.

The science of transmutations is called alchemy. The basic foundation of alchemy is the Arcanum A.Z.F.

Mind, heart, and sex are the perfect triangle of holy alchemy. The struggle is terrible: brain against sex, sex against brain, and even more terrible and painful, heart against heart. You know this!

Many are those who blaspheme against the divine life, against God. They accuse the unknowable and divine of being

BRAIN: INTELLECT

HEART: EMOTION

SEXUAL ORGANS

THE THREE BRAINS

the cause of all their sufferings and pains. The great divine life
has nothing to do with all the errors of the "I."

Any man or woman desires something; thereafter, they
form their plans and projects. These plans and projects are
very beautiful when they think about them; yet, the problems
come when they want to fulfill them. When our plans are fulfilled we say, "God is very good to me, as he granted me what
I desired." Yet, when those plans and projects fail, then the
desire is frustrated and the devotee feels himself disappointed.
He then blames God and blasphemes against the eternal one.
However, if they are occultists or Theosophists, etc., then they
blame the lords of karma, or they blaspheme against them.
This is how humanity is!

People do not want to realize that what is divine is absolute happiness and has nothing to do with pain. The "I" creates its own pain. The "I" is Satan.

Those who convert pain into mysticism are masochists.

Pain ends when we dissolve the "I."

There is total revolution when we dissolve the "I."

We only annihilate the "I" based on alchemical operations.

The incessant transmutations of alchemy are performed
in exact arithmetical operations.

Many masochistic students of occultism, Theosophy, etc., consider misery, pain, and even sickness as an inexhaustible fountain of light and wisdom. Those wretched people adore the "I." Those people are Satanic. God or that which is God, the divinity, is happiness, peace, and abundance. Misery and pain belong to Satan.

Other people wait, believing that through evolution and time they will one day attain perfection. Those people are even worse, because they want to perpetuate Satan throughout the centuries. They are worse, because they want to perfect Satan (Satan is the "I"). Satan enjoys when he reincarnates in order to satisfy his desires. Satan enjoys when he gets more experience. The experiences of life complicate and strengthen the "I."

As adolescence, youth, and maturity pass away, the innocent and beautiful child gains experiences that complicate him and finally transform him into a sly, malicious, distrustful, etc., old man.

The innocent human being of eighteen million years ago is now the human being of cabarets and the atomic bomb, the human being of embezzlement and crime.

This is what the evolution of the "I" is. It is a complication and a fortification of the myself. It is the projection of error throughout the centuries.

Therefore, evolution ends when the "I" is dissolved. This is what total revolution is.

The Absolute does not know itself. The Absolute needs to know itself. Each super-divine atom needs to know itself in order to have consciousness of its own happiness. Unconscious happiness is not happiness.

The human being, in his last synthesis, is just a super-divine atom from the Abstract Absolute Space. That atom is known by the Kabbalists by the name Ain Soph. It is urgent to know that the Ain Soph sends its spirit to the world of matter with the purpose of acquiring that which is called self-cognizance of its own happiness.

When the spirit, after having passed through the mineral, plant, and animal states of consciousness, attains the human state, it can return into the Ain Soph to fuse with it. This is how the Ain Soph becomes conscious of its own happiness.

Unfortunately, the human being allows himself to be confused by matter and by the fatal voices of desire. This is how the "I" is born.

The worst disgrace is the continuity of the "I." Satan complicates himself through reincarnation. Satan suffers the consequences of his own errors through reincarnation (karma). Satan is born in time and dies in time. Satan is time.

To want to perfect Satan is an absurdity. To want to become liberated with time is the same as to adore Satan. That which is God, the divine, the truth, is non-temporal.

The human being organizes mystical schools with the great pain of Satan. The human being converts pain into mysticism. This is masochism.

We created the complicated theory of evolution based on a mistake.

The human being committed a mistake when he ate the forbidden fruit. This is how the "I" was born. The forbidden fruit that Adam ate was sex. Since then, the error continues reincarnating. This is how pain continues.

We dissolve the "I" only through incessant transmutations. This is how evolution ends. This is total revolution.

Economical and political revolution is partial revolution. We need total revolution.

After the absolute death of the "I," the spirit of the human being returns unto his interior star that has always smiled upon him. That star is a super-divine atom from the Abstract Absolute Space. The spirit of the human being is the ray of that interior star.

The horrible dragon of desire trapped that ray. Therefore, when the ray liberates itself from the horrible beast of desire, he then returns into his interior star. This is how the star becomes conscious of its own happiness.

The ray returns into its star by climbing the symbolic ladder of Jacob. In its return, the ray acquires angelic, archangelic, seraphic, etc., types of consciousness. Therefore, the divine hierarchies are the outcome of tremendous interior revolutions.

Partial revolution is another type of pain.

We need total revolution.

Total revolution is supreme happiness.

Chapter 31
Intellectual Criminology

Intellectual criminology is so profound and complex that we would need millions of volumes in order to study this single subject; therefore, we will touch on a few points only.

Intellectual criminology is found in books, magazines, bull fighting arenas, movie theaters, pamphlets, etc.

There are pornographic magazines that prostitute the minds of male and female youngsters in different countries.

When a pornographic representation reaches the mind, the unconsciousness traps that representation and elaborates its conceptual content. The conceptual content elaborated by the unconsciousness is the exact outcome of the quality of the representation. The psychological "I" traps that representation within the depths of the mind's unconsciousness and elaborates its conceptual content with it. The conceptual content is translated as semi-conscious images within the world of the cosmic mind. These are the effigies of the mental world. The psychological "I" fornicates and commits adultery with those images within the plane of the cosmic mind. This is what the prostitution of the mind is. Nocturnal pollutions (wet dreams) are the morbid outcome of the prostitution of the mind.

There are also magazines [now matchmaking websites] for failures. In the magazines for the failures, women announce themselves. They solicit for a husband who is short, fat, skinny, with money, etc. Many young ladies are following that ultramodern example. This is mental prostitution. The outcome of this mental prostitution is critical. The interchange of writing begins. They start falling in love with someone they do not know and they start projecting plans. Yet, in the end, on the day when the couple meets, failure is the inevitable outcome.

Ladies who have never been prostitutes—honorable and distinguished young ladies—allow themselves to be cheated by modernism and fall into the crime of mental prostitution.

If a clairvoyant were to study in the mental plane the announcements of love of all of those magazines [match-making websites], one will see houses of prostitution. Each announcement of love corresponds in the mental world to a horrible mental bedroom of a whorehouse. Every clairvoyant is astonished when seeing those whorehouses of the mental plane.

Within each bedroom of those horrible dens a prostitute is found lying there. Men enter and leave from those bedrooms. Each announcement of the magazine corresponds to one of those bedrooms. The woman who placed the announcement is lying down in her bedroom. This is what the prostitution of the mental plane is.

True love has nothing to do with those whorehouses of the mental plane.

Thousands of young and distinguished ladies are perverting themselves with those types of magazines [and websites].

True love begins always with a flash of delectable affinity. It is substantiated with the force of tenderness, and it is synthesized in infinite, supreme adoration.

True love is natural, without artifices, like the love of birds, like the love of the fish of the immense sea, like the love of the savage creature from the impenetrable jungle.

Another intellectual crime is "bull fighting." The first critical symptoms are shown among those women who in their emotional climax hurl even their intimate underwear or pantyhose to the torero. It is ludicrous to see women's shoes or any type of dressing garments falling down into the arena. Those women look insane.[36]

Violent emotion causes transitory mental disturbances. The violent emotion is a function of the instinctive "I." Antisocial and highly criminal acts are the outcome of violent emotions. Violent emotions originate instantaneous psychic traumas. The violent sensation transmitted by the torero, the bullfighter, produce internal criminal reflexes within the depths of the mind.

---

36 This is common at celebrity appearances, musical performaces, etc.

The mental criminal reflexes evolve within the psychobiological field of the human infraconsciousness. Internal criminal reflexes that evolve within the field of the infraconsciousness are the secret causes of criminal sadism.

There are three types of emotions: light, optima, and puissant.

The first does not reach total alteration of the mind.

The second activates the sensual imagination, inhibiting intellectual analysis. This is when we see hysterical emotional episodes, like those in the black masses of the Middle Ages. The hysterical emotional episodes in bull fighting arenas and those in black masses during the Middle Ages are similar. In both cases we find out-of-control shouting, women hurling their underwear, the loss of intellectual analysis, etc.

The third type, puissant emotion, annuls any type of reasoning and the victim falls into a state of coma or stupor.

Oftentimes in the bull fighting arenas, some otherwise very sensible people fall unconscious, senseless. During black masses, many women—extremely hyper-emotional, with an evolving epileptic type of emotion—fall on the floor senseless with epileptic convulsions. Then, everybody is satisfied, because they consider these women to be possessed by the devil.

We believe that people who are mediums are easily obsessed by hyper-sensory microbes: astral larvae, incubi, elementals, and every type of inferior entity of the astral plane.

Mental disturbances of traumatic origin are the fatal outcome of violent emotions.

Bull fighting arenas have their origin in Pagan Rome. Later, those barbarian circuses planted their roots in Spain. It is lamentable that such a sad spectacle had been transplanted to Latin America. Animal protection societies should fight against those types of bloody spectacles.

The fault of this type of spectacle falls one hundred percent upon the Roman Catholic Church. The Roman sect is the intellectual author of that criminal spectacle, because that sect denied animals the legitimate right of having an immortal soul.

The torero believes that the animal has no soul. This is why without ever feeling charity or mercy they stab picks into the afflicted flesh of the innocent victim. The torero is an executioner of innocents. The torero is worse than the sanguinary tiger of Bengal, because the torero does not kill by a savage instinct of self-defense nor to satiate his hunger. The torero kills innocent animals in order to entertain the multitudes, who are avid and thirsty for blood and pleasure. The torero is similar to the Roman gladiator who after impaling the heart of his victim exclaimed, "Hail, Caesar!"

The word animal comes from the word anima, "soul." The word anima remains just by taking the letter L from the word animal.

The animal is an anima. The anima of the animal is an innocent and beautiful elemental.[37]

Every atom is a trio of matter, energy, and consciousness.

The consciousness of every atom is always an intelligent elemental.

If the materialists are not capable of seeing those elementals, it is because they still do not know the scientific procedures that allow us to see them.

We have special methods in order to see those creatures.

Indeed, the atom is a truly infinitely small planetary system. Those planetary systems of the atoms are formed by ultra-atomic ternaries that spin around their centers of gravitation.

The atom with its alpha, beta, and gamma rays is a trio of matter, energy, and consciousness.

The monistic doctrine of the Haeckelian materialist states that force and matter are the same thing. The materialist Haeckel asseverates that consciousness is latent in everything that exists and he states that we must search for it within our brain cells.

We, the Gnostics, go further, because we know esoteric anatomy and the astral body.

---

37 The intelligence or soul of non-human creatures, whose physical bodies are the minerals, plants and animals, but whose souls are called variously gnomes, sprites, elves, fairies, devas, etc.

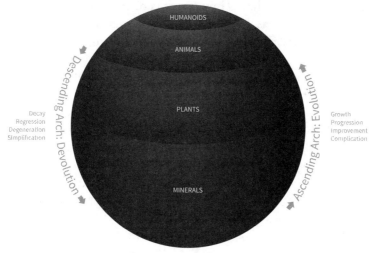

SOULS EVOLVE AND DEVOLVE THROUGH THE FOUR MECHANICAL KINGDOMS OF NATURE.

The cosmic consciousness reflects itself in the whole panorama of the universe.

We know that cosmic consciousness acts upon force, and force acts upon matter.

The coordinates of every biological, physiological, atomic, etc., phenomena are intelligent. Every directive intelligence is conscious.

We cannot have biomechanical phenomena without conscious coordinates.

You can be sure that the fanatic, conservative, and retarded materialist dogmatically rejects the former affirmations.

The psychological trauma of the fanatics of dialectical materialism is reactionary.

The organism of the animal is a synthesis of matter, energy, and consciousness.

The animal consciousness is an intelligent elemental.

The mineral, plant, animal, and human being have soul. That soul is the cosmic consciousness. There is only one soul; this is the cosmic consciousness. That is the Anima Mundi of Plato. The great consciousness is coexistant with Abstract Absolute Space. You can call that great consciousness God, Allah, Parabrahman, or whatever you like; in the end it does not matter a bit. What is important is to comprehend the reality of the great consciousness. Human words are smoke that cloud the starry heaven of the spirit. What is important is the great reality.

The torero who assassinates the unhappy beast commits a horrible crime against the great universal fraternity. Within the universal spirit of life we, all beings, are one. The hunter who kills his minor brothers (the animals) commits also the cowardly crime of fratricide. The boxer who punches his brother in order to entertain the multitudes is also a fratricide. The wrestling fighters, boxers, the toreros, the sly and perverse hunters, etc., are assassins. The intellectual author of all of those crimes is the Catholic religion.

Chapter 32
Combative Psychosis

The press, radio, magazines, etc., have created the state of combative psychosis.

The Gnostic Movement, AGLA, and Sivananda Aryavarta Ashrama fight against argumentative necro-neurosis.

Combative psychosis evolving within the human infra-consciousness finally converts itself into violence, hatred, and war.

Combative psychosis originates sicknesses.

While in the middle of a battle in the Second World War, a soldier became blind. The cause of his blindness was his self-guilt. The man saw a hand grenade coming; thus, he threw himself to the ground and sheltered behind a boulder. If he had warned his comrades, they would have not died; therefore, he felt guilty and became blind. When the doctors examined him, they did not find any wound in his eyes. The psychiatrist who hypnotized him could cure him because he discovered the cause. The psychiatrist commanded the man to see and he saw. Naturally, the psychiatrist had to persuade him with good arguments in order for the man to forget his guilt.

Gnosis is promoting the advent of a new civilization and culture.

Gnosis unites all philosophical and spiritual schools, all religions and sects, to study at a round table all the economical and social problems of humanity.

Gnosis works longing for the day in which each citizen becomes truly free and just.

Gnosis is a universal revolutionary movement that fights for the advent of the new Aquarian Era.

Cultural-spiritual labor must replace argumentative propaganda.

Gnosis performs a gigantic cultural-spiritual labor in many parts of the world.

Combative propaganda is destructive and dangerous.

The human being must resolve all of our problems without wars and without argumentative propaganda.

Chapter 33
Paranoia

The paranoid appears normal.

The reasoning and completely lucid madness is named paranoia.

Great personages are always in danger of being assassinated by paranoids. Many presidents and statesmen have been assassinated by paranoids.

Commonly, the paranoid is delirious, with false ideas.

We knew the case of a paranoid Rosicrucian boss. That man intended to monopolize the Rosicrucian science. He was a paranoid with deliriums of grandeur. He considered himself the single priest of the truth. The distrust and pride of that Rosicrucian paranoid were tremendous. The truth is the unknowable from moment to moment. However, that Rosicrucian paranoid was convinced of being the absolute owner of the truth. He believed that he knew the truth.

Many are the occultist, Theosophist Rosicrucians who become paranoids. Every mystic-paranoid considers himself as the very incarnation of the truth.

The "I" cannot recognize the truth, because the "I" has not experienced the truth.

We can only recognize what we know; yet, we cannot recognize what we do not know.

The "I" does not know the truth. The "I" is born in time and dies in time.

The "I" is time itself.

The truth does not belong to the "I," because the truth is not of time.

The truth is non-temporal; it is eternal.

The paranoid has deliriums about the truth and believes that he has the truth.

The human being can rack his brain searching for the truth, yet he will not find it.

The paranoid believes that he has the truth. Indeed, he only projects opinions about the truth. The mind is bottled up within the "I."

Some stubborn people say that God exists; others say that God or the truth does not exist. Those who say that the truth exists and those who deny it are both stubborn. To affirm or to deny the existence of the truth is opinion. Every opinion is a mental projection of the "I," of the myself.

JOSEPH STALIN
There is significant evidence that the highly intelligent Joseph Stalin, the leader of Communist Russia from the 1920's to1953, was a paranoid, responsible for killing at least as many people as Hitler did.

Every affirmation and negation of the truth does not increase or take away an atom from the infinite.

Those who search for the truth are imbeciles, because no one can search what he does not know.

The occultist, Theosophist, etc., paranoid believes that he can find and recognize the truth.

A person can never recognize another person whom he has never known.

Therefore, no one can recognize the truth, because no one has ever known it.

Let us not talk about the truth. It is better to talk about alchemy.

The "I" can die only by transmuting desire into wisdom and love.

The truth comes into us only when the "I" dies.

The esotericists need to be careful to not fall into paranoia.

The delirium of paranoids is very dangerous. Hitler was a paranoid. The Quixote of Cervantes is an example of what a paranoid is.

The delirious ideas from paranoids do not resist logical analysis. Many paranoids like to be inventors. Others like to be great businessmen, illustrious reformers, extraordinary prophets, etc. When we analyze their delirious ideas, we see then that they do not resist analysis. When their errors are shown to them, they are filled with supreme pain. Afterwards, they react against the person who showed them their error and accuse that person as being unjust and envious, etc.

The Rosicrucian paranoid, mentioned by us in previous paragraphs, asked forgiveness of one of his critics. Afterwards, confused, he wept. When it was demanded to him to retract himself in public, he then reacted and accused his critic. This is how the paranoids are.

The occultist, Theosophist Rosicrucians must study the sacred science without loosing their mental balance. Unfortunately, many esotericist students become paranoids. Commonly, they feel themselves to be reincarnations of Jesus Christ, Buddha, Mohammed, Marie Antoinette, Napoleon, etc. This is how they convert themselves into Quixotes, into authentic paranoids. This is the danger of esoteric studies.

Many esotericists are assaulted by the delirium of grandeur; they seem to perform gigantic things, etc. They fill themselves with malice and distrust. They believe that the whole world is bewitching them. They slander others by accusing them of being black magicians, etc. This is what a Theosophist occultist paranoid is.

The paranoid who did not study esoteric doctrines thinks that he descends from Napoleon or from some Count or very famous sage. He assumes that he is a superman. He believes himself to be a great businessman, etc.

In Mexico, we knew the case of a paranoid who assassinated many women. Finally, when they discovered that he assassinated his fiancée, the daughter of a lawyer, he was caught and put in jail. That paranoid was burying his victims in the garden of his home. In the penitentiary he said that he only needed one more victim in order to find the secret with which the human being can mock death and never die. This is how the paranoids are: very intelligent and dangerous people.

According to clinical criteria, there are many paranoids who live normally and who are not dangerous. However, among them are psychopaths who are terribly dangerous!

Commonly, the paranoid is essentially malicious and distrustful. The paranoids are so sly that they even cheat the psychiatrists themselves.

The constellation of paranoia has many degrees. The most socially dangerous paranoid psychosis is the one that deprives some of these individuals of rationalism. Consequently, when they become demented, they commit the most terrible crimes.

Chapter 34
Educational Psychotherapy

There are two types of criminal authors.

The first are those who lead others into delinquency by means of hypnotism, spiritualism, intimidation, coaction, witchcraft, psychological constriction, etc. These are the mediate authors.

The second ones are the immediate authors, those who commit the concrete crime, the factual situations, the criminal situational reactions, etc.

We, the partisans of expanded psychiatry, expanded with Theosophical and Rosicrucian matters, believe that criminology is a very profound science.

Adler, Jung, and Freud have given psychiatry the A, B, C's of scientific criminology.

The penal code is not criminology. The penal code is only a human covenant in order to defend themselves from society.

The satyrs, for instance, are criminals even if they are not enclosed within a jail.

The endocrine pathologies lead to crime; nonetheless, the penal code has nothing to do with it.

Eroticism, accompanied by personal pain, is related with the instinct of power and with the sexual instinct. This is masochism. The sadist inflicts pain to his/her sexual partner in order to feel pleasure. Those forms of sexual perversion constitute that which is called algolagnia.[38]

The instinct of power and the sexual instinct are related with the diencephalon[39] and the gray cerebral nucleus that control their manifestations.

Anger, the origin of too many bloody cases, corresponds to the instinct of power.

---

38 "A perversion (as sadism or masochism) characterized by pleasure and especially sexual gratification in inflicting or suffering pain." – Merriam-Webster.com

39 "The central, lower part of the brain that contains the basal ganglia, the thalamus, the hypothalamus, the pituitary gland." –Collins Dictionary of Medicine

Love is related with the sexual glands. How many times both love and anger unite, mix, and condition each other until becoming crime!

Love and anger, sexual instinct, and instinct of power have their plusses and minuses in the biorhythm of our glands of internal secretion. We recommend the book *Biorhythm* by Dr. Krumm-Heller.

Love and anger have their mutual transferences and their most capricious psychic combinations.

Traumas and nervous impressions often disturb the functions of the central nervous system and the functions of the autonomic nervous system, as well as the glands of internal secretion.

The sexual psychopathic personality has, for instance, very complex origins. The deviation of the sexual instinct and the instinct of power originates an infinite variety of psychopathic, schizoid, and compulsive personalities.

The sadists and masochists are the best example of what the deviation of the sexual instincts and the instincts of power signifies. The sadomasochists commit the bloodiest crimes that overwhelm by their monstrosity.

Fetishism,[40] with its black masses and witchcraft, form part of this criminal constellation. Nevertheless, one is overwhelmed when one sees the judges laughing when faced with witchcraft, its "voodoo dolls" and fetishism.

On a certain occasion, a sick individual presented himself before the Public Ministry. He came to place a complaint against his lover who he thought was bewitching him. He was exhibiting, as a corpus delicti, a doll filled with pins. Of course, the authorities laughed at the denouncer, and in order to be rid of him for that moment, they came up with a sophism of distraction, promising to arrest that woman. When that man left the office of the Public Ministry, an employee, while laughing, removed the pins from the doll and afterwards hurled the "embo" into a water pot. The next day, the man full of happiness and health, presented himself again

---

40 The word fetishism is used here in the original sense, as "religious worship of a material object—a fetish—believed to be endowed with supernatural properties."

before the authorities. The man gave thanks to the authorities, since he firmly believed that they had cured him. He was feeling himself completely sane. What is this? What does this signify? What does the penal code state about this? The penal code does not understand anything about this.

The study of the scientific part of fetishism and witchcraft corresponds to the science of criminology. It is impossible to laugh before demonstrated facts. In this epoch of radioactivity and in instants in which we are studying atomic physics, it is indeed stubborn and absurd to laugh about "voodoo dolls." The case that we have narrated here could be included in psychobiology.

The employee who removed the pins from the "doll" and afterwards hurled it into the water pot was indeed the "doctor" of that sick man.

What hurt that man was the imagination of that man's lover, focused by the pins of that doll. There was a psychobiologic, energetic, and subtle relationship between the doll and the sick man. Those subtle energies are as real as the waves of a radio or as the emanations of radium and cobalt.

The employee who took the pins from the doll and threw it into water altered the instrument of torture, thus he cured the sick man. The employee was the doctor of the sick man.

It is necessary to awaken clairvoyance in order to study psychobiology in depth, to study it profoundly at its base.

We need to transcend the barbaric law of retaliation[41] and study criminology in the light of expanded psychiatry.

It is necessary to take into account and to study the hereditary "I," the unconscious "I," the infraconscious "I," the subconscious "I," the epileptic "I," the phenotypic "I," etc.

It is necessary to profoundly explore the "I" within the depths of the mind, and thereafter organize a transcendental psychotherapy in order to cure those unhappy delinquents.

The law of retaliation does not reform anybody. Pain is useless.

We need psychotherapy.

41 From the Code of Hammurabi, Babylon, 1792-1750 BC. Used in the Bible, Exodus 21:24 and Matthew 5:38, "An eye for an eye, a tooth for a tooth."

It is necessary to study the syndromes or psychic sicknesses. The criminological diagnostics must be based on expanded psychiatry.

It is necessary to analyze the mental alterations of ourselves based on Theosophy.

It is urgent to know the mental body.

It is necessary to expand forensic psychiatry.

It is necessary to study, in a didactic way, psychobiology and psychopathology.

The valuable work of Lombroso[42] and Marro[43] is incomplete without Theosophy. The studies of criminal anthropology, perfected by Vervaeck,[44] when applied to the purely penitentiary system, are incomplete when psychiatry very well expanded with Theosophical wisdom is not studied.

It is necessary to make a psychosomatic analysis of the delinquent. It is urgent to know the psychophysiology of the delinquent. It is indispensable to study the endocrine glands of the delinquent. It is necessary to analyze the purely psychic functions of the endocrine glands of the delinquent.

Endocrinology and criminology are intimately correlated.

It is urgent to study the nervous systems of central relation and the vegetative organs.

After all of these studies about the delinquent, we must explore in depth his psychological "I," the most profound depths of his mind.

When we know the Theosophy and Rosicrucian subject matter, the diagnosis[45] and prognosis[46] of the personality of the delinquent are exact.

Any science is incomplete when one does not know the esoteric wisdom, that is to say, Gnosis.

---

42 Cesare Lombroso, considered the founder of criminology.

43 Antonio Marro, psychiatrist and sociologist, disciple of Lombroso, who believed crime has a biological origin.

44 Dr. Louis Vervaeck, founder of the world's first criminal-biological diagnostic clinic in Belgium in the early twentieth century.

45 (Greek "to know, to discern") A critical analysis of the nature or cause of something.

46 (Greek "fore-knowing, foreseeing") A term for predicting the likely outcome or future development.

The diagnosis and prognosis of the delinquent must be exact, otherwise the law of retaliation will continue.

The penitentiaries must be converted into psychiatric clinics, hospitals, universities, schools, workshops, agriculture farms, etc.

Psychotherapy is a polyphase system.

Each delinquent needs specialized professors.

Educational corrective treatment, educational psychotherapy, must be led by psychiatrists who truly have studied Theosophy, Rosicrucianism, hermeticism, yogic philosophy, etc.; that is to say, they must be Gnostics.

Materialist psychiatrists do not achieve the reformation of delinquents. They are an absolute failure.

Materialism already failed in Soviet Russia. It is demonstrated by the evident fact that fifteen million Muslims are living in the heart of Russia.

Practically, only a few fanatics of the Creole materialism have remained who still live, in this day and age, as if this was the eighteenth century.

Good music, conferences, educational and highly spiritual movies, baths, hiking, a sexually healthy life, etc., can reform and cure delinquents.

The law of retaliation has routinely failed.

Now we need corrective psychotherapy.

Conclusions

Endocriminology is a science that is still in an embryonic state.

Criminology is stagnated by materialistic science.

The powers of clairvoyance, clairaudience, intuition, telepathy, omniscience, etc., are in a latent state within the endocrine glands.

The mistaken use of powers is criminal.

Ignorance is the cause of the evil use of psychic powers.

Psychiatry, expanded with Theosophical and Rosicrucian matters, will take criminology from the stagnant state in which it is found.

The penal code must be reformed with arrangements based on scientific criminology.

Psychobiology without Theosophy is like a garden without water.

Every esotericist student must have discipline and intellectual culture.

The esotericist without discipline and intellectual culture converts himself into a delinquent.

The upright use of powers is a blessing for the whole world. The unjust use of powers is a damnation for the whole world.

The ignoramus who wants to educe and develop the psychic powers latent in the glands of internal secretion is like a child who wants to play with dynamite.

The esotericist without intellectual culture converts himself into a delinquent.

This book is a codex of scientific ethics for all the Rosicrucian Gnostics, yogis, esotericists, spiritualists, etc.

The esotericist who studies and accepts this book as a codex of scientific ethics will not fall into the abyss of delinquency.

This book opens a new field of investigations for psychiatry and criminology.

Glossary

Absolute: Abstract space; that which is without attributes or limitations. The Absolute has three aspects: the Ain, the Ain Soph, and the Ain Soph Aur.

"The Absolute is the Being of all Beings. The Absolute is that which Is, which always has Been, and which always will Be. The Absolute is expressed as Absolute Abstract Movement and Repose. The Absolute is the cause of Spirit and of Matter, but It is neither Spirit nor Matter. The Absolute is beyond the mind; the mind cannot understand It. Therefore, we have to intuitively understand Its nature." - Samael Aun Weor, *Tarot and Kabbalah*

"In the Absolute we go beyond karma and the gods, beyond the law. The mind and the individual consciousness are only good for mortifying our lives. In the Absolute we do not have an individual mind or individual consciousness; there, we are the unconditioned, free and absolutely happy Being. The Absolute is life free in its movement, without conditions, limitless, without the mortifying fear of the law, life beyond spirit and matter, beyond karma and suffering, beyond thought, word and action, beyond silence and sound, beyond forms." - Samael Aun Weor, *The Major Mysteries*

Alchemy: Al (as a connotation of the Arabic word Allah: al-, the + ilah, God) means "The God." Also Al (Hebrew) for "highest" or El "God." Chem or Khem is from kimia which means "to fuse or cast a metal." Also from Khem, the ancient name of Egypt. The synthesis is Al-Kimia: "to fuse with the highest" or "to fuse with God." Alchemy is one of the oldest sciences in the world, and is the method to transmute our inner impurity into purity. It is also known in the East as Tantra.

Aryan race: "(Sanskrit) arya [from the verbal root to rise, tend upward] Holy, hallowed, highly evolved or especially trained; a title of the Hindu rishis [initiates]. Originally a term of ethical as well as intellectual and spiritual excellence, belonging to those who had completely mastered the aryasatyani (holy truths) and who had entered upon the aryamarga (path leading to moksha or nirvana). It was originally applicable only to the initiates or adepts of the ancient Aryan peoples, but today Aryan has become the name of a race of the human family in its various branches. All ancient peoples had their own term for initiates or adepts, as for instance among the ancient Hebrews the generic name Israel, or Sons of Israel." —Theosophical Glossary

"From Sanskrit [=a]rya excellent, honorable; akin to the name of the country Iran, and perh. to Erin, Ireland, and the early name of this people, at least in Asia. 1. One of a primitive people supposed to have lived in pre-historic times, in Central Asia, east of the Caspian Sea, and north of the Hindoo Koosh and Paropamisan Mountains, and to have been the stock from which sprang the Hindoo, Persian, Greek, Latin, Celtic, Teutonic, Slavonic, and other races; one of that ethnological division of mankind called also Indo-European or Indo-Germanic." - Webster's Revised Unabridged Dictionary

While formerly it was believed that the ancient Aryans were European (white), most scientists now believe that the ancient people commonly referred to as Aryan were the original inhabitants of India, which Manu called Aryavarta, "Abode of the Aryans."

However, in universal Gnosticism, the word Aryan refers not to "white people" or to an ancient, dead civilization, but instead refers to to the vast majority of the population of this planet. In Gnosis, all modern races are "Aryan."

Astral Body: What is commonly called the astral body is not the true astral body, it is rather the lunar protoplasmatic body, also known as the kama rupa (Sanskrit, "body of desires") or "dream body" (Tibetan rmi-lam-gyi lus). The true astral body is solar (being superior to lunar nature) and must be created, as the Master Jesus indicated in the Gospel of John 3:5-6, "Except a man be born of water and of the Spirit, he cannot enter into the kingdom of God. That which is born of the flesh is flesh; and that which is born of the Spirit is spirit." The solar astral body is created as a result of the Third Initiation of Major Mysteries (Serpents of Fire), and is perfected in the Third Serpent of Light. In Tibetan Buddhism, the solar astral body is known as the illusory body (sgyu-lus). This body is related to the emotional center and to the sephirah Hod.

"Really, only those who have worked with the Maithuna (White Tantra) for many years can possess the astral body." - Samael Aun Weor, *The Elimination of Satan's Tail*

Bodhisattva: (Sanskrit; Tibetan: changchub sempa) Literally, Bodhi means "enlightenment" or "wisdom." Sattva means "essence" or "goodness," therefore the term Bodhisattva literally means "essence of wisdom." In the esoteric or secret teachings of Tibet and Gnosticism, a Bodhisattva is a human being who has reached the Fifth Initiation of Fire (Tiphereth) and has chosen to continue working by means of the Straight Path, renouncing the easier Spiral Path (in Nirvana), and returning instead to help suffering humanity. By means of this sacrifice, this individual incarnates the Christ (Avalokitesvara), thereby embodying the supreme source of wisdom and compassion. This is the entrance to the Direct Path to complete liberation from the ego, a route that only very few take, due to the fact that one must pay the entirety of one's karma in one life. Those who have taken this road have been the most remarkable figures in human history: Jesus, Buddha, Mohammed, Krishna, Moses, Padmasambhava, Milarepa, Joan of Arc, Fu-Ji, and many others whose names are not remembered or known. Of course, even among bodhisattvas there are many levels of Being: to be a bodhisattva does not mean that one is enlightened. Interestingly, the Christ in Hebrew is called Chokmah, which means "wisdom," and in Sanskrit the same is Vishnu, the root of the word "wisdom."

It is Vishnu who sent his Avatars into the world in order to guide humanity. These avatars were Krishna, Buddha, Rama, and the Avatar of this age: the Avatar Kalki.

Chakra: (Sanskrit) Literally, "wheel." The chakras are subtle centers of energetic transformation. There are hundreds of chakras in our hidden physiology, but seven primary ones related to the awakening of consciousness.

"The Chakras are centres of Shakti as vital force... The Chakras are not perceptible to the gross senses. Even if they were perceptible in the living body which they help to organise, they disappear with the disintegration of organism at death." - Swami Sivananda, *Kundalini Yoga*

"The chakras are points of connection through which the divine energy circulates from one to another vehicle of the human being." - Samael Aun Weor, *Aztec Christic Magic*

Chastity: Although modern usage has rendered the term chastity virtually meaningless to most people, its original meaning and usage clearly indicate "moral purity" upon the basis of "sexual purity." Contemporary usage implies "repression" or "abstinence," which have nothing to do with real chastity. True chastity is a rejection of impure sexuality. True chastity is pure sexuality, or the activity of sex in harmony with our true nature, as explained in the secret doctrine. Properly used, the word chastity refers to sexual fidelity or honor.

"The generative energy, which, when we are loose, dissipates and makes us unclean, when we are continent invigorates and inspires us. Chastity is the flowering of man; and what are called Genius, Heroism, Holiness, and the like, are but various fruits which succeed it." - Henry David Thoreau, *Walden*

Christ: Derived from the Greek Christos, "the Anointed One," and Krestos, whose esoteric meaning is "fire." The word Christ is a title, not a personal name.

"Indeed, Christ is a Sephirothic Crown (Kether, Chokmah and Binah) of incommensurable wisdom, whose purest atoms shine within Chokmah, the world of the Ophanim. Christ is not the Monad, Christ is not the Theosophical Septenary; Christ is not the Jivan-Atman. Christ is the Central Sun. Christ is the ray that unites us to the Absolute." - Samael Aun Weor, *Tarot and Kabbalah*

"The Gnostic Church adores the saviour of the world, Jesus. The Gnostic Church knows that Jesus incarnated Christ, and that is why they adore him. Christ is not a human nor a divine individual. Christ is a title given to all fully self-realized masters. Christ is the Army of the Voice. Christ is the Verb. The Verb is far beyond the body, the soul and the Spirit. Everyone who is able to incarnate the Verb receives in fact the title of Christ. Christ is the Verb itself. It is necessary for everyone of us to incarnate the Verb (Word). When the Verb becomes flesh in us we speak with the verb of light. In actuality, several masters have incarnated the Christ. In secret India, the Christ Yogi Babaji has lived for millions of years; Babaji is immortal.

The great master of wisdom Kout Humi also incarnated the Christ. Sanat Kumara, the founder of the great College of Initiates of the White Lodge, is another living Christ. In the past, many incarnated the Christ. In the present, some have incarnated the Christ. In the future many will incarnate the Christ. John the Baptist also incarnated the Christ. John the Baptist is a living Christ. The difference between Jesus and the other masters that also incarnated the Christ has to do with hierarchy. Jesus is the highest Solar initiate of the cosmos..." - Samael Aun Weor, *The Perfect Matrimony*

Clairvoyance: A term invented by occultists, derived from the French clair "clear," and voyance "seeing."

"There is clairvoyance and pseudo-clairvoyance. The Gnostic student must make a clear differentiation between these two forms of extrasensory perception. Clairvoyance is based on objectivity. However, pseudo-clairvoyance is based on subjectivity. Understand that by objectivity we mean spiritual reality, the spiritual world. Understand that by subjectivity we mean the physical world, the world of illusion, that which has no reality. An intermediate region also exists, this is the astral world, which can be objective or subjective according to the degree of spiritual development of each person." - Samael Aun Weor, *The Perfect Matrimony*

"Positive clairvoyance is achieved only with a great intellectual culture and a great esoteric discipline. The highest cultured people, who are submitted to the most rigorous intellectual disciplines, only achieve the truly positive clairvoyance. The illuminated intellect is the outcome of positive clairvoyance." - Samael Aun Weor, *Fundamental Notions of Endocrinology and Criminology*

The two main categories of consciousness are objective (positive, related with free consciousness) and subjective (negative, related to the deluded perception and opinions of the psychological "I"s). Further, there are five types of clairvoyance, as explained in *Fundamental Notions of Endocrinology and Criminology*.

1. Conscious clairvoyance: to perceive any given phenomenon (whether internal phenomenon related with the psyche and internal worlds or external phenomenon related to the circumstances of the physical world and nature) through the intelligence of the Monad which is essence or consciousness. Conscious clairvoyance is experienced when one is able to perceive a physical or psychological phenomenon how it really is, in all of its causes and multiple dimensions.

2. Supra-conscious clairvoyance: This is the level of Logoic consciousness. This is only for those venerable masters who finish The Great Work. This level of consciousness is Turiya, those masters who have no ego, who have resurrected, and for those who never dream.

3. Subconscious clairvoyance: This is related to the perception of the egos who are related with memories of past experience. These egos are the most superficial egos whose inherent pattern was defined during the formation of the personality (birth to seven years old). These egos can be created at

any time in our lives but the pattern is related to the false personality and the PCPF. An example of a subconscious ego is the one who avoids broccoli for their entire lives because they remember the disgust they had when they were forced to eat it by their parents. Remember that subconscious clairvoyance is the way the ego perceives that particular experience; as in the example, it was the way the ego perceives the impression of broccoli and that example.

4. Unconscious clairvoyance: This is the type of perception that develops through the frustration of desires. Pride constantly talks about himself and how great he is because it if frustrated that nobody else talks about him; this is an unconscious habit. Lust becomes frustrated because it was never able to satisfy its sexual desire to fornicate with a particular movie star, etc. This desire becomes frustrated and in the astral plane projects its frustrated desires in the form of sexual dreams with the image/impression of the movie star.

5. Infra-conscious clairvoyance: The deepest aspects of our egos, related to the spheres of Lilith in the Klipoth. Remember that everything in the universe has its antithesis. The antithesis of the angel of love, Anael, is Lilith, the demon of fornication, black magic and homosexuality. This region is usually only experienced during nightmares. A minority of people bring these egos to the surface, incorporating these elements in action and with the personality. Sadly, this humanity has more and more people who bring the elements of black magic, homosexuality and brutality to the surface of their psychological world.

Consciousness: "Wherever there is life, there is consciousness. Consciousness is inherent to life as humidity is inherent to water." - Samael Aun Weor, *Fundamental Notions of Endocrinology and Criminology*

From various dictionaries: 1. The state of being conscious; knowledge of one's own existence, condition, sensations, mental operations, acts, etc. 2. Immediate knowledge or perception of the presence of any object, state, or sensation. 3. An alert cognitive state in which you are aware of yourself and your situation. In universal Gnosticism, the range of potential consciousness is allegorized in the Ladder of Jacob, upon which the angels ascend and descend. Thus there are higher and lower levels of consciousness, from the level of demons at the bottom, to highly realized angels in the heights.

"It is vital to understand and develop the conviction that consciousness has the potential to increase to an infinite degree." - The 14th Dalai Lama

"Light and consciousness are two phenomena of the same thing; to a lesser degree of consciousness, corresponds a lesser degree of light; to a greater degree of consciousness, a greater degree of light." - Samael Aun Weor, *The Esoteric Treatise of Hermetic Astrology*

Divine Mother: "Among the Aztecs, she was known as Tonantzin, among the Greeks as chaste Diana. In Egypt she was Isis, the Divine Mother, whose veil no mortal has lifted. There is no doubt at all that esoteric Christianity has never forsaken the worship of the Divine Mother Kundalini. Obviously she is Marah, or better said, RAM-IO, MARY. What orthodox religions did not specify, at least with regard to the exoteric or public circle, is the aspect of Isis in her individual human form. Clearly, it was taught only in secret to the Initiates that this Divine Mother exists individually within each human being. It cannot be emphasized enough that Mother-God, Rhea, Cybele, Adonia, or whatever we wish to call her, is a variant of our own individual Being in the here and now. Stated explicitly, each of us has our own particular, individual Divine Mother." - Samael Aun Weor, *The Great Rebellion*

"Devi Kundalini, the Consecrated Queen of Shiva, our personal Divine Cosmic Individual Mother, assumes five transcendental mystic aspects in every creature, which we must enumerate:

1. The unmanifested Prakriti

2. The chaste Diana, Isis, Tonantzin, Maria or better said Ram-Io

3. The terrible Hecate, Persephone, Coatlicue, queen of the infernos and death; terror of love and law

4. The special individual Mother Nature, creator and architect of our physical organism

5. The Elemental Enchantress to whom we owe every vital impulse, every instinct." - Samael Aun Weor, *The Mystery of the Golden Blossom*

Ego: The multiplicity of contradictory psychological elements that we have inside are in their sum the "ego." Each one is also called "an ego" or an "I." Every ego is a psychological defect which produces suffering. The ego is three (related to our Three Brains or three centers of psychological processing), seven (capital sins), and legion (in their infinite variations).

"The ego is the root of ignorance and pain." - Samael Aun Weor, *The Esoteric Treatise of Hermetic Astrology*

"The Being and the ego are incompatible. The Being and the ego are like water and oil. They can never be mixed... The annihilation of the psychic aggregates (egos) can be made possible only by radically comprehending our errors through meditation and by the evident Self-reflection of the Being." - Samael Aun Weor, *The Gnostic Bible: The Pistis Sophia Unveiled*

Elemental: The intelligence or soul of non-human creatures, whose physical bodies are the minerals, plants and animals, but whose souls are called variously gnomes, sprites, elves, fairies, devas, etc. (Strictly speaking, even intellectual animals remain as elementals until they create the soul; however in common usage the term elementals refers to the creatures of the three lower kingdoms: mineral, plant, and animal).

"In the times of King Arthur and the Knights of the Round Table, elementals of Nature were manifest everywhere, deeply penetrating our physical atmosphere. Many are the tales of elves, leprechauns and fairies, which still abound in green Erin, Ireland. Unfortunately, all these things of innocence, all this beauty from the soul of the Earth, is no longer perceived by humanity. This is due to the intellectual scoundrel's pedantries and the animal ego's excessive development." –Samael Aun Weor, *The Great Rebellion*

Ens Seminis: (Latin) Literally, "the entity of semen." A term used by Paracelsus.

Ens Virtutis: (Latin) A term used by Paracelsus. Literally, ens is "army; host; mighty works (pl.);" and virtutis is "strength/power; courage/bravery; worth/manliness/virtue/character/excellence." Virtutis is derived from Latin vir, "man." So, we can translate this as "power entity."

Paracelsus stated that the ens virtutis must be extracted from the ens seminis, thus saying that all virtue and excellence is developed from the force within the sexual waters.

Essence: "Without question the Essence, or Consciousness, which is the same thing, sleeps deeply... The Essence in itself is very beautiful. It came from above, from the stars. Lamentably, it is smothered deep within all these "I's" we carry inside. By contrast, the Essence can retrace its steps, return to the point of origin, go back to the stars, but first it must liberate itself from its evil companions, who have trapped it within the slums of perdition. Human beings have three percent free Essence, and the other ninety-seven percent is imprisoned within the "I's"." - Samael Aun Weor, The Great Rebellion

"A percentage of psychic Essence is liberated when a defect is disintegrated. Thus, the psychic Essence which is bottled up within our defects will be completely liberated when we disintegrate each and every one of our false values, in other words, our defects. Thus, the radical transformation of ourselves will occur when the totality of our Essence is liberated. Then, in that precise moment, the eternal values of the Being will express themselves through us. Unquestionably, this would be marvelous not only for us, but also for all of humanity." - Samael Aun Weor, *The Revolution of the Dialectic*

Fornication: Originally, the term fornication was derived from the Indo-European word gwher, whose meanings relate to heat and burning (the full explanation can be found online at http://sacred-sex.org/terminology/fornication). Fornication means to make the heat (solar fire) of the seed (sexual power) leave the body through voluntary orgasm. Any voluntary orgasm is fornication, whether between a married man and woman, or an unmarried man and woman, or through masturbation, or in any other case; this is explained by Moses: "A man from whom there is a discharge of semen, shall immerse all his flesh in water, and he shall remain unclean until evening. And any garment or any leather [object] which has semen on it, shall be immersed in water, and shall remain unclean until evening. A woman with whom a man cohabits, whereby there was [a discharge of] semen, they shall immerse in water, and they shall remain unclean until evening." - Leviticus 15:16-18

To fornicate is to spill the sexual energy through the orgasm. Those who "deny themselves" restrain the sexual energy, and "walk in the midst of the fire" without being burned. Those who restrain the sexual energy, who renounce the orgasm, remember God in themselves, and do not defile themselves with animal passion, "for the temple of God is holy, which temple ye are."

"Whosoever is born of God doth not commit sin; for his seed remaineth in him: and he cannot sin, because he is born of God." - 1 John 3:9

This is why neophytes always took a vow of sexual abstention, so that they could prepare themselves for marriage, in which they would have sexual relations but not release the sexual energy through the orgasm. This is why Paul advised:

"...they that have wives be as though they had none..." - I Corinthians 7:29

"A fornicator is an individual who has intensely accustomed his genital organs to copulate (with orgasm). Yet, if the same individual changes his custom of copulation to the custom of no copulation, then he transforms himself into a chaste person. We have as an example the astonishing case of Mary Magdalene, who was a famous prostitute. Mary Magdalene became the famous Saint Mary Magdalene, the repented prostitute. Mary Magdalene became the chaste disciple of Christ." - Samael Aun Weor, *The Revolution of Beelzebub*

Gnosis: (Greek) Knowledge.

1. The word Gnosis refers to the knowledge we acquire through our own experience, as opposed to knowledge that we are told or believe in. Gnosis - by whatever name in history or culture - is conscious, experiential knowledge, not merely intellectual or conceptual knowledge, belief, or theory. This term is synonymous with the Hebrew "daath" and the Sanskrit "jna."

2. The tradition that embodies the core wisdom or knowledge of humanity.

"Gnosis is the flame from which all religions sprouted, because in its depth Gnosis is religion. The word "religion" comes from the Latin word "religare," which implies "to link the Soul to God"; so Gnosis is the very pure flame from where all religions sprout, because Gnosis is knowledge, Gnosis is wisdom." - Samael Aun Weor from the lecture entitled The Esoteric Path

"The secret science of the Sufis and of the Whirling Dervishes is within Gnosis. The secret doctrine of Buddhism and of Taoism is within Gnosis. The sacred magic of the Nordics is within Gnosis. The wisdom of Hermes, Buddha, Confucius, Mohammed and Quetzalcoatl, etc., etc., is within Gnosis. Gnosis is the doctrine of Christ." - Samael Aun Weor, *The Revolution of Beelzebub*

Holy Spirit: The Christian name for the third aspect of the Holy Trinity, or "God." This force has other names in other religions. In Kabbalah, the third sephirah, Binah. In Buddhism, it is related to Nirmanakaya, the "body of formation" through which the inner Buddha works in the world.

"The Holy Spirit is the Fire of Pentecost or the fire of the Holy Spirit called Kundalini by the Hindus, the igneous serpent of our magical powers, Holy Fire symbolized by Gold..." - Samael Aun Weor, *The Perfect Matrimony*

"It has been said in *The Divine Comedy* with complete clarity that the Holy Spirit is the husband of the Divine Mother. Therefore, the Holy Spirit unfolds himself into his wife, into the Shakti of the Hindus. This must be known and understood. Some, when they see that the Third Logos is unfolded into the Divine Mother Kundalini, or Shakti, She that has many names, have believed that the Holy Spirit is feminine, and they have been mistaken. The Holy Spirit is masculine, but when He unfolds Himself into She, then the first ineffable Divine Couple is formed, the Creator Elohim, the Kabir, or Great Priest, the Ruach Elohim, that in accordance to Moses, cultivated the waters in the beginning of the world." - Samael Aun Weor, *Tarot and Kabbalah*

"The Primitive Gnostic Christians worshipped the lamb, the fish and the white dove as symbols of the Holy Spirit." - Samael Aun Weor, *The Perfect Matrimony*

Innermost: "Our real Being is of a universal nature. Our real Being is neither a kind of superior nor inferior "I." Our real Being is impersonal, universal, divine. He transcends every concept of "I," me, myself, ego, etc., etc." - Samael Aun Weor, *The Perfect Matrimony*

Also known as Atman, the Spirit, Chesed, our own individual interior divine Father.

"The Innermost is the ardent flame of Horeb. In accordance with Moses, the Innermost is the Ruach Elohim (the Spirit of God) who sowed the waters in the beginning of the world. He is the Sun King, our Divine Monad, the Alter-Ego of Cicerone." - Samael Aun Weor, *The Revolution of Beelzebub*

Internal Worlds: The many dimensions beyond the physical world. These dimensions are both subjective and objective. To know the objective internal worlds (the astral plane, or Nirvana, or the Klipoth) one must first know one's own personal, subjective internal worlds, because the two are intimately associated.

"Whosoever truly wants to know the internal worlds of the planet Earth or of the solar system or of the galaxy in which we live, must previously know his intimate world, his individual, internal life, his own internal worlds. Man, know thyself, and thou wilt know the universe and its gods. The more we explore this internal world called "myself," the more we will comprehend that we simultaneously live in two worlds, in two realities, in two confines: the external and the internal. In the same way that it is indispensable for one to learn how to walk in the external world so as not to fall down into a precipice, or not get lost in the streets of the city, or to select one's friends, or not associate with the perverse ones, or not eat poison, etc.; likewise, through the psychological work upon oneself we learn how to walk in the internal world, which is explorable only through Self-observation." - Samael Aun Weor, *Treatise of Revolutionary Psychology*

Through the work in Self-observation, we develop the capacity to awaken where previously we were asleep: including in the objective internal worlds.

Kabbalah: (Hebrew קבלה) Alternatively spelled Cabala, Qabalah from the Hebrew קבל KBLH or QBL, "to receive." An ancient esoteric teaching hidden from the uninitiated, whose branches and many forms have reached throughout the world. The true Kabbalah is the science and language of the superior worlds and is thus objective, complete and without flaw; it is said that "All enlightened beings agree," and their natural agreement is a function of the awakened consciousness. The Kabbalah is the language of that consciousness, thus disagreement regarding its meaning and interpretation is always due to the subjective elements in the psyche.

"The objective of studying the Kabbalah is to be skilled for work in the internal worlds... One that does not comprehend remains confused in the internal worlds. Kabbalah is the basis in order to understand the language of these worlds." - Samael Aun Weor, *Tarot and Kabbalah*

"In Kabbalah we have to constantly look at the Hebrew letters." - Samael Aun Weor, *Tarot and Kabbalah*

Karma: (Sanskrit, literally "deed"; derived from kri, "to do, make, cause, effect.") Causality, the Law of Cause and Effect.

"Be not deceived; God is not mocked: for whatsoever a man soweth, that shall he also reap." - Galatians 6:7

"Buddha said there are three eternal things in life: 1. The Law (Karma), 2. Nirvana, 3. Space." - Samael Aun Weor, *Tarot and Kabbalah*

Kundalini: "Kundalini, the serpent power or mystic fire, is the primordial energy or Sakti that lies dormant or sleeping in the Muladhara Chakra, the centre of the body. It is called the serpentine or annular power on account of serpentine form. It is an electric fiery occult power, the great pristine force which underlies all organic and inorganic matter. Kundalini is the cosmic power in individual bodies. It is not a material force like electricity, magnetism, centripetal or centrifugal force. It is a spiritual potential Sakti or cosmic power. In reality it has no form. [...] O Divine Mother Kundalini, the Divine Cosmic Energy that is hidden in men! Thou art Kali, Durga, Adisakti, Rajarajeswari, Tripurasundari, Maha-Lakshmi, Maha-Sarasvati! Thou hast put on all these names and forms. Thou hast manifested as Prana, electricity, force, magnetism, cohesion, gravitation in this universe. This whole universe rests in Thy bosom. Crores of salutations unto thee. O Mother of this world! Lead me on to open the Sushumna Nadi and take Thee along the Chakras to Sahasrara Chakra and to merge myself in Thee and Thy consort, Lord Siva. Kundalini Yoga is that Yoga which treats of Kundalini Sakti, the six centres of spiritual energy (Shat Chakras), the arousing of the sleeping Kundalini Sakti and its union with Lord Siva in Sahasrara Chakra, at the crown of the head. This is an exact science. This is also known as Laya Yoga. The six centres are pierced (Chakra Bheda) by the passing of Kundalini Sakti to the top of the head. 'Kundala' means 'coiled'. Her form is like a coiled serpent. Hence the name Kundalini." - Swami Sivananda, *Kundalini Yoga*

"Kundalini is a compound word: Kunda reminds us of the abominable "Kundabuffer organ," and lini is an Atlantean term meaning termination. Kundalini means "the termination of the abominable Kundabuffer organ." In this case, it is imperative not to confuse Kundalini with Kundabuffer." - Samael Aun Weor, *The Great Rebellion*

These two forces, one positive and ascending, and one negative and descending, are symbolized in the Bible in the book of Numbers (the story of the Serpent of Brass). The Kundalini is "The power of life."- from the Theosophical Glossary. The Sexual Fire that is at the base of all life.

"The ascent of the Kundalini along the spinal cord is achieved very slowly in accordance with the merits of the heart. The fires of the heart control the miraculous development of the Sacred Serpent. Devi Kundalini is not something mechanical as many suppose; the Igneous Serpent is only awakened with genuine Love between husband and wife, and it will never rise up along the medullar canal of adulterers." - Samael Aun Weor, *The Mystery of the Golden Blossom*

"The decisive factor in the progress, development and evolution of the Kundalini is ethics." - Samael Aun Weor, *The Revolution of Beelzebub*

"Until not too long ago, the majority of spiritualists believed that on awakening the Kundalini, the latter instantaneously rose to the head and the initiate was automatically united with his Innermost or Internal God, instantly, and converted into Mahatma. How comfortable! How comfortably all these theosophists, Rosicrucians and spiritualists, etc., imagined High Initiation." - Samael Aun Weor, *The Zodiacal Course*

"There are seven bodies of the Being. Each body has its "cerebrospinal" nervous system, its medulla and Kundalini. Each body is a complete organism. There are, therefore, seven bodies, seven medullae and seven Kundalinis. The ascension of each of the seven Kundalinis is slow and difficult. Each canyon or vertebra represents determined occult powers and this is why the conquest of each canyon undergoes terrible tests." - Samael Aun Weor, *The Zodiacal Course*

Mantra: (Sanskrit, literally "mind protection") A sacred word or sound. The use of sacred words and sounds is universal throughout all religions and mystical traditions, because the root of all creation is in the Great Breath or the Word, the Logos. "In the beginning was the Word..."

Meditation: "When the esotericist submerges himself into meditation, what he seeks is information." - Samael Aun Weor

"It is urgent to know how to meditate in order to comprehend any psychic aggregate, or in other words, any psychological defect. It is indispensable to know how to work with all our heart and with all our soul, if we want the elimination to occur." - Samael Aun Weor, *The Gnostic Bible: The Pistis Sophia Unveiled*

"1. The Gnostic must first attain the ability to stop the course of his thoughts, the capacity to not think. Indeed, only the one who achieves that capacity will hear the Voice of the Silence.

"2. When the Gnostic disciple attains the capacity to not think, then he must learn to concentrate his thoughts on only one thing.

"3. The third step is correct meditation. This brings the first flashes of the new consciousness into the mind.

"4. The fourth step is contemplation, ecstasy or Samadhi. This is the state of Turiya (perfect clairvoyance). - Samael Aun Weor, *The Perfect Matrimony*

Medium: In the 1840s in upstate New York arose a belief that it is possible to communicate with the spirits of the dead. Sessions (séances) were held by "mediums" (intermediaries) who would convey information back and forth. The primary in uences and methods of this system were derived from Mesmer and hypnotism, a technique that manipulates the sleeping consciousness, which is black magic. Mediumism is a technique of black magic that is more commonly known now as channelling. Channellers are either cunning hoaxes or outright states of possession by demons. No genuine spiritual master needs to communicate through the body of another person.

"We have frequently heard of so many unbalanced individuals who state that they "channel" entities from beyond! Usually, those "channelers" are mediums." - Samael Aun Weor, The Divine Science

"Any Master of Samadhi can clearly verify when in the state of ecstasy the following: that which is manifested through the mediums of Spiritism are not the souls or the spirits of the dead, but the devil-"I"s of the dead, which are the psychic aggregates that continue beyond the burial chamber. It has been said to us with much emphasis that during the postmortem (after death) states the mediums continue to convert themselves into beings who are possessed by a demon or demons. It is unquestionable that after a certain time the mediums conclude by divorcing themselves from their own divine Being. Then they enter into the submerged devolution of the infernal worlds." - Samael Aun Weor, The Three Mountains

"Remember that spiritualist mediums often serve as vehicles for black en- tities. These entities pose as saints and advise against the perfect marriage. Usually, they declare themselves Jesus Christ or Buddha, etc., to cheat the fools." - Samael Aun Weor, The Perfect Matrimony

Mental Body: One of the seven bodies of the human being. Related to Netzach, the seventh sephirah of the Tree of Life; corresponds to the fifth dimension. In Egyptian mysticism, it is called Ba. In Hinduism, is it called vijnanmayakosha or kama manas (some Hindu teachers think the mental body is "manomayakosha," but that is the astral body).

"The mental body is a material organism, yet it is not the physical organism. The mental body has its ultra-biology and its internal pathology, which is completely unknown to the present men of science." - Samael Aun Weor, *The Revolution of Beelzebub*

Personality: (Latin personae: mask) There are two fundamental types of personality:

1. Solar: the personality of the inner Being. This type is only revealed through the liberation of the mind from samsara.

2. Lunar: the terrestrial, perishable personality. We create a new lunar personality in the first seven years of each new physical body, in accordance with three influences: genotype, phenotype and paratype. Genotype is the influence of the genes, or in other words, karma, our inheritance from past actions. Phenotype is the education we receive from our family, friends, teachers, etc. Paratype is related to the circumstances of life.

"The personality is time. The personality lives in its own time and does not reincarnate. After death, the personality also goes to the grave. For the personality there is no tomorrow. The personality lives in the cemetery, wanders about the cemetery or goes down into its grave. It is neither the astral body nor the ethereal double. It is not the Soul. It is time. It is energetic and it disintegrates very slowly. The personality can never reincarnate. It does not ever reincarnate. There is no tomorrow for the human personality." - Samael Aun Weor, *The Perfect Matrimony*

"Our personality has to become more and more passive..." - Samael Aun Weor, from the lecture "Knowing How to Listen"

"The human personality is only a marionette controlled by invisible strings... Evidently, each one of these I's puts in our minds what we must think, in our mouths what we must say, and in our hearts what we must feel, etc.Under such conditions the human personality is no more than a robot governed by different people, each disputing its superiority and aspiring to supreme control of the major centers of the organic machine... First of all, it is necessary, urgent and imperative that the Magnetic Center, which is abnormally established in our false personality, be transferred to the Essence. In this way, the complete human can initiate his journey from the personality up to the stars, ascending in a progressive, didactic way, step by step up the Mountain of the Being.As long as the Magnetic Center continues to be established in our illusory personality we will live in the most abominable psychological dens of iniquity, although appearing to be splendid citizens in everyday life... These values which serve as a basis for the Law of Recurrence are always found within our human personality."- Samael Aun Weor, *The Great Rebellion*

Ray of Creation: The light of the Ain Soph Aur, also known as the Okidanokh, Quetzalcoatl, Kulkulcan, Krestos, and Christ. This ray decends as a lightning bolt, creating and illuminating all the levels of existence.

"The proper arrangement of the Ray of Creation is as follows:

1. Absolute - Protocosmos

2. All the worlds from all of the clusters of Galaxies - Ayocosmos

3. A Galaxy or group of Suns - Macrocosmos

4. The Sun, Solar System - Deuterocosmos

5. The Earth, or any of the planets - Mesocosmos

6. The Philosophical Earth, Human Being - Microcosmos

7. The Abyss, Hell - Tritocosmos

"The brothers and sisters of the Gnostic Movement must deeply comprehend the esoteric knowledge which we give in this Christmas Message, in order for them to exactly know the place that they occupy in the Ray of Creation." - Samael Aun Weor, *The Elimination of Satan's Tail*

Semen: In the esoteric tradition of pure sexuality, the word semen refers to the sexual energy of the organism, whether male or female. This is because male and female both carry the "seed" within: in order to create, the two "seeds" must be combined. In common usage: "The smaller, usually motile male reproductive cell of most organisms that reproduce sexually." English semen originally meant 'seed of male animals' in the 14th century, and it was not applied to human males until the 18th century. It came from Latin semen, 'seed of plants,' from serere, 'to sow.' The Latin goes back to the Indo-European root *se-, source of seed, disseminate, season, seminar, and seminal. The word seminary (used for religious schools) is derived from semen and originally meant 'seedbed.' That the semen is the source of all virtue is known from the word "seminal," derived from the Latin "semen," and which is defined as "highly original and influencing the development of future events: a seminal artist; seminal ideas."

"According to Yogic science, semen exists in a subtle form throughout the whole body. It is found in a subtle state in all the cells of the body. It is withdrawn and elaborated into a gross form in the sexual organ under the influence of the sexual will and sexual excitement. An Oordhvareta Yogi (one who has stored up the seminal energy in the brain after sublimating the same into spiritual energy) not only converts the semen into Ojas, but checks through his Yogic power, through purity in thought, word and deed, the very formation of semen by the secretory cells or testes or seeds. This is a great secret." - Sri Swami Sivananda, *Brahmacharya* (Celibacy)

Vital body: (Also called Ethereal Body) The superior aspect of the physical body, composed of the energy or vital force that provides life to the physical body.

"It is written that the vital body or the foundation of organic life within each one of us has four ethers. The chemical ether and the ether of life are related with chemical processes and sexual reproduction. The chemical ether is a specific foundation for the organic chemical phenomena. The ether of life is the foundation of the reproductive and transformative sexual processes of the race. The two superior ethers, luminous and reflective, have more elevated functions. The luminous ether is related with the caloric, luminous, perceptive, etc., phenomena. The reflective ether serves as a medium of expression for willpower and imagination." - Samael Aun Weor, *The Gnostic Bible: The Pistis Sophia Unveiled*

In Tibetan Buddhism, the vital body is known as the subtle body (lus phra-mo). In Hinduism, it is known as pranamayakosa.

White Brotherhood or Lodge: That ancient collection of pure souls who maintain the highest and most sacred of sciences: White Magic or White Tantra. It is called White due to its purity and cleanliness. This "Brother-hood" or "Lodge" includes human beings of the highest order from every race, culture, creed and religion, and of both sexes.

Yoga: (Sanskrit) "union." Similar to the Latin "religare," the root of the word "religion." In Tibetan, it is "rnal-'byor" which means "union with the fundamental nature of reality."

"The word YOGA comes from the root Yuj which means to join, and in its spiritual sense, it is that process by which the human spirit is brought into near and conscious communion with, or is merged in, the Divine Spirit, according as the nature of the human spirit is held to be separate from (Dvaita, Visishtadvaita) or one with (Advaita) the Divine Spirit." - Swami Sivananda, *Kundalini Yoga*

"Patanjali defines Yoga as the suspension of all the functions of the mind. As such, any book on Yoga, which does not deal with these three aspects of the subject, viz., mind, its functions and the method of suspending them, can be safely laid aside as unreliable and incomplete." - Swami Sivananda, *Practical Lessons In Yoga*

"The word yoga means in general to join one's mind with an actual fact..." - The 14th Dalai Lama

"The soul aspires for the union with his Innermost, and the Innermost aspires for the union with his Glorian." - Samael Aun Weor, *The Revolution of Beelzebub*

"All of the seven schools of Yoga are within Gnosis, yet they are in a synthe-sized and absolutely practical way. There is Tantric Hatha Yoga in the prac-tices of the Maithuna (Sexual Magic). There is practical Raja Yoga in the work with the chakras. There is Gnana / Jnana Yoga in our practices and mental disciplines which we have cultivated in secrecy for millions of years. We have Bhakti Yoga in our prayers and Rituals. We have Laya Yoga in our meditation and respiratory exercises. Samadhi exists in our practices with the Maithuna and during our deep meditations. We live the path of Karma Yoga in our upright actions, in our upright thoughts, in our upright feel-ings, etc." - Samael Aun Weor, *The Revolution of Beelzebub*

"Yoga does not consist in sitting cross-legged for six hours or stopping the beatings of the heart or getting oneself buried underneath the ground for a week or a month. These are all physical feats only. Yoga is the science that teaches you the method of uniting the individual will with the Cosmic Will. Yoga transmutes the unregenerate nature and increases energy, vital-ity, vigour, and bestows longevity and a high standard of health." - Swami Sivananda, *Autobiography*

"Brahmacharya [chastity] is the very foundation of Yoga." - Swami Sivananda

"The Yoga that we require today is actually ancient Gnostic Christian Yoga, which absolutely rejects the idea of Hatha Yoga. We do not recommend Hatha Yoga simply because, spiritually speaking, the acrobatics of this discipline are fruitless; they should be left to the acrobats of the circus." - Samael Aun Weor, *The Yellow Book*

"Yoga has been taught very badly in the Western world. Multitudes of pseudo-sapient Yogis have spread the false belief that the true Yogi must be an infrasexual (an enemy of sex). Some of these false yogis have never even visited India; they are infrasexual pseudo-yogis. These ignoramuses believe that they are going to achieve in-depth realization only with the yogic exercises, such as asanas, pranayamas, etc. Not only do they have such false beliefs, but what is worse is that they propagate them; thus, they misguide many people away from the difficult, straight, and narrow door that leads unto the light. No authentically initiated Yogi from India would ever think that he could achieve his inner self-realization with pranayamas or asanas, etc. Any legitimate Yogi from India knows very well that such yogic exercises are only co-assistants that are very useful for their health and for the development of their powers, etc. Only the Westerners and pseudo-yogis have within their minds the belief that they can achieve Self-realization with such exercises. Sexual Magic is practiced very secretly within the Ashrams of India. Any true yogi initiate from India works with the Arcanum A.Z.F. This is taught by the great Yogis from India that have visited the Western world, and if it has not been taught by these great, initiated Hindustani Yogis, if it has not been published in their books of Yoga, it was in order to avoid scandals. You can be absolutely sure that the Yogis who do not practice Sexual Magic will never achieve birth in the superior worlds. Thus, whosoever affirms the contrary is a liar, an impostor." - Samael Aun Weor, *Alchemy and Kabbalah in the Tarot*

Index

Glands, 3, 10, 21, 36, 41, 43, 45,
   51-53, 55, 64-66, 68-70, 72,
   74-78, 91-92, 99, 161, 234,
   236, 239
Glandular, 69, 74
Glossopharyngeal, 159
Glucose, 89
Glycogen, 89
Gnosis, 27, 125, 187, 196, 200, 202-
   203, 206, 227, 236, 242, 248,
   255
Gnostic, 27, 70, 75, 77, 116, 183,
   186-187, 190, 194, 205, 208,
   212, 227, 243-244, 246, 249,
   251-252, 254-256
Gnosticism, 27, 29, 242, 245
Gnostic Movement, 186, 227, 254
Gnostics, 64, 108-109, 111, 184, 200-
   201, 203, 208, 213-214, 224,
   237, 239
Goddesses, 36
Gods, 23, 36, 83, 133, 136, 241, 249
Goiter, 72
Gold, 22, 118, 133, 187, 249
Golden, 22, 133, 246, 251
Gonads, 43-44
Good, 8, 31, 36, 39, 53-55, 70, 118,
   131, 175, 177, 217, 227, 237,
   241
Gorillas, 116
Gospel, 124, 143, 193, 242
Gossip, 215-216
Government, 16, 54, 162, 213
Grail, 37
Grains, 180
Grand, 13, 64, 70, 74, 79-80, 110,
   118
Grandmother, 136-137
Grandmothers, 73
Gravitate, 27, 32
Gravitation, 4-5, 224, 250
Gravity, 27, 185
Great Work, 185, 244
Greece, 3, 101
Greed, 172, 174, 182, 215-216
Greek, 43, 65, 130, 172, 242-243, 248
Greeks, 245

Green, 129, 180, 246
Grenade, 227
Guilty, 17, 227
Gurdjieff, 138
H. P. B., 187
H. P. Blavatsky, 68
Habits, 33-34, 58, 176, 245
Haeckel, 224
Haiti, 105-106
Hallucination, 70, 103-105, 141,
   176, 210
Hamsa, 4
Hamsa-upanishad, 83
Happiness, 3, 8, 23, 34-35, 45, 51,
   164, 216-220, 234
Happy, 24, 34, 38, 241
Harlots, 169
Hatred, 5, 22, 129, 153, 163, 169,
   172, 182-183, 215-216, 227
Heal, 112, 118, 198, 210, 216
Health, 52, 54, 78, 201, 205-206,
   210, 234, 237, 255-256
Heart Lotus, 81
Heartbeat, 84, 134
Hearts, 80, 92, 117-118, 253
Heat, 36, 247
Heaven, 56-57, 226
Hebrew, 135, 241-242, 248, 250
Hegel, 186, 200
Heindel, 145
Helena Petrovna Blavatsky, 117, 147,
   157, 189
Hell, 30, 167, 254
Hemispheres, 161
Hepatic, 88-90
Hercolubus, 19, 23
Hereditary, 111, 206, 235
Hermaphrodite, 116
Hermes, 3, 11, 22, 24, 28, 45, 179,
   248
Hermetic, 159, 206, 245-246
Hermeticism, 205, 237
Hindbrain, 157
Hindu, 189-190, 192-193, 241, 252,
   255
Hindus, 249

Meditation, 57, 74, 82, 86, 130-131,
134, 181-182, 246, 251-252,
255
Medium, 94, 145-147, 149, 158, 196,
200, 223, 252, 255
Medulla, 45, 47, 92, 114-116, 157,
161, 215, 251
Melancholy, 35, 154, 205
Memories, 163, 167, 172, 176-177,
209, 244
Memory, 17, 19, 37, 97, 121, 127,
133, 141, 157
Men, 8-9, 16-20, 23-24, 28, 33, 35,
38-40, 44-45, 48, 51, 54-55,
59, 100, 107, 113, 116-117,
152, 168-169, 222, 250, 253
Menstrual, 198
Mental, 14, 52-53, 117-118, 141,
147, 149, 155, 157, 159-160,
167, 196-199, 201-202, 205-
206, 209-211, 216, 221-223,
230-231, 236, 245, 252, 255
Mental Body, 14, 149, 157, 159, 209-
210, 236, 252
Mentalist, 195, 197
Mentally, 33, 72, 83, 149, 155, 161,
185, 195, 197-203
Mercury, 51, 56-57, 59, 129
Mercy, 170, 183, 224
Mesencephalon, 157, 165
Messiah, 189
Metabolism, 71, 74, 85, 97
Metal, 72, 133, 241
Metallic, 59
Metamorphosis, 11, 44
Metaphysical, 16, 45, 186, 199
Method, 11-12, 39, 42, 241, 255
Methods, 47, 207-208, 224, 252
Mexican, 28, 40, 102
Mexico, 10, 23, 47, 70, 103, 113, 209,
231
Micro-laboratories, 43
Micro-organisms, 79
Micro-voltage, 197
Microbes, 126, 199-201, 208, 211,
223
Microcosmos, 55, 76, 88, 254

Microscope, 64, 70, 126, 128, 199,
208
Midbrain, 157, 161, 165
Middle Ages, 37, 155, 223
Milarepa, 24, 242
Milk, 20-21, 77, 132
Million, 76, 104, 218, 237
Millions, 23, 38, 48, 54, 79, 107, 113,
199, 201, 221, 243, 255
Mind, 1, 12, 56-57, 66, 73, 83, 117-
118, 121-127, 137-138, 153,
157, 159-163, 168, 171, 175-
176, 181, 185, 199, 201, 211-
212, 215-216, 221-223, 230,
235-236, 241, 251-253, 255
Minds, 57, 84, 121, 123-124, 138,
190, 199, 212, 221, 253, 256
Mineral, 180, 218, 225, 246
Minerals, 99, 136, 246
Minor, 69, 79, 226
Minors, 168
Miracle, 4, 5, 251
Mirror, 129, 131-132, 162
Modest, 40, 187
Mohammed, 28, 231, 242, 248
Molecule, 4-5, 79
Monad, 135, 243-244, 249
Money, 29, 221
Mongolia, 86, 207
Monkeys, 116
Monsters, 167, 199, 214
Monstrosity, 59, 234
Monstrous, 18, 54, 59
Moon, 4, 23, 38, 51, 56, 59, 73, 77,
136-137
Moor, 37, 112
Moral, 18, 143, 155, 163, 175, 181,
199-200, 243
Moses, 135, 242, 247, 249
Mother, 43, 55, 78, 111, 136-137,
149, 151, 166, 195, 203, 215,
245-246, 249-250
Motor, 32-34, 58, 97
Mountains, 8, 133, 241, 252-253
Mouth, 8-9, 177, 205, 253
Movement, 32, 35, 44, 107, 183-184,
186, 197, 212, 227, 241, 254

About the Author

His name is Hebrew סמאל און ואור, and is pronounced "sam-ayel on vay-or." You may not have heard of him, but Samael Aun Weor changed the world.

In 1950, in his first two books, he became the first person to reveal the esoteric secret hidden in all the world's great religions, and for that, accused of "healing the ill," he was put in prison. Nevertheless, he did not stop. Between 1950 and 1977 – merely twenty-seven years – not only did Samael Aun Weor write over sixty books on the most difficult subjects in the world, such as consciousness, kabbalah, physics, tantra, meditation, etc., in which he deftly exposed the singular root of all knowledge — which he called Gnosis — he simultaneously inspired millions of people across the entire span of Latin America: stretching across twenty countries and an area of more than 21,000,000 kilometers, founding schools everywhere, even in places without electricity or post offices.

During those twenty-seven years, he experienced all the extremes that humanity could give him, from adoration to death threats, and in spite of the enormous popularity of his books and lectures, he renounced an income, refused recognitions, walked away from accolades, and consistently turned away those who would worship him. He held as friends both presidents and peasants, and yet remained a mystery to all.

When one reflects on the effort and will it requires to perform even day to day tasks, it is astonishing to consider the herculean efforts required to accomplish what he did in such a short time. But, there is a reason: he was a man who knew who he was, and what he had to do. A true example of compassion and selfless service, Samael Aun Weor dedicated the whole of his life to freely helping anyone and everyone find the path out of suffering. His mission was to show all of humanity the universal source of all spiritual traditions, which he did not only through his writings and lectures, but also through his actions.

Your book reviews matter.

Glorian Publishing is a very small non-profit organization, thus we have no money to spend on marketing and advertising. Fortunately, there is a proven way to gain the attention of readers: book reviews. Mainstream book reviewers won't review these books, but you can.

The path of liberation requires the daily balance of three active factors:

- · birth of virtue
- · death of vice
- · sacrifice for others

Writing book reviews is a powerful way to sacrifice for others. By writing book reviews on popular websites, you help to make the books more visible to humanity, and you might help save a soul from suffering. Will you do your part to help us show these wonderful teachings to others? Take a moment today to write a review.

Donate

Glorian Publishing is a non-profit publisher dedicated to spreading the sacred universal doctrine to suffering humanity. All of our works are made possible by the kindness and generosity of sponsors. If you would like to make a tax-deductible donation, you may send it to the address below, or visit our website for other alternatives. If you would like to sponsor the publication of a book, please contact us at (844) 945-6742 or help@gnosticteachings.org.

Glorian Publishing
PO Box 110225
Brooklyn, NY 11211 US
Phone: (844) 945-6742

VISIT US ONLINE AT gnosticteachings.org